# INSIGHT GUIDES

*Created and Directed by Hans*

GW00367369

# aMERICan SOUTHWEST

Edited by Virginia Hopkins

Update Editor: John Gattuso

Managing Editor: Martha Ellen Zenfell

Editorial Director: Brian Bell

## WEST SUSSEX LIBRARIES

| Copy No 74285 | Class No 917.9 | |
|---|---|---|
| Supplier B | Date Invoiced 17 JAN 1997 | |
| 1st Loc RW | Initials | 2nd Loc Initials |
| 3rd Loc | Initials | 4th Loc Initials |

WEST SUSSEX COUNTY LIBRARY WITHDRAWN

APA PUBLICATIONS

# ABOUT THIS BOOK

*Höfer*

**A**rtist Georgia O'Keeffe said about her first visit to New Mexico, "I loved it immediately." It's a common reaction among travelers in the Southwest. They are enchanted by the region's stunning landscapes and fascinating mix of Hispanic, Indian and Anglo cultures and, like O'Keeffe herself, are often compelled to return again and again.

*Insight Guide: American Southwest* is an invitation to explore the natural beauty, cultural heritage and contemporary life of America's most colorful corner. It's part of the award-winning travel series created in 1970 by Hans Höfer, now chairman of Apa Publications. Each of the 190 titles encourages readers to celebrate the essence of a place rather than try to tailor it to their expectations, and is edited according to Hofer's conviction that, without insight, travel can narrow the mind rather than broaden it.

*Hopkins*

**A**pa Publications bided its time until it could assemble the perfect team of experts and insiders. Heading this book's project team was **Virginia Hopkins**, who has lived in Aspen, Colorado, and New York City after graduating from Yale University, Connecticut. It was her love for the region that won her the role as project editor of the book. She spent months traveling the Southwest, collecting material and information, and coordinating the writers and photographers. Her experience as editor of *Aspen Magazine* and as writer for *Life* and *Outside* was invaluable in the production of this book.

Best selling author **Tony Hillerman** set the right mood with his introduction to the book. He also takes readers on a tour of northern Arizona's Indian Country, home of the Navajo

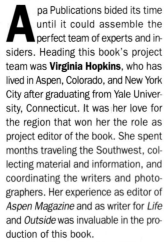

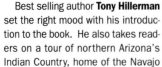

*Hillerman*

and Hopi tribes. The author of more than a dozen books, including a series of award-winning mystery novels featuring Navajo Tribal Police officers, Hillerman has been writing about the Southwest for more than 35 years.

**Bruce Berger** contributed much wit and insight to the book in his articles on geology, history and people. He also covered Phoenix and central Arizona. Berger has written for *New York Times, Poetry, Aspen Magazine* and *The Yale Review*, and has published two books on the Southwest: *There was a River* and *Hangin' On: Gordon Snidow portrays the Cowboy Heritage*.

**Buddy Mays** is a former resident of New Mexico and a well-known sportsman, travel writer and photographer who brought his eclectic talents to "Indian Prehistory" and "The Great Outdoors." Most of the pictures in this book were gathered from his photo agency. **Stan Steiner** authored "Spanish Exploration" and "Arrival of the Anglos." Steiner has written many books and articles on the Southwest. Four of his books: *The New Indians, La Raza, The Vanishing White Man*, and *The Ranchers* discuss the relationship between people and the environment.

The author of several books on the Southwest, **Richard Erdoes** is well-qualified to write about "Early 20th Century," "Hispanics" and "The Navajo," all as erudite and charming as the author himself. His photographs are featured throughout the book.

Award-winning author **Leslie Marmon Silko** penned "Native Americans" and "The Pueblo." Silko, a Pueblo Indian raised on the Laguna reservation in New Mexico, has published three novels, *Storyteller, Ceremony* and *Almanac of the Dead*, and was a recipient of the prestigious MacArthur Foundation Fellowship.

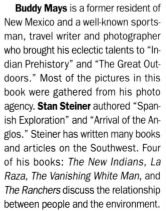

*Berger*

*Mays*

*Steiner*

*Silko*

**Rudolfo Anaya**, co-author of the "Hispanics," is one of the most lyrical and renowned Hispanic writers of the Southwest. His list of honors includes a national literary award for his first novel, *Bless Me, Ultima*.

**Randy Udall**, who covered The Grand Canyon and Southern Utah, is an Outward Bound instructor whose great passion is exploring that country by foot, raft and four-wheel-drive vehicle. **Ruth Armstrong**'s "Pueblo Country," "Albuquerque," "Santa Fe," "Taos," "The Southeast" and "The Southwest" gave New Mexico the rich and varied coverage it deserves. A writer with more than 40 years of experience in the Southwest, Armstrong has been published in major American newspapers, *Reader's Digest* and *Travel and Leisure*.

*Armstrong*

**Suzi Barnes** wrote the sidebar on "Adobe." She also has a few photographic representations in the book. **Tom Miller**, whose droll view of "Tucson and the Border County" appears in this volume, is an accomplished writer. His book, *On the Border*, has led *Swank* magazine to declare him "a Southwestern John McPhee." **Barbara Chulick** wrote about the zany neon world of Las Vegas. Her work has been published in *The Nevada* (the Sunday supplement of *Las Vegas Review/Journal*), and the *Las Vegas Magazine*.

*Miller*

Hopi writer **Alison Sekaquaptewa** covered "The Hopi," said to be the most culturally intact tribe in the country. Reporting on the "Apache" was **Ned Anderson**, former Chairman of the San Carlos Apache Tribe; and **Ofelia Zepeda**, a Tohono O'odham Indian poet and a Professor of Linguistics at the University of Arizona in Tuscon, wrote about the Tohono O'odham and Pima tribes.

In the sunny climes of California,

*Chulick*

**Matthew Jaffe**, a staff writer at *Sunset Magazine*, took a look at Western movies and the impact they've made the world over.

In addition to those mentioned earlier, several other photographers are represented in this volume. **Mireille Vautier** traveled the Southwest and shot 1,000 rolls of film. **Terrence Moore**, published in *Newsweek* and *New York Times*; **Allan Morgan**, Tucson; and **Kathleen Cook**, California; contributed some lovely images. Other photographers were **Donald Young**, **Karl Kernberger**, **Ronnie Pinsler**, **Joseph Viesti**, **Lee Marmon**, **David Ryan**, **Sam Curtis**, **Harvey Caplin**, **Dick Kent Photography**, **Stephen Trimble** and **Jack Hollingsworth**.

The original version of this book was helped to completion by **John Anderson** and **Adam Liptak**. **John Gattuso**, project editor of *Insight Guide: Wild West*, *Insight Guide: Native America* and *Insight Guide: National Parks West*, updated this version and contributed pieces on Georgia O'Keeffe and the Gunfight at the O.K. Corral. **Edward Jardim** assisted with copy editing.

*Gattuso*

In the London editorial offices, **Martha Ellen Zenfell**, editor-in-chief of Apa's North American titles, aided in the overall project while **Martin Rosser** took charge of the details. The book was proofread and indexed by **Caroline Radula-Scott**.

*Zenfell*

Back in the US, Apa is also grateful for assistance from the native population of the Southwest who, even though generally wary of outsiders, took the time to tell their story, and whose courage, independence and hardy cultures gave many of our contributors inspiration that had made this book a reality.

# CONTENTS

**Preceding pages:** detail, old Navajo rug; noble bearing.

## Maps

Preceding pages: detail, old Navajo rug, double beading.

# A BEAUTIFUL VALLEY

Makers of maps like to keep things orderly and tend to define the American Southwest in terms of state boundaries. But those who live there, and love it, and consider time spent elsewhere as a sort of exile, know that another type of boundary must be applied. The Southwest begins where the land rises out of that vast ocean of humid air which covers midland America and makes it the fertile breadbasket of half the world. And it ends along that vague line where winter cold wins out over sun and even the valleys are buried under snow. There is one ever more essential requirement. Wherever you stand in the Southwest there must be, on one horizon or another, the spirit-healing blue shape of mountains. Thus you have Arizona and New Mexico, a slice of southern Colorado, much of southern Utah, and part of Nevada.

The Southwest is high – an immense tableland broken by the high ridges of the southern Rocky Mountains – and dry, with annual precipitation varying drastically with altitude. Thus Albuquerque, New Mexico, 5,200 ft (1,585 meters) above sea level, measures an arid 8 inches (20 cm) of rainfall per year, while the crest of Sandia Mountain only 15 miles (24 km) away but a mile higher receives more than triple that amount. The few minutes required to go from the Rio Grande in downtown Albuquerque to the top of the Sandia Ski Basin ski run via tramway takes one through five of North America's biological life zones – from Upper Sonoran Desert to the cool spruce forests of the Arctic-Alpine zone.

This highness and dryness has another effect which endears it to the hearts of Southwesterners. Air loses 1/30th of its density with each 900 ft (274 meters) of altitude gained. Therefore, a resident of Flagstaff, Arizona, or Santa Fe, New Mexico, more than 7,000 ft (2,134 meters) above sea level, looks through air which is not just humidity-free. It has also lost about a quarter of its weight in oxygen and carbon dioxide. Looking through this oddly transparent air adds a clarity to everything one sees.

But what attracted artists Frederic Remington (and scores of other artists) to Taos was not the beauty but the culture. The Southwest was Spanish Colonial country – the very outer limit of the immense empire of Carlos II. It is also the heartland of America's Indian country. America has been called a melting pot, but in the Southwest this homogenizing process didn't work efficiently. The inhospitable land didn't attract men like Cortes and Pizarro, who gutted Aztec Mexico and destroyed Inca Peru, or like the English, who eradicated Indians from the Eastern seaboard.

The Spanish who settled the Southwest were milder men, softened by the Church's insistence that Indians had souls and the Crown's decision that they should, therefore, be treated humanely. The complex culture of the Pueblo Indians has survived in centuries-old adobe villages scattered up and down the Rio Grande. And so has America's largest tribe, the Navajo. Some 150,000 strong, they occupy a 14-million-acre (5.7-million-hectare) reservation which sprawls across the heart of the Southwest in Arizona, New Mexico and Utah. These original Americans give the Southwest a Holy Land, a territory of shrines and sacred mountains.

A man tries to explain why he has returned to this empty land after finding loneliness in crowded California cities. He looks down into the immense sink which spreads below the southwest slope of the Chuska Mountains. A wilderness of sun-baked stone stretches into the dim distance – gray caliche, wind-cut clay as red as barn paint, great bluish outcrops of shale, the cracked salt flats where the mud formed by the "male rains" of summer tastes as bitter as alum. Everything here is worn, eroded and tortured. It is axiomatic that the desert teems with life, but there is no life here. Not even creosote brush or cactus survives, not even a lizard, nor an insect for it to feed upon. White mapmakers would call it "Desolation Sink."

"The Navajo name for this," he says, "is Beautiful Valley."

**Preceding pages:** tying the knot; Monument Valley; Albert Skukalski's *The Last Supper* in the Nevada desert; San Xavier Mission on Tohono O' odham Indian Reservation; hacienda near Taos. **Left**, keeping an eye on the beautiful valleys.

The forces that created the geology of the Southwest also laid it bare. The region lies in the latitude of the world's great deserts, where air currents thrown skyward by equatorial heat, drained of their tropic rains, descend in dry, evaporative winds. Moisture-laden Pacific storms slam into the Sierras and the Peninsular ranges in California, drop their rain and snow, and continue dry over the inland basins. The resulting lack of vegetation accelerates erosion, gouging out history-revealing canyons, scarps and mesas.

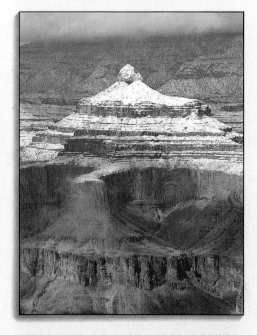

Bear in mind that of the earth's 4.5 billion years of history, only the last half billion is documented in any detail. The first 89 percent of early time is known collectively as the Precambrian, and the oldest Southwestern evidence of its events are the dark metamorphic rocks of the Grand Canyon's inner gorge. They began as sediments and igneous rocks deposited 2 billion years ago near the edge of a large continent. Some 1.7 billion years ago, the area underwent a collision between continental plates, lifting the formations into high mountains, heating and buckling the layers, and metamorphosing them into gneiss and schist. Granitic magma

infiltrated the cracks, leaving the rocks marbled like beef. Later the sea came in from the west, beveled the mountains flat, and added thick layers of sandstone, limestone and shale.

The area remained little changed through the Paleozoic Era, which began 570 million years ago. The Southwest bathed in shallow seas that rose gently into land, then sank back into water, so that deposits alternate between marine sediments, deltas and dunes.

The Mesozoic, beginning 200 million years ago, was a time of upheaval and transformation. The Sierra Nevada burst forth, its enormous rain shadow creating deserts far more severe than those of today. Sandstone and shale from dunes and rivers have weathered into the spectacular slick-rock country of southern Utah, along with the phantasmagoria of such parks as Arches, Canyonlands, Capitol Reef, Zion, and Mesa Verde. Volcanic ash from the Mesozoic created the painted deserts of northern Arizona.

Toward the end of the Mesozoic, North America broke away from Europe, collided with and overrode the Pacific plate, initiating 25 million years of mountain-building. The Arizona Highlands and Rocky Mountains derive from this time. Hot mineral-bearing magma seeped through the fractures, depositing the copper now extensively mined in Utah and Arizona.

Uplift continued into the Cenozoic, beginning 65 million years ago, elevating the Colorado Plateau. The Colorado River cut into the Plateau as it rose, giving us perfect core samples of the Plateau's interior, and revealing quite a surprise: despite plate collisions, volcanoes and other calamities, the strata of the Grand Canyon lie in calm horizontals, what geologists call layer-cake geology. It is believed that the crust beneath the Colorado Plateau is unusually thick, and while many layers have been worn away, what remains is on solid ground and gives the Grand Canyon a sense of uncanny peace.

The Cenozoic Era sheared the Colorado Plateau from the Southwest's other major contemporary land form, the basin and range. Beginning at the north in central Oregon and southwest Idaho, basin and range takes in

Nevada and western Utah, curls around the Colorado Plateau to include southern Arizona and southwestern New Mexico, and stretches into Mexico. With the Great Plains, it is one of the two major land forms in the US. The fault-block mountain ranges, separated by long narrow valleys, are caused by crustal plates slowly pulling apart. As the land widens, the bedrock splits along the faults. The great blocks of stone tip toward their heavier ends in the relatively shallow magma, creating ranges often sloped on one side and precipitous on the other. Valleys sink into the gaps of stretched land, so that some ranges gain more height from dropped valleys than from their own tilting.

more important than the forces of creation is that slow artist of decay called erosion. The wearing away of stone can be accomplished by blowing sand, seismic shift, and the roots of plants, but the primary force is water.

Water enters cracks and fissures then freezes and expands, chiseling rock apart. Water seeping through a soft permeable layer atop a hard one will hollow caves and even chip away at the ceiling until the entrance stands as an arch. The Colorado River system, working the Mesozoic sandstones of southeastern Utah, has created a labyrinth of canyons so high and narrow that some gorges pinch to human width while continuing to soar hundreds of feet overhead. Snowmelt

Explosions across southern Arizona heaved up such ranges as the Superstitions and the Kofa Mountains. Volcanism extended to the Colorado Plateau. The high volcanoes of the San Francisco Peaks, and such ranges as the Henrys, Abajos, and Navajo Mountain in southern Utah, all formed when magma welled up without breaking the surface.

Although the events of the Cenozoic shaped the current Southwestern landscape, perhaps

**Preceding pages:** prickly *Opuntia bigelovii* cacti find homes in Southwest deserts. <u>Left</u>, a late winter storm in Grand Canyon. <u>Above</u>, a horned toad at Gila River Valley.

scours canyon bottoms with its annual burden of silt, until entire mountains and plateaus are reduced to level plains.

Collaborating with erosion to give the Southwest its hold on the human imagination is color. The foremost colorist is iron. Occurring naturally in volcanic material, iron gradually seeps into sedimentary layers. Highly oxidized iron creates the family of reds, while iron in an oxygen-deprived or reducing environment can create blues and greens associated with coppers and cobalts.

When we look out at these ruddy landscapes, we are looking deeply into the long history of creation.

In the final stages of the Pleistocene Epoch came the Ice Age. Nearly one-sixth of the earth's surface was blanketed with ice, making possible the arrival of humans in North America. Massive glaciers formed from billions of tons of water, and so the oceans receded. In some areas the sea level dropped as much as 300 ft (91 meters) and long-submerged fragments of sea bottom were exposed. One of these – a 56-mile (90-km) strip of rocky earth between northeastern Siberia and northwestern Alaska – was an early gateway to this continent.

Exact dates of New World penetration are simply unobtainable with present technology. We can, however, say that aboriginal Asians probably arrived upon North American shores between 15,000 and 40,000 years ago. Human arrival was not sudden. Late in the Pleistocene, interglacial sub-ages (warm trends) began to occur, causing sea-level ice to melt. As the climate slowly mellowed, grass and low shrubs flourished, even on the newly exposed land bridge. This forage attracted grazing animals from the Asian continent, and following the mammoth and bison came hunters. So began the Paleo-Indian Period in North America.

When did humans first reach the Southwest? Archaeological evidence – mostly the datable artifacts found with bones of extinct animals – suggests that they were firmly entrenched in relatively large numbers 10,000 or 12,000 years ago. This same evidence has allowed scientists to reach some logical conclusions about early humans.

Paleo-Indians were meat-eaters (although they probably gathered wild plants for food as well). Using flint or bone-tipped weapons of their own creation and design, Paleo-Indians could kill animals 20 times their size. At least in part, early humans were social creatures; they hunted in organized groups in order to kill not just a single animal but an entire herd at one time for the good of the community. Because constant expansion of

**Preceding pages:** reminders of the Southwest's prehistoric culture. **Left**, Wetherill Mesa, a huge Anasazi cliff dwelling in Mesa Verde National Park, Colorado.

hunting range was necessary, fixed habitations were seldom constructed.

From about 7000 BC until the time of Christ, human life-styles in the Southwest were changing significantly. This span of cultural amplification has been named the Desert Archaic period. Among the most important changes to occur during the Archaic period were these: acquisition of the fire-drill and the grinding stone; utilization of foods other than meat – mainly seeds, wild grains, tubers and berries; construction of semipermanent, seasonal dwelling places – primarily "pithouses," round or rectangular holes in the earth that were covered with brush and mud; and the practice of spiritual ceremonies.

The development of the Paleo-Indian into the Archaic Indian was a sluggish process at best, dependent upon interaction between groups of people sometimes separated by hundreds of miles. This was not true, however, of the next period of cultural expansion – the Pithouse-Pueblo Period – which began shortly after the time of Christ and ended with the arrival of Europeans in the Southwest in the mid-16th century. If humans had crept out of their shells before, they were now free and running.

**Cultural divisions:** Of the many changes occurring during the 1,500-year-long Pithouse-Pueblo Period, none exceeded in importance, and indeed all were connected to, the development of discrete human societies over a wide area.

By AD 700, five distinct groups of people had evolved and were inhabiting the Southwest. In the north were the Anasazi – an intelligent, artistic, peaceful society of farmers whose cliff palaces and sprawling canyon cities were so well constructed that many have survived nearly intact for a thousand years. To the south, near the San Francisco Peaks area of present-day Arizona, were the Sinagua, an agricultural people whose culture later became a melting pot of building techniques and increasingly complex social development. In the Gila and Salt River valleys near present-day Phoenix, Arizona, were the Hohokam, at their peak perhaps the greatest canal builders in North America. To the east were Hohokam cousins, the Salado; and in the rich mountain country of present-day New Mexico, the Mogollon.

We can only guess how and why these divisions of culture came about. One important factor was probably the introduction and development of agriculture – a new concept to primitive humans that demanded huge changes in social structures. Because agricultural products could be stored for the winter, dependence upon hunting and gathering was drastically reduced. In turn, habitations became more permanent so that farmers could tend their fields. Permanency demanded security from enemies, and security required a large and stable population.

weaving implements were also in use. More important (as far as archaeologists can determine), none developed an aristocracy, of a kind that marked the Aztec and Inca civilizations to the south.

Similarities among the cultures occurred also in their people's physical appearance, clothing, and daily activities. From burial evidence, scientists think that most prehistoric Indians were about the same size and build; men averaged 5 feet 4 inches (1.6 meters), the women slightly less. They were muscular, stocky people with sparse body hair. Head hair was thick, however. Men wore it long; women preferred it bobbed or fashioned into elaborate coiffures.

Whatever the reason or combination of reasons, there arose these five major cultures and many minor ones. Geographically they were separated by hundreds of miles, yet each bore striking similarities to the others. They were all agricultural societies, heavily dependent for survival upon crops of maize (corn), beans, squash, and melons. In their early stages of development, all lived in underground pithouses or in caves, later moving to above-ground, apartment-style, multistoried homes called pueblos by the Spaniards. By AD 700, they all used pottery extensively and they had acquired the bow and arrow. Three centuries later, cotton and

Clothing varied, but variations depended less upon tribal affiliation than upon time of year. In hot weather, most Indians wore nothing but sandals woven from plant fiber or plaited from yucca leaves. As the seasons changed and the days cooled, skirts and aprons made from vegetable material or animal skins were added. In winter, hide cloaks, shirts and blankets – the latter made from rabbit skin, dog fur or turkey feathers – were probably sufficient to turn the chill. When cotton was introduced and Indians learned the art of weaving, more elaborate forms of winter clothing – mainly heavy cloaks – came into vogue.

**The Golden Age:** These similarities were not coincidental. Throughout the 15-century span of the Pithouse-Pueblo Period, interaction undoubtedly occurred among all prehistoric cultures in the Southwest as well as in northern Mexico, with each contributing something to the cultural pot. So rapidly, in fact, did new ideas and methods spread among the five major cultures that by the mid-11th century a Golden Age existed among Southwest Indians. Building techniques and irrigation systems had progressed to a point far ahead of their time. Frivolities – such as ball games and contests with dice – were common. In addition, increased rainfall had mellowed the sometimes harsh environment;

many plausible explanations as to why the Golden Age was cut short, one of the most feasible is that by the middle of the 12th century, cyclic weather patterns had once again changed and the region saw the beginning of drought. Where water was permanently available, farmers were little affected; but in areas where agriculture depended upon rainfall and not irrigation, existence once again became difficult. Many towns and outlying family dwellings were abandoned, the inhabitants migrating to larger centers of population that had been constructed near natural groundwater sources. What possessions could be carried were taken along; all else was left behind. This sudden influx of

natural springs and streams ran full, and game and wild plants flourished. Because of the added moisture and new agricultural techniques, farming increased, and with surplus food available, populations grew. New farming projects were started in areas that could hardly have supported cactus a century before. Existing towns grew more complex.

This new life of relative comfort was only temporary, however, and although there are

**Left**, stone points such as these are found throughout the Southwest. **Above**, dioramas realistically represent primitive lifestyles, in this case a Mesa Verde Pueblo of about AD 850.

refugees must have created hardships for the already settled population but, in most cases, room was found.

**Drastic changes:** Then a new threat appeared in the Southwest. Shoshonean raiders (probably the ancestors of present-day Ute) suddenly arrived uninvited from the north, and local Indians found themselves the targets of continual harassment. Few in number, the Shoshone dared not attack a fully protected town, but they easily raided fields, stole harvests and picked off an occasional farmer or his family. In addition, towns and villages had, probably out of necessity, begun to prey on one another.

Sometime during the late 12th century, the combination of harassment, thievery and steadily worsening drought conditions brought about a drastic change in life-styles for most of the Southwestern cultures. The people began to leave their traditional valleys or mesa-top homes for the security of isolated caves and protected canyon amphitheaters. Whether the move ended the Shoshone threat or only prolonged it, archeologists don't know. They do know, however, that it did little to ease internal strife or to alleviate the need for water.

Midway through the 13th century, even as the great cliff cities of Mesa Verde, Mancos Canyon, Betatakin, Keet Seel and others like

them were under construction, the drought was reaching its peak. Even permanent water sources began to go dry, and life became a matter of day-to-day survival. The soil was worn out and turned to dust; crops failed year after year. Hunting and gathering had never been fully abandoned, but wild food supplies decreased in direct proportion to the decrease in moisture. There was simply not enough food and water for the population. Although we have no idea of its exact nature, some type of social upheaval undoubtedly took place – perhaps a universal uprising against the blameless but available leadership. Migrations began. By 1299, when the

drought finally ended, most villages and towns of the Anasazi and Mogollon had been abandoned. Hohokam, Salado and Sinagua communities (near permanent streams) survived longer; however, they met the same fate within a century.

It is here that the real mystery begins. Where did the refugees go? It is believed that some journeyed east to join or start pueblos on the Rio Grande River in present-day New Mexico. Others went east but not as far, stopping at the pueblos of Zuni and Acoma, also in New Mexico. Some may have gone south to Mexico or west to California, and a good many simply changed their life-styles to meet current requirements for survival and remained nearby. These refugees are the ancestors of today's Pima and Hopi.

The Hopi mesas in Arizona, in fact, were perhaps a major refuge for both the Sinagua and Anasazi. Hopi people claim ancestral ownership of many of the great population centers such as Mesa Verde, Betatakin, Keet Seel, Wupatki. Prehistoric Hopi clan signs found in these ruins give validity to the claims, though many archaeologists argue the point. Pictographs (prehistoric rock paintings) and petroglyphs (rock carvings) similar to those the Hopi claim as clan symbols were once freely used throughout both North and South America. This certainly suggests widespread interaction among early cultures but not necessarily the traditional ownership of the signs that Hopi legends proclaim. Hopi ancestors were probably an aggregation of several different cultures.

Wherever these early people went, they were gone, for the most part, by AD 1400. They abandoned to the wind the homes they had so painstakingly constructed. Many of these prehistoric dwellings, preserved by dry desert air, and in some cases by the stabilization and restoration technology of modern science, still exist and may be easily visited. Remember, though, that when viewing these ancient ruins, you are examining a short but important piece of the earth's history. Take nothing when you leave but knowledge, and leave nothing that was not already there. Allow those who come after you the privilege of viewing that history unmarred.

**Left, early fire making. Right, by 1400, many civilizations had disappeared. Others were incorporated into the Catholic church.**

*The worst lay in parting little by little with the thoughts that clothe the soul of the European, and most of all the idea that man attains his strength through dirk and dagger and serving in your Majesty's guard. We had to surrender such fantasies until our inward nakedness was the nakedness of an unborn baby, starting life anew in a womb of sensations which in themselves can mysteriously nourish.*

—Cabeza de Vaca, *His Relation of the Journey* (1528–36). Edited by Haniel Long.

On an autumn day late in November of 1528 four half-drowned seamen, survivors of the ill-fated Spanish expedition of Pánfilo de Narváez, were washed ashore onto the beaches of Texas by the unfriendly sea. Naked, chilled and starving, they were fortunate to be found alive by Native Americans, who fed and clothed them. These naked conquistadors were the first Spaniards to set foot in the Southwest.

**The Gods' messengers:** So began one of the most remarkable journeys in American history. The shipwrecked, led by Nuñez Cabeza de Vaca, walked for thousands of miles through the desert until, eight years later, they reached Mexico City.

On the way, they learned to live and behave like Indians. They adopted not only the clothes but the habits of the tribes they met along the way. The Indians most often feted the men as messengers of the gods, as the Aztecs had regarded Cortés. Especially welcome in this group of four men was Estéban, the black Moor, a Christianized slave of the Spaniards who was favored by the Indian women even more than the others.

Although no records exist to document the theory, historians conjecture that the first *mestizos*, half Spanish and half Indian, were born of the lost conquistadors and the Indians. In his memoirs, de Vaca mused wryly about "the possibility of life in which to be deprived of Europe was not to be deprived of too much."

On his arrival in Mexico City, de Vaca told tales of walled cities with houses four and five stories tall and of Indians who were more civilized than the Spaniards. To the conquistadors of Cortés, who had conquered most of Mexico and fallen into fighting among themselves over the spoils, the reports meant new treasures of gold might be found in the desert. The cry went up: *Otro Mexico! Otro Peru!* Here is another Mexico! Another Peru!

Enticed by de Vaca's tale, the restless and bored conquistadors polished their rusting armor and prepared themselves for battle. They would conquer the entire continent.

The Viceroy, Antonio de Mendoza, sent forth an *entrata* – an expedition – led by

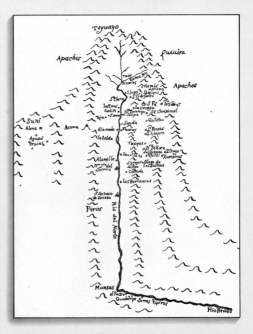

Father Marcos de Niza and guided by the black Moor, Estéban. Its aim was to find the legendary Gran Quivira and the fabled Seven Cities of Cíbola that de Vaca had heard about but never seen.

**Cities of gold:** For months, Father Marcos and his men wandered through the desert but found no cities of gold. They returned to Mexico City empty-handed. In the course of their ordeal, Estéban had been killed by the men of Zuni Pueblo, who said he had "assaulted their women." (For reasons no one understands, a statue of Saint Estéban was raised in the nearby pueblo of Acoma, where it stands even today.)

Despite the failure of Father Marcos' expedition, the Spanish were not discouraged. The deaths, the hardships, the dangers challenged their sense of adventure and manhood, and, when that failed, the promise of great riches spurred them on. "To possess silver and gold the greedy Spaniards would enter Hell itself," said the Franciscan Father Zarate Salmeron of New Mexico. He could not dissuade them from becoming the Don Quixotes of the New World.

**The Knight of El Dorado:** Of all the conquistadors who set forth in search of the Seven Cities of Cíbola and Gran Quivira, none behaved with more grandeur and nobility than Francisco Vazquez de Coronado, the

and so poor he had to borrow from his wife to fund the expedition. His pretension of courtly nobility in the inhospitable wilderness, epitomized by his wearing armor in the burning desert sun, made him the American Don Quixote; he was one of those rare men who perfectly fit his moment in history.

The men of Coronado's army, on the other hand, were the riffraff, cutthroats and adventurers of Mexico City. It was an epic irony. The image of the conquistadors riding forth in resplendent armor of gold, with flags and plumes proudly flying as in a knightly pageant, is largely a myth, created in retrospect. The contemporary description of Coronado's men is not nearly so grand.

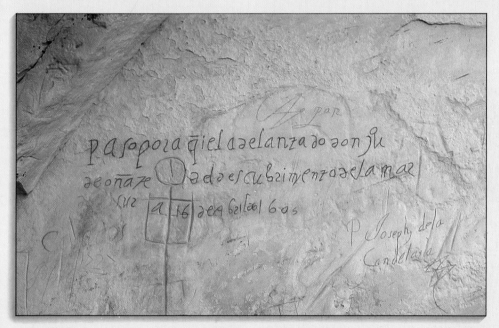

governor of the Kingdom of Nuevo Galicia, the "Knight of El Dorado." With the blessing of the emperor and the viceroy, Coronado marshaled a small army and crossed half a continent. He alone among the conquistadors created a romantic legend.

Coronado was the image of the poor *hidalgo* (gentleman): dignified, handsome

**Preceding pages: San Jose de Gracia church boasts the best Pueblo architecture in New Mexico. Left, map of New Mexico, 1680. Above, the oldest inscription, other than Indian petroglyphs, was made by Don Juan de Oñate on El Morro Rock in 1605.**

Most of Coronado's men wore "American" rather than European clothing, said one observer, and another noted that "many more [wore] buckskin coats than coats of armor." And while the majority were horsemen, few were high-born. In Spain, only a gentleman was permitted – by royal decree – to ride a horse, and any knight found on a mule was subject to punishment. But in Mexico, anyone could ride. In 1554, the viceroy Velasco complained, "Very few [of the horsemen] are *caballeros* [knights] or *hijosdalgos* [sons of gentlemen]. They are *gente comun* [common people]. In these provinces, the *caballero* is a merchant." The nobleman Don Juan

Garray added in total disgust, "Even beggars ride horses in Mexico."

According to Francois Chevalie, writing in *Land and Society in Colonial Mexico*, most of these pretenders to knighthood were "rustics who had left their villages [in Spain] under a cloud or children who had left families incapable of supporting them." Whatever their background, de Oñate summed up the general feeling about Coronado's men by saying that those "who were going on the expedition would do more good than harm by departing, for they were all idle and without means of support."

**Coronado's army:** For his *entrata*, Coronado mustered nearly 400 men, almost all of them

wranglers, herdsmen, *vaqueros* (cowboys) and bridge builders. All of them were well armed with lances, spears, and bows and arrows. Were it not for these Mexican Indians and the American Indians who later joined the troops, it is doubtful that there could have been an expedition at all.

Coronado's army traveled north from Mexico for some 1,500 miles (2,415 km), through the Apache lands of what is now Arizona into present-day New Mexico. On the Rio Grande, Coronado asked directions from a man he called The Turk (because he was dark-skinned) who explained that his people had no gold – it was all farther east in what is now Kansas, where the people were

volunteers. There were officially 235 mounted men and 62 on foot, but unofficially there were many more, ranging from teenagers to old men. It was a motley troop.

Not only were the soldiers not conquistadors, some of them weren't even Spaniards. The company bugler was a German, there were two Italians, five Portuguese, a Frenchman and a Scotsman, Thomas Blake, who had changed his name to Tomas Blaque. And there were hundreds of Indians.

No one knows how many Indians marched with Coronado, but it is known that they were not simply bearers and carriers. Most of them were hired to be scouts, guides, horse

so rich that even their canoes were made of glittering gold.

Coronado headed for Kansas. He crossed the Pecos River into West Texas and went northward through Oklahoma. He finally reached Kansas near the present-day town of Abilene, but found no gold canoes there. Frustrated, he turned back to Mexico after first ordering the execution of "The Turk."

Neither Coronado nor any of the other conquistadors found the gold and jewels they sought. Most of them returned to Mexico City in disappointment, and, after their discouraging reports, few followed them into the desert in search of fabulous treasure. The conquistadors themselves, weary and aging, had come to that time of life when even old soldiers have to settle down and retire. The conquest was over. Even the mighty Cortés lamented, "I am wasted, and exhausted, by all I have done…"

By themselves, the conquistadors could never have conquered the Southwest. In the rugged mountains and deserts, their medieval military tactics and armor were of little use, nor did they have the spirituality needed to comprehend the deep religiousness of the Native Americans. So disillusioned were the latter-day conquistadors that they even forgot their discovery of California. Not until more than two centuries after the voyage of

down their plowshares, took up swords, and forced their rule on the native tribes.

The Franciscan padres in New Mexico and the Jesuits in Arizona and Texas did more than baptize and make Christians of these Indians (from 1591 to 1631, the Jesuits baptized 151,240 Indians). They tried to transform the Indians into Spanish peasants, to "attract the nomadic tribes to a peaceful, sedentary life." As the Jesuit Father Juan Nentuig wrote in 1763, the Christian Indians were "more inclined to work…[and]…to till their lands."

The missions of the Jesuits were more than churches. Into their hands was placed the responsibility for the government and the

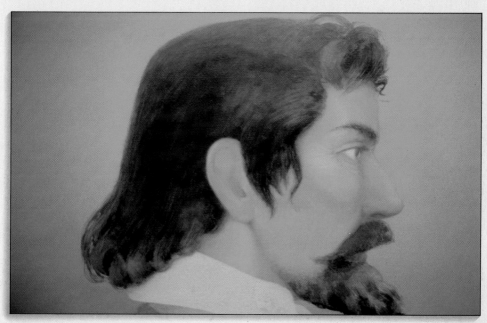

Cabrillo did Juan Bautista Anza set forth to settle California in 1777. In the end, it was left to the Spanish missionaries to accomplish what the conquistadors could not: to conquer the land.

**Onward Christian missionaries:** The missionaries came to conquer not by force of arms but by settlement and their religious fervor. Of course, when the Indians rejected "peaceful" conquest, the new conquistadors set

**Left**, a 19th-century engraving showing the interior of the Acoma Church. **Above**, Diego de Vargas Zapata, governor of New Mexico (1688–97, then again 1703–04).

economy. The missions became the centers of farming, commerce and education.

To the suspicious Spanish officials, the Jesuits seemed to be building an ecclesiastical empire within the Spanish provinces. What was worse, many of the Jesuits – Pfefferkorn, Benz, Kino, Stiger, Nentuig and others – were not even Spaniards.

Nevertheless, when Jesuits asked for permission to raise their own troops, the Spaniards often agreed. (In one case, prisoners were released from the jails of Mexico City and sent out to protect the missions.) In New Mexico, the mission churches of the Franciscans were more like fortresses than places of worship. The walls were sometimes 7 ft (2 meters) thick. After the Pueblo revolt of 1680, when Indians killed 22 Franciscans, the missionaries protected themselves with Indian slaves and mercenaries.

Even so, in 1792, the Franciscan Juan Domingo Arricivita called for the "protection of troops in order to propagate the faith." It was "impossible without them," he said. And from 1744 to 1745, when the Visitador to Sonora, Juan Antonio Balthasar, had visited the San Xavier de Bac mission of the Papago at Tucson, he requested "soldiers to force these Indians to live in the Pueblo," for "just a hint of soldiering is necessary" to make them go to church.

made of two calf skins, and his pillow was a saddle. His eulogist Father Luis Velarde said Kino died as he lived: as one with the Indians. (His bones, are displayed under glass in the center of Magdalena, Mexico.)

With the missionaries came settlers, people escaping their lives in Mexico. They, more than the conquistadors, were the true explorers of the land. Once settled, they began detailed surveys of the countryside. As farmers, they had to know the flow and direction of every stream and river, the precise rise and fall of every canyon and valley, the grass and trees of every pasture and forest. The settlers explored the land the ways soldiers could not; the conquistadors, riding swiftly for

But not all the missionaries were so eager to take up arms against their parishioners. Father Eusébio Francisco Kino, the Jesuit who founded the San Xavier de Bac mission, would have objected to such a policy. He wanted the Indians treated as brothers. One of the most courageous of the missionaries, he was said to have made 40 *entratas* into the deserts and established many missions and the first cattle ranches in Arizona. (There is currently a move to have Kino canonized.)

**The Padre on Horseback:** A true folk hero, Kino was known as the Padre on Horseback. At the age of 70, he died at the mission of Magdalena in Sonora; his death bed was

safety in hostile territory, mapped from horseback. But settlers walked the earth, foot by foot, and explored the territory intimately, surveying every inch of land. The old Spanish land grants were measured, and so were the village deeds.

Many of the settlers were poor farmers and shepherds, Mexicans from Sonora and Chihuahua. Few wealthy noblemen or old conquistadors in Mexico or Spain had any desire or need to endure the desert's severe hardships to establish a new life. As always, the immigrants were poor men and women seeking new opportunities, hoping to escape a life of poverty.

But on the poor lands of the desert, the poor settlers became poorer. The dry farming and small mines they established offered a meager existence. "Not only have the settlers of New Mexico not enjoyed riches, but the scourge of God has been upon them always, and they are the most oppressed and enslaved people in the world," the Franciscan Father Zarate de Salmeron wrote of them in 1626. "As long as they have a good supply of tobacco to smoke, they are very contented and they do not want riches, for it seems as if they have made a vow of poverty."

In the palatial mansions in Mexico City, the Southwest was known as the "Land of the *Barbarosos*" – the barbarians – and that

referred not only to the American Indians but to the "Spanish" settlers as well.

Few of the settlers who came on the *entrata* of Juan de Oñate into New Mexico were born in Spain. Most were Mexicans and *mestizos*, half-Indians, who, like de Oñate himself, were born in Sonora; he was married to an Indian woman said to be a granddaughter of Montezuma. Typical of the expeditions of the Southwest, de Oñate's *entrata* included

**Santa Fe is the heart of Hispanic New Mexico, and annual fiestas relive the days when "the Spanish came to town." <u>Left</u>, Spanish priests. <u>Above</u>, conquistadors.**

as many as 1,000 Mexican Indians, who outnumbered the "Spanish" settlers by 10 to one. Since these Indians lived on similar land across the invisible borders of Mexico, they knew the terrain and survived more easily than the settlers.

**Exodus of the Jews:** During the height of the Spanish Inquisition, many Jews fled to Mexico to escape persecution. Originally settling on ranches along the coast of Mexico, nearer Panuco, the Jewish ranchers, led by Don Juan de Caravajal, were granted land in the Kingdom of Nuevo Leon by Philip II that extended for 600 to 800 miles (966 to 1,288 km) to the Rio Grande and into West Texas. One of the largest cattle ranches in Mexico was established by Jews.

By 1545, more than one quarter of the residents of Mexico City were admitted Jews, and historians estimate that, by the late 16th century, there were more Jews in Mexico than Catholics. Even Archbishop de Vitoria of Mexico had been born of Jewish parents.

Alarmed by the great number of Jews posing as Catholics, the Holy Inquisition came to Mexico to ferret them out. The Governor of Nuevo Leon, de Caravajal, was among the many who died. Once more escaping the Inquisition, many Jews fled north. Often in disguise, they joined many of the *entratas* into the Southwest, where they mixed in with missionaries and poor farmers in settling the desert lands.

So it was that the explorers and settlers of New Mexico and Arizona were Moorish, Spanish, Mexican, Italian, Portuguese, Indian, Jesuit and Jewish – a mixed lot, but one with a decidedly Spanish accent.

**A modern reenactment:** Today, in the foothills of the Sangre de Cristo Mountains (the Mountains of the Blood of Christ) high in northern New Mexico, there nestles the village of Chimayo. Poor farmers, the villagers every year reenact the conquest of the Southwest by their ancestors. They dress as conquistadors and Indians, wearing plastic armor and headdresses of polyester plumes. In the field they perform a ritual battle on horseback, turning the conquest into a pageant.

The fiesta is called *Los Cristianos y Los Indios*, The Christians and The Indians, and it bears a remarkable similarity to a medieval drama known in Spain as *Los Cristianos y Los Moros*, The Christians and The Moors. All that has changed is the name.

Cow boy, going

41

Famous Med War Chief Chiricahua Apaches now raiding.

In the East, they were contemptuously known as "Squaw Men" and "White Indians." No one quite like them had ever lived on the American frontier before, and certainly no one ever will again. The mountain men who came to New Mexico and Arizona in the early 1800s were "a rare moment in history," wrote the Native American author Vine Deloria. These men not only crossed the continent, they crossed over from one culture to another.

The first Anglos to settle in the Southwest came to hunt beaver and to trade, not to conquer. In the mountain wilderness where they made their homes, they most often lived in peace with the Mexicans and Indians who were there before them.

Paradoxically, the mountain men, who went West to escape the civilization of the East, brought it with them in their saddle-bags and wagons. The trade goods they offered the native people forever changed the wilderness and paved the way for the shop-keepers who replaced them. The mountain men made themselves obsolete.

**Colorful figures:** By necessity, mountain men were multicultural and multilingual, and by nature they were invariably colorful figures. The flamboyant Pauline Weaver, a hunter and agent of the Hudson Bay Company, was a two-gun-toting adventurer who is sometimes called the "Founder of Arizona." Christopher "Kit" Carson, one of the fathers of Anglo New Mexico, began his career as a grizzled mountain man, then became a US Army scout and officer, a respected citizen of Taos and a civic leader who personally united the three cultures of the territory by marrying, in turn, a Mexican, an Indian and an Anglo wife.

One of the first mountain men in the Southwest, Baptiste le Land of the Missouri Fur Company came to Santa Fe, New Mexico, in 1804, the same year as the Lewis and Clark expedition. The first Anglo the Mexicans

and Indians had ever seen, Le Land was, in fact, a French Creole who married an Indian woman and settled in Santa Fe. He was followed by James Pursell in 1805 and, in 1809, Zebulon Pike, a mapmaker and government agent who first arrived in Santa Fe as a prisoner on his way to trial in Mexico City. Pike built the first Anglo fort, of cotton-wood trees, on the Conejos branch of the *Rio del Norte*, the Rio Grande River.

The empire of Spain then ruled the land, but just barely. It was sparsely inhabited by

Spaniards, and the royal authorities were nervous about the Anglo traders and wanderers who had entered their domain. Between 1812 and 1821, several merchant adventurers were arrested by Spanish soldiers and locked up in Chihuahua's dungeons.

Not until the Mexican War of Independence in 1822 and the founding of the Mexican Republic in 1824 did the atmosphere change. The Territory of Nuevo Mexico was established, a vast terrain that included New Mexico and Arizona, where the Anglo mountain men and merchants were welcomed in a friendlier manner. In his "Report on Foreigners," in 1825, the Governor of New

**Preceding pages:** *Cowboys Going to Dinner*, Mora County, New Mexico, from around the turn of the century. **Left**, Apache chief Geronimo and, **right**, Kit Carson were two heroes of the West fighting for what they believed.

Mexico, Antonio Narbona, wrote of 20 Anglos arriving in a single month, half of them merchants. By 1827, a similar monthly report listed 36 Anglos, of whom 31 were merchants who "to sell their goods remain for some time in the towns," but have "no intentions of settling themselves."

**Santa Fe Trail:** With the establishment of the old Santa Fe Trail from Missouri, wagon trains and caravans crowded the trails that led West. By 1821, the Missouri frontiersman William Becknell led his "company of men destined to the westward" to New Mexico. Of these traders, George Sibley wrote in 1825: "the first adventurers were hardy, enterprising men who, being tired of

an estimated $15,000 yearly up to $450,000.

The merchant wagons brought a new way of life into the Southwest. Not merely champagne and beer, whiskey and rum, but oranges, lemons, cherries, whale-oil candles, tobacco, Epsom salts, straw hats, silk handkerchiefs, dried fish and hundreds of other items. In their dusty wake, the merchant wagons also brought settlers. They homesteaded, planted crops, established ranches and built towns – all on Mexican and Indian land grants to which they had no title. For generations afterward, the ownership of the land would be under dispute; it still is.

The settlers were soon followed by soldiers. In 1846, President Polk sent General

the dull and profitless pursuits of husbandry, were determined to turn merchants and traders in the true spirit of Western enterprise," for these men believed the "many strange and marvelous stories of inexhaustible wealth" that were told about the West.

Becknell's expedition opened the way West. In Congress, Senator Thomas Benton introduced a bill to maintain a road to New Mexico. Since the distance was much shorter from Missouri than from Mexico City, goods could be sold more cheaply by the Anglo traders than by the Mexican *entratas*. From 1822 to 1844, the value of the merchandise carried on the Santa Fe Trail increased from

Stephen Watts Kearny to the West to conquer New Mexico, but the anticipated war with Mexico became more an occupation than a conquest. In a treaty signed with Mexico in 1848, the United States paid $15 million for New Mexico, Arizona, Utah, Nevada, California and part of Colorado.

After the Mexican War, few federal troops besides General Kearny's small detachment were stationed in New Mexico and Arizona. With so few troops to defend them, the territories were nearly lost to the Confederacy during the Civil War.

The supplying of merchandise and food to the troops became the region's largest and most profitable business. Many an old family fortune was built on government contracts, something of an irony for people who prided themselves on rugged individualism. "Almost the only paying business the white inhabitants of the territory have is supplying the troops," General Edward Ord wrote to President Johnson after the Civil War. "Hostilities are therefore kept up [against the Apache] with a view of supporting the inhabitants…" Even that irony was compounded by the sending of the 10th Cavalry, composed largely of former slaves, to subdue and control the Indians.

Arizona presented a dramatic contrast to New Mexico: the settlers who populated the

into Arizona. From the 1600s on, the Apache, fighting from their mountain strongholds, successfully held back the European invaders. In 1630, Padre Alonzo Benavides called them, "A people fiery and bellicose and very crafty in war." In fact, the Apache were a nomadic people, less interested in conquering places and capturing people than in taking horses and cattle.

By the 1760s, in spite of the efforts of the staunch Jesuit missionaries, the Spaniards had to abandon nearly 50 settlements and 126 ranches throughout Arizona. By 1775, Padre Bartolomo Ximeno reported that there were only 10 horses and 56 cows left in the territory that the Apache had not stolen.

western desert were of a different breed from those in New Mexico. Few people chose to venture into the lands of the Apache, thus, few trading centers, farm towns and ranches were established in Arizona. The main settlements were mining towns, such as Tombstone, Jerome and Prescott, that were to yield billions of dollars in silver and copper ore.

Even in the early centuries of colonization by the Spaniards, few settlers had ventured

**Left**, an 1840 map of the Republic of Mexico. **Above**, painting shows a Comanche raid for booty and captives on an emigrant train using the Santa Fe Trail.

Those Anglos who did settle in Arizona were mostly Southerners, and, although there were few slaves in the area, there was a lively slave trade in Apache children. During the Civil War, Arizona, unlike New Mexico, sided with the slave states. The citizens of Tucson voted to join the Confederacy, and in 1862 the Confederate Congress proclaimed Arizona a Confederate territory.

Despite their former rebel sympathies, the Anglo settlers in Arizona were happy to welcome the US Army after the Civil War had ended. The Indian Wars, fought to open more territory for settlement, were largely conflicts between nomads and settlers, and when faced with Western-style military campaigns, they often chose surrender.

In 1865, the Mescalero headman Victorio told Lieutenant Colonel N.H. Davis, "I and my people want peace. We are tired of war. We are poor and have little to eat and wear. We want to make peace."

Davis replied, "Death to the Apache, and peace and prosperity to this land, is my motto." General Edward Ord added his agreement; the Apache, he declared, were "vermin to be killed when met."

Not everyone among the conquering forces agreed. General George Crook, who led in the capture of Geronimo, said of the Apache, "I wish to say most emphatically that [this]

Billy the Kid (born in Brooklyn) earned his reputation as a gunman. In reality, The Kid worked as a busboy and waiter in a café in the town of Shakespeare; he was no more a cowboy than was Wyatt Earp, Bat Masterson or Doc Holliday, the dentist. Few, if any, cowboys ever fought in the Range Wars.

On the ranches of the Southwest, the cowboy of English-Irish-Scottish-German ancestry inherited the older western traditions of the Mexican and Indian *vaquero*. Southerner and Easterner, Mexican and Native American, Spaniard and Anglo, they all merged into a new and unique figure known as the Westerner. Perhaps more than anything else, it was the earth and sky that

American Indian is the intellectual peer of most, if not all, the various nationalities who have assimilated to our laws…"

During the 1870s, ranching became a new way of life in the west. Huge cattle outfits spread out over the horizons; ranches such as the vast Matador, XIT, King and Lumpkin ran tens of thousands of cattle on hundreds of thousands of acres.

**The Range Wars:** Not many years after the Civil War and the Indian Wars had ended, the Range Wars began. These were battles between sheepmen and cattlemen over grazing lands. One of the most famous was the Lincoln County War, in New Mexico, where

shaped cowboy culture. There was nothing in their experience back East to prepare the Anglos for the awesome vistas.

In the beginning, the cattle ranches resembled those of Sonora and Chihuahua in northern Mexico, built in the adobe styles of the Southwest. And during the old days of Spanish rule, the ranches were feudal fiefdoms with *haciendas* that were entire towns. But later ranches of the Anglos were rough frugal buildings, reflecting the pioneering life of their owners.

In time, with the meeting of divergent cultures under the inhospitable desert sun, a new breed – the buckaroo – was created: he was, as the old saying goes, "Tough as a longhorn cow, and just as dumb."

**What the cowboys and the cowgirls say:** One of the old cowboy yells of the Southwest says it all. The cowboy yell was a way by which a cowhand proclaimed his manhood:

*Whe-ee-o, I'm a bad man! Whoopeee! Raised in the backwoods, suckled by a polar bear, nine rows of jaw teeth, a double coat of hair, steel ribs, wire intestines and a barbed wire tail, and I don't give a dang where I drag it. Whoop-whee-ha!*

Ranch women of those days were not about to be outdone by their men. They thought themselves to be as tough. One proper cowboys of the Southwest were lusty, ribald, raucous men who lived with a gusto that reflected the Victorian appetites of the era. With the passing of the open range and the fencing of the New Mexico and Arizona range, the Anglo ranchers and cowboys were doomed. The turn of the century turned their memories into nostalgia. The last of the old-time cowboys, together with the lawmen and outlaws, joined Buffalo Bill's Wild West Show or Teddy Roosevelt's Rough Riders, largely recruited in New Mexico and Arizona.

When the cattle drives ended and the stagecoach trails faded, the desert silence was shattered by the din of railroads and motorcars that brought thousands of newcomers.

lady described herself like this in 1887:

*My bonnet is a hornet's nest, garnished with wolves' tails and eagle feathers. I can wade the Mississippi without getting wet, out scream a catamount [mountain lion], jump over my own shadow… and cut through the bushes like a pint of whiskey among forty men.*

The modest, laid-back, low-key, taciturn style of the 20th-century cowboy was not that of his 19th-century ancestor. The first

**Left**, early miners and prospectors at Faro game session. **Above**, four outlaws who went on a trail drive to Dodge City, Kansas.

These were the new Anglos from the East, the sick seeking the sun, the land developers and the artists.

As the 19th century ended, artists discovered the Southwest. Ernest Blumenschein and Bert G. Phillips settled in Taos, New Mexico, in 1898. In 1916, Mabel Dodge Luhan moved her New York salon to Taos. A few years later, novelist D.H. Lawrence, a temporary resident, was to proclaim, "There are all kinds of beauty in the world, but for a greatness of beauty I have never experienced anything like New Mexico."

The old-timers were to become a part of the artists' scenery and the writers' stories.

The era between the turn of the century and World War I was an in-between time. The old frontier life was gone – but not quite. The new technological age was as yet a faint outline on the horizon. Gone were the long-horns and the great cattle drives on the Goodnight Trail. Gone were most of the gunslingers and *bandidos*, but by no means all. Gone was the colorful prospector with his burro, pickaxe and pan, though a few aged optimists lingered on. Gone were the covered wagons, to be replaced by railroads, which had their own mythology.

Peculiar to the American West was the dizzying speed with which history unfolded and life changed. A man born in 1820 who came out West in 1840 to be a mountain man and trap the beaver was still essentially a pre-industrial creature. He had a strike-a-lite – flint and tinder to light his pipe; an old muzzle-loader and bowie knife to defend himself against marauding Apaches. His sole transportation in a roadless empty land was his horse and, when that died under him, his two legs. In 1890, aged 70, the same man might be sitting with his biographer at Delmonico's, having traveled to New York by train and gone to the restaurant by the elevated rail after having made his appointment via telephone.

For Indians the change was even more bewildering. Geronimo, born in 1829, had grown up as a technological stone-age man, his first weapons stone-tipped lances and arrows. Shortly before his death in 1909, as a member of the Dutch Reformed Church, he attended a convention of cattlemen in Tucson, Arizona. In his hotel room he found himself confronted by those newfangled symbols of civilization – electric lights and the flush toilet. He did not know how to use them. As nobody had told him how to turn off the lamp at his bedside, he simply put his boot over it. Later, he was photographed at the wheel of an early Ford automobile.

**The old frontier spirit:** Even so, there was still a lot of the frontier atmosphere left.

**Preceding pages:** the first passenger train through the Grand Canyon in 1901. **Left,** officers picnic under saguaro near Fort Thomas, Arizona.

Many of the old gunfighters, those who had not died of "lead-poisoning", were still alive. Pat Garrett, the sheriff who killed Billy the Kid, was himself dry-gulched in 1908 with a bullet in his head, at a time when such goings-on were presumably a thing of the past.

As late as 1911, a classic six-gun shoot-out between two gentlemen who had discovered that they were sharing the favors of the same married lady took place. The battle was fought in Denver's Brown Palace, the "Abode of Luxury and Refinement."

The great gambling saloons of the Southwest closed their doors sometime between 1900 and 1911, outlawed due to an influx of "good women", but in the red-light districts the "soiled doves of the prairie" still did a land-office business. Mexican *bandidos* still strayed across the border to raise havoc on the wrong side of the Rio Grande. And trains were still robbed at gunpoint until the outbreak of World War I.

**The Mexican Revolution:** The Mexican Revolution (1910–23) brought plenty of excitement. It actually started on American soil when, in 1911, Francisco Madero led a few hundred followers across the Rio Grande to start the civil war which would topple the dictator, the "Old Cacique" Porfirio Díaz. A decisive battle was fought at Juarez between the revolutionary army, led by Pancho Villa and Pascual Orozco, and the *Porfiristas* led by Vásquez Gómez. Shouting "*Viva Madero!, Viva la Revolucion!*" the rebels won a brilliant victory, while Americans on the El Paso side across the river had a grandstand view, watching the battle from their roofs and the top of railroad cars.

The Revolution had a way of spilling over onto American soil. In 1912, freshly escaped from jail and fleeing for his life, Villa holed up in a fleabag hotel in El Paso's Chamizal district. Soon he was back in Mexico to lead his famous Division of the North to meet up with Zapata in Mexico City. Sometimes relations between the revolutionaries and the American Government were good, and sometimes bad. At a time when they were bad, in 1916, Villa made his famous raid on Columbus, a sleepy New Mexico frontier town where the only previous excitement in the town's history was a plague of rattlesnakes.

The battle in the streets and houses of Columbus between the *Villistas* and American soldiers and citizens grew into one of the greatest shoot-outs the Southwest had ever experienced. It resulted in the death of 16 American citizens and brought on a punitive expedition of the US cavalry under "Black Jack" Pershing in a fruitless pursuit of the elusive "Centaur of the North."

The time up to the outbreak of World War I and beyond has been described as the "Time of the Gringo." It was a period of racial tension as Anglo newcomers engulfed the Spanish-speaking communities. The Anglos looked down upon the Hispanics.

before Anglo and Hispanic learned to live with each other in friendship. In some mountain villages resentment toward outsiders persists to this day.

Development proceeded slowly. After all, New Mexico's state motto is *Crescit Eundo* – it grows as it goes. Frontier manners remained rough for many years. In the early 1900s it was still necessary to make laws against a man having more than one wife. In Flagstaff, Sandy Donohue, barkeep at the Senate Saloon, greeted President Teddy Roosevelt: "By God, you are a better looking man than your picture, you old son-of-a-bitch." Teddy, the one-time cowboy, took it as the compliment it was.

Racial hatred held up the statehood of both Arizona and New Mexico until 1912.

Lawmakers and preachers alike opposed statehood. One congressman argued: "We don't want any more states until we civilize Kansas!" Protestant parsons thundered against statehood which would bring in its wake "Greaser" legislators who would "put the yoke of Romishness and popery upon the morally and mentally superior man from the North." The Arizona Legislature passed the Alien Labor Law stipulating that 80 percent of all workers in the state had to be American born, a measure directed against the influx of Mexicans and Asians. It was some time

Modern amenities were slow to arrive in the Southwest. Flagstaff got its first telephone in 1900, with 85 subscribers throughout the county. The first steam-powered automobile arrived in 1902. Electricity came in 1904. Teachers were scarce as their salaries were fixed at $75 a month, while room and board cost $40.

**Minerals and miners:** In the mid-19th century, prospectors had searched for gold. They found some, but gold never really became important. Gold's best year was 1915 when New Mexico produced $1,461,000 worth of what the ancient Indians had called the "Dung of the Gods."

Silver came after gold and was found in some abundance throughout the region, though never rivaling the famed silver lodes of Nevada and Colorado. The most silver produced in New Mexico was $1,162,200, in 1910. By 1950 this had dwindled to about $100,000 per year.

Luckily, the Southwest had a wealth of other desirable minerals, and copper soon became king. The industry is still flourishing, though its peak has passed. When American industries began demanding copper, mines and mining towns once again grew up overnight like mushrooms – in New Mexico, 25 copper mines within a decade. Coal also became important, particularly with the ever

conditions for miserable wages, living in shacks for which the company asked outrageous rents. They had to buy their goods at the company store and were little better than slaves. This led to a number of spectacular clashes between management and labor during the early 1900s, culminating in armed battles between the mine workers on one side and the company police, supported by National Guardsmen, on the other. Martial law was declared and a substantial number of deaths resulted. Eventually laws protecting the workers were passed and unions became established.

After copper and coal came potash and a number of more exotic minerals such as

expanding networks of railroads which needed the black silver for their engines.

The coal and copper miners were a very different breed from the independent spirits who had gone after gold. They were mere proletarians, often imported Mexicans, Germans, Irishmen, Greeks, Hungarians and Slavs who were shamelessly exploited by the mining barons, "who made the laws though nobody had ever elected them to public office." Miners worked in miserable

**Left**, man and Metz automobile on the rim of the Grand Canyon, 1914. **Above**, Zuni Indian and his beast of burden.

cobalt, antimony and molybdenum. As one kind of metal gave out to be replaced by another, new communities sprang up and old ones faded to become ghost towns.

"This would be great country if only it had water," a visitor to the Southwest once exclaimed. "So would hell!" was the native son's answer. The early Anglo settlers had come to till the soil. In 1900, in New Mexico alone, 5 million acres (2 million hectares) were under cultivation, and by 1910 the state had 35,000 farms. Lack of rain in the years 1906–12 wiped out many of these farmers. In 1911 the first of the big dams – Roosevelt Dam – was built in Arizona, followed in

1916 by Elephant Butte Dam in New Mexico. Irrigation brought farming back, though the small farmer was replaced by agribusiness.

Some 90 percent of the land in the Southwest is unsuited for cultivation but is good cattle country. Cattle do not grow fat on southwest ranches. They are raised to be sold to cattle feeders in the Midwest and elsewhere. By 1910 there were 40,000 miles (64,374 km) of four-strand barbed wire in Arizona alone. The end of the open range also meant the end of the old-fashioned cowboy. In 1892 a Western writer lamented that "railroads and bobwire spell the demise of that colorful character." After the end of World War I, in 1918, the Southwest was set to become the New West.

Among those affected for the better were the area's oldest inhabitants – Native Americans. In 1919 Indian men who had enlisted in the army to fight the country's enemies became eligible for US citizenship. Oil was discovered on the Navajo reservation, bringing income to the tribe which was wisely invested in education and other projects beneficial to all. In 1922 Pueblo Indians formed the "All Pueblo Council" to fight the so-called Bursum Bill, which was designed to secure the right to Indian land for white squatters. In 1924 American citizenship was conferred upon all Indians born within the borders of the United States.

In 1934 the Indian Reorganization Act gave the right of partial self-government to the tribes. As a result tribal constitutions were framed and tribal presidents and councils democratically elected. It was a mixed blessing. The elected leaders often represented the more assimilated, educated and English-speaking people, while the traditional Indians saw no reason to adopt forms of self-rule patterned after the system of government practiced by whites. They adhered to their old dependence on elders or religious chiefs. This led in some places to a simmering conflict between the "Progressives" and the "Traditionals."

Lagging behind the Anglos in economic gains and the professions, Hispanic Americans of New Mexico concentrated on politics and wound up effectively running the state. One author, Francis Stanley, wrote:

"Politics is a religion above the family. It streams into the nino from his mother's breasts; it is patted into the tortilla, and ladled with the frijole, masticated with every mouthful of chili, washed down with every glass of beer. Sacred, ingrained, ritualistic, mysterious, it is its race, color, creed – POLITICS."

The experiment with Prohibition wrought less havoc in the Southwest than elsewhere. Authorities winked at the citizen imbibing his *vino* and *cerveza* as they themselves indulged. Hard liquor never played the role it did among Anglos, and gangsterism was rarely a factor in this relaxed atmosphere.

Gold and silver mining was a memory and many coal mines were shut down as unproductive, but potash mining started in a big way in 1931. Natural gas became a source of income in the 1920s, and the Southwest enjoyed a number of moderate oil booms. Large copper mines opened in Arizona and New Mexico. In 1936 Hoover Dam was completed. Water, or rather the lack of it, was becoming a problem. Old-timers complained that modern industry, farming, ranching, tourists and the increased population were "pumping the West dry."

In 1942, the Army took over land belonging to a boys' school at Los Alamos. In the words of Erna Ferguson:

"No secret was ever better kept than that of Los Alamos. The schoolboys had it that they were moving out for the Ethiopian Ski Corps or the Scandinavian Camel Artillery. Santa Feans saw lights against the Jemez peaks, but knew nothing."

A town of 8,000 inhabitants was springing up almost overnight in the vicinity of the state capital without anybody being aware of it. On a plateau dotted with hundreds of cave dwellings carved from the soft tufa rock by prehistoric Pueblo Indians, the atomic bomb was built. It was first exploded at the Trinity site, near Alamogordo, New Mexico, in 1945…"A blind girl saw the flash of light, a rancher thought the end of the world had come," but the country at large did not know that a major force in world history had been engendered here. It was a New Mexican officer who "armed" the bomb before it was flown to Japan and dropped on Hiroshima, and it was Paddy Martinez, a Navajo Indian who, in 1950, found the first lump of uranium in the Arizona desert. Thus the Nuclear Age was born in the American Southwest.

**Right, Hopi Indians enjoy the view.**

54

Landlocked and chronically thirsty, the Southwest at the end of World War II was remote but hardly unknown. Railroads, highways and scheduled flights made access easy. Inhabitants shipped out iron, T-bones and grapefruit, and got back dude ranchers and tourists doing the national park circuit. Yet each state seemed in a private trance. Arizona, locus of frantic Air Force activity during the War, returned to its three Cs: cotton, cattle and copper. New Mexico, with its Pueblo and Hispanic agricultural traditions, changed primarily with the seasons. Southwest Nevada, in decline since the silver boom of the 1800s, was a polity of sand and collapsing buildings. And southern Utah deliberately stayed out of the postwar mainstream to preserve the isolation and purity of its Mormon culture. The Southwest in 1945 resembled the Great Basin of Utah and Nevada, whose rivers dead-end in separate valleys instead of reaching out to the sea. Like the Great Basin it encompassed, the Southwest faced inward, fixed on its several selves.

**Great and mighty dams:** The federal role was crucial in developing what all Southwesterners demanded: water. Reclamation was hardly a new idea. The Southwest had already got the Reclamation Act in 1902, the Hoover Dam on the Colorado River in 1935 and countless dams by federal, state and private concerns. But with the war effort over, the Bureau of Reclamation could direct its attention westward in a major way, and it made proposals for every watercourse. Its grandest single monument was Glen Canyon Dam, completed in 1963 and backing water 180 river miles into some of the Colorado's least known and most spectacular canyons; and its most ambitious scheme is the ongoing Central Arizona Project, to hoist water from the Colorado River to Phoenix and Tucson at a cost of more than four times the original estimate of a billion dollars.

Federal stimulation of the Southwestern economy developed a wide spectrum of activities and shifted the balance of power in

the Southwest. Contracts for reclamation projects went primarily to regional companies, allowing them at last to escape eastern domination. Agriculture benefited from reclamation and crop subsidies, but the most benefits went to big agribusiness, often squeezing out the small farmer. Cheap leasing on public lands favored expansive ranching operations and often led to overgrazing. Oil and gas industries were subsidized through depletion allowances. Conservative politicians rallied against federal intrusion

and Washington bureaucrats – and snared all the public works money they could. Such support made commercial development of the Southwest possible, but often at the expense of homegrown independent operators.

Much of the driest and least productive land had been allotted to the military during World War II, and the military kept it. During the 1950s, the salt and alkali basins of Nevada became the site of hundreds of underground nuclear tests, and Hill Air Force Base in Utah became the West's leading missile center. Towns like Yuma and Sierra Vista, in Arizona, are virtual adjuncts to the military, and many of the most empty reaches

**Preceding pages: rush hour in Monument Valley. Left, a thoroughly modern cowboy. Right, the commercialization of Native American culture.**

of the Southwest are off-limits to civilians.

Ironically, much of the land in the hands of the military – scarred by tanks, pounded by artillery, glittering with shrapnel – has remained relatively intact, while the drive for minerals, timber and cheap energy has caused the more lasting devastation. Mining on federal land was encouraged by minimal fees and scant regulation, while timber contracts didn't – and still don't – make that most basic requirement that a new tree be planted for each cut down. In the early 1950s, uranium prospectors gouged roads at random across southern Utah, leaving permanent scars. Uranium was developed more systematically in northwestern New Mexico in the

States could no longer rely on undependable foreign companies for its energy needs and had to develop its own resources to become self-sufficient.

A far-reaching plan, with great potential profits, was conceived for the Colorado Plateau. Cities like Los Angeles and Phoenix badly needed new energy but had to generate it elsewhere because their pollution levels were already intolerable. Coal that abounded in southern Utah and northern Arizona could be burned on the spot, sending fly ash over a sparsely populated area. Power would surge through transmission lines to cities hundreds of miles away. A consortium of 21 utilities, representing seven states, banded together in

1970s, leaving behind carcinogenic mill tailings for the Indian inhabitants.

**"Black gold" – a source of energy:** But it was coal, abundant and often lying near the surface, that became the most coveted resource. In 1957 a Utah company made the first contract with the Navajo Tribal Council for coal on the Navajo Reservation. The major oil companies, sensing that the coal beds of the Colorado Plateau, would become a vital energy source, began acquiring coal companies and turning them into subsidiaries. The future of coal was given a further boost with President Nixon's Project Independence speech in 1973, which argued that the United

1974 and proposed a mesh of strip mines, power plants and transmission lines of unprecedented complexity. Not all of the proposed grid came into being, but major coal-fired power plants went up in Farmington, New Mexico, and Page, Arizona. The Page plant, near Glen Canyon Dam, was linked by a company railroad to a strip mine 70 miles (113 km) east on Black Mesa, a formation sacred to the Hopi.

By the time of the assault on the Colorado Plateau, large-scale development was no longer wholly popular. Many of the Southwest's new residents had fled from industrial devastation elsewhere. In the late

1960s, environmentalists were strong enough to kill a proposal to build two hydroelectric dams in the Grand Canyon.

The fight came to a head over a plan to strip-mine coal on the Kaiparowits Plateau. The idea was to combust it and then scatter ash across southern Utah's national parks. Feelings on both sides ran high. Lawsuits and lobbying delayed the project until California, realizing it had overestimated its need for energy in the first place, pulled out; the Kaiparowits scheme collapsed.

**Retirees and real estate:** While energy battles were being fought on the Colorado Plateau, the warmer lands to the south were filling up with humanity. With the introduction of air-

querque, Phoenix and Tucson drew ambitious young people to the area, balancing the demographics and at the same time inflating the population.

The real estate industry was the prime beneficiary, and development exploded from the cities. Mesquite gave way to mobile home communities, to pseudo-adobe duplex compounds, to townhouse labyrinths around artificial lakes that obliterated the desert. One developer brought the London Bridge to the Colorado River and ran the world's tallest fountain on subsiding groundwater merely to promote his ventures. Easier on the terrain was outright land fraud, wherein development took place on paper and the land, if any,

conditioning during World War II, suddenly no desert was too hot for colonization. Snow-belt retirees settled in vast retirement communities like Sun City, Green Valley and Youngtown, in tracts and trailer parks along the Colorado River from Boulder City, Nevada, to Yuma, Arizona, and even in the small towns of southern New Mexico.

While traditional industries like copper mining and small-scale ranching fell into decline, high-technology industries in Albu-

**Left**, telescopes at Kitt Peak National Observatory, Arizona. **Above**, *Columbia 3* lands at White Sands Missile Range, New Mexico.

was spared. During the 1970s, Phoenix, Albuquerque and El Paso grew by more than 30 percent. By the 1980s, Phoenix was swelling by more than 100,000 people a year and Las Vegas was America's fastest-growing city. The collapse of the savings-and-loan industry, with Arizona's Charles Keating Jr. as one of the main villains, halted much development, although in the mid-1990s the pace has again picked up a bit.

In the 1970s, President Carter put forth a proposal to place MX missiles on a railroad maze running through 4,600 shelters in vast reaches of western Utah and eastern Nevada. Southern Utahns, who formerly would have welcomed the jobs, were less willing to embrace the scheme – especially as many of them had started showing up with cancer attributed to underground nuclear testing in Nevada 20 years back. Local politicians who routinely supported construction and national defense sensed new qualms among their constituents. They stalled for time and then turned against the project after it was attacked by the Mormon Church. The MX racetrack plan collapsed.

**Art and nature:** While recent changes in the Southwestern landscape represent the works of man, what most visitors still come for are the works of nature. The tourist industry is thus torn between the need to accommodate the visitor and the need to preserve those features the visitor comes to see. Efforts on behalf of the Southwestern terrain have been a holding action. What has been protected in parks is well-known enough to be threatened by overvisitation. A few corners are surprisingly intact: relatively unvisited are the area north of the Grand Canyon known as the Arizona Strip, southern New Mexico, and the restful Texas hill country north of Big Bend National Park – which is full of little towns, unmechanized ranches and lava-crowned mesas.

But not all the novelties of man need be avoided, even in the Southwest. The art enclaves of Santa Fe, Taos and Scottsdale, the Flagstaff Summer Festival of the Arts, the Santa Fe Opera, the dense-pack experimental communities of Paola Soleri and the superb buildings of Frank Lloyd Wright scattered through Phoenix – all prove that good weather has not entirely numbed the artistic spirit. Probably the most significant artistic work currently being produced is that of Native Americans, who are reviving and extending such traditions as weaving and ceramics, sculpture and painting, combining traditional motifs with the latest innovations from New York.

Farther reaching if less visible are advances in the sciences. Los Alamos, which continues to hone weaponry in top secret, has branched into such life-oriented pursuits as solar and geothermal energy, cancer research, laser surgery and astrophysics. Kitt Peak National Observatory, west of Tucson, has the world's foremost concentration of advanced telescopes, and has collected much of our stunning news about pulsars, quasars, black holes and storms on the sun. The Very Large Array, a collection of radio telescopes in an empty stretch of western New Mexico, is probing what may be the very edge of the universe and peering backward in time to the Big Bang itself. The White Sands Missile Range, near Alamogordo, New Mexico, has been the site for many NASA (National Aeronautics and Space Administration) experiments and plays alternate host to the Space Shuttle. In Alamogordo itself is the International Space Hall of Fame, whose displays of moon memorabilia and John Glenn's space suit prove that even the cutting edge of science needn't preclude a little kitsch.

Finally, among the works of man, there is Las Vegas. Nevada legalized gambling in 1931, in time to welcome the construction workers for Hoover Dam, and the little Mormon town of Las Vegas enjoyed a fleeting boom as the cement was poured. But Las Vegas only became *Vegas* in 1946 with the opening of the Flamingo, first of the clubs to feature heroically bad architecture and superstar entertainment. Clubs on the Strip reached new summits of commercial flamboyance, while merely gaudy casinos catered to the common man in downtown's Glitter Gulch. However hard to take seriously, Las Vegas has become a major convention center, and is an important Southwestern crossroads of economic and political power. Las Vegas is an object of pilgrimage for connoisseurs of the surreal as well as those with loose change, and if neon signs are an art form, as some folklorists claim, Las Vegas is its Louvre.

Such assaults upon a formerly remote landscape make recent Southwestern history seem a whirlwind of population sprawl and resource development. But new factors could radically alter its course. Nature, for instance, could foreclose on the increasing defiance of heat and drought. Culturally, the deluge of legal and undocumented aliens from Latin America, seeking jobs and political asylum, has encouraged speculation that the Southwest may face a Spanish-speaking separatist movement similar to that of the Quebecois in Canada. Rather than being at risk of losing its regional flavor, the Southwest may be about to witness its flowering.

**Right, it takes a lot of neon to get noticed in Las Vegas these days.**

So diffuse is the Southwestern cultural majority known as the Anglos that it is difficult to say who is included, except that very few actually descend from the Angles, a small German tribe that invaded England in the 5th century. The label was given currency by Spanish-speaking Southwesterners, and it generally includes all white Americans of European descent who do not happen to have Spanish surnames.

The first Anglos to reach the Southwest were explorers, fur trappers and traders who brought long-coveted goods along the Santa Fe Trail and introduced a dominant Anglo cultural strain: commerce. That small breach through the formerly self-enclosed New Spain soon became a flood. The American military presence began with forts and garrisons to protect trade routes from outlaws and raiding Apache, but it was soon engaged in the largely trumped-up war with Mexico that resulted in Arizona and New Mexico being ceded to the United States by treaty in 1848. Before long the Southern Pacific and Santa Fe railroads had opened the Southwest to the American public.

**The great move:** The enterprising Yankees who built the railroads also built the first grand hotels, and the pleasure-seeking self-indulgent Southwesterner of the future was imported. Within decades paved highways, air services and national promotion opened the Southwest to tourism. Respiratory patients discovered the clean dry air, and northerners found an ideal place to resettle. By the 1960s, a national migration had been launched that organized Southwestern retirement into vast planned communities. By the 1970s, resorts had passed through the grand-hotel and dude-ranch phases to emerge as lavish resort complexes with golf and tennis, restaurants, discos and national convention facilities. Mobile home communities and trailer parks staked out mile after mile, motorcycles and dune buggies roared across the open desert, and motorboats plied

**Preceding pages: hitting the trail in Bryce Canyon; cowgirls at Santa Fe. Left, a typical Anglo face – young girl on ranchland in Artesia, New Mexico, with her roping horse.**

the reservoirs. Organized leisure became the Southwest's most visible industry.

Traditional agriculture and manufacturing, meanwhile, went into relative decline. Mining, subject to falling demand, foreign competition, shrinking deposits and labor disputes, suffered the most, and many smelters and open-pit mines closed. Ranches, faced with expensive mechanization, have further consolidated into large spreads. Cattle are fattened more in feedlots than on the open range, and cowboys work machines or they don't work. Water-intensive surplus crops like cotton no longer make economic sense, and municipalities are clamoring for water. Ranches, citrus groves and cotton fields increasingly have been bought out by agribusiness or have given way to the walled-in multiplex developments now radiating from most Southwestern cities.

The industrial slack has been taken up by the leisure boom, and by aerospace and electronics. Arizona has a major stake in high-tech industries, which together employ a considerable proportion of the manufacturing work-force. In addition, defense-oriented research into microbiology and particle physics are major employers at Los Alamos and Sandia Laboratories in New Mexico. What has become known as the silicon desert has resulted in the upwardly mobile career-oriented subculture represented by singles bars and club-like apartment complexes, all epitomized by "lifestyle" magazines.

Such a fast-moving, fun-centered culture has had a drastic impact on stable minorities. Native Americans have the deepest ties to the region, yet more than half have left their jobless homelands for cities. Even reservation communities are divided between those favoring development and those trying to shore up traditional ways. Reservation boundaries, originally drawn by Anglos around presumably worthless land, are now invaded by Anglo corporations mining newly-discovered coal, oil and uranium – often in areas traditional Indians hold to be sacred, and under contracts that confer few benefits on members of the tribes. Strange cultural alliances have developed: Kitt Peak, sacred to the Tohono O'odham god I'itoy, was available to astronomers only after assurances that telescope-wielding Anglos were practicing their own form of sky-worship; Navajo, worried that the new generation is learning only English, are planning to teach Navajo by computer. Less appropriately, ceremonial dances are mobbed by Anglo tourists who treat them as camera fodder, and a band of 300 Prescott businessmen calling themselves the Smokis dress up annually as Hopi, present the sacred snake dance as a tourist pageant, and shrug off protests by Hopi elders. Most humiliated is the Tohono O'odham Nation in southern Arizona, which has been rendered nearly uninhabitable by hundreds of sonic booms a

the three-martini lunch. Anglo-Hispanic relations are more peaceful in Arizona, where illegal immigration from Mexico is pronounced – and where a promising example is being set by south Phoenix, in which Anglos, Hispanics and African-Americans in nearly equal numbers live in relative harmony.

The trend toward consumerism and resource exploitation finds its strongest opposition within the Anglo community itself. Mormons, powerful in Arizona as well as Utah, have held out for conservative, family-oriented values, though even they have had to strike compromises that allow them, for instance, to own or manage gambling casinos, though not to deal cards or gamble

day from military aircraft that perform war games at low levels, ignoring complaints.

Problems experienced by Hispanics are less severe as a result of a partly shared culture, differences that are largely linguistic, and bilingual education. Tensions run deepest in New Mexico, where 25 percent of the population have Spanish surnames, and resentment dates from the transfer of the Southwest from Mexican to American control, when many Hispanics were cheated out of their Spanish and Mexican land grants. Hispanics complain of Anglo bigotry, while Anglos allege political corruption in which contracts and appointments are made over

themselves. Environmentalism, which grows increasingly passionate as the landscape disappears, is a primarily Anglo movement that runs counter to Anglo materialism. Curiously, environmentalists look to traditional Indians, particularly the Hopi and Navajo elders, as philosophical allies, and often join tribal councils in suing outside corporations.

Even as it is fought from without and within, the Anglo assault of resource extraction and organized leisure seems to devastate everything in its path. The landscape has been wasted by strip mines, deforestation, overgrazing, fly ash, transportation grids, sprawl, and above all by the redistribution of water. Water has been impounded behind dams, sluiced through canals, hauled out of aquifers and tunneled from basin to basin until rivers as fierce as the mighty Colorado have been turned into careless plumbing. Fast travel, franchise marketing and the mania to sell are leveling cultural differences just as radically.

**Southwestern retirees:** The phrase "retired to the Southwest" invariably conjures up images of the swimming pool and deck chairs, the golf and hot sun of a Snow-Belter's afterlife. The reality, while including those items, is fortunately far livelier and far more reflective of the American spectrum.

The terrain itself does not permit uniformity. Much of the Southwest is higher in elevation than outsiders realize and suffers classic northern winters. A few individuals settle in such mountainous small towns as St George, in Utah and Flagstaff, in Arizona, knowing that they will enjoy temperate summers while their contemporaries are holed up with their air-conditioning. A few more will strike some compromise like Santa Fe and Taos, in New Mexico, or Sedona and Prescott, in Arizona, where the summers are slightly too warm and the winters just overchilled. But most of the incoming retirees have spent previous Januaries numb to their very bones, and so they go to the opposite extreme, demanding perfect winters and the summer discomfort be damned. Given the sunward tilt of the Southwest – high in the north and falling as the Rio Grande and Colorado River Basins drain southward – retirement country thickens in southern New Mexico and reaches peak density in the Sonoran Desert of central and southern Arizona, where the winters are celestial.

Most responsible for the popular image of Southwestern retirement is Sun City, west of Phoenix, invented by Del Webb Corporation in 1960 and the granddaddy of American planned retirement communities. Some 46,000 people now inhabit this walled-in labyrinth of curving streets, single-story dwellings, golf courses, artificial lakes, recreational centers, churches, medical centers and subdued commercial areas. To own a

home you must be at least 50 years old. Residents gather in travel clubs, bicycle clubs, alumni clubs, even a club for retired union members, and a giant Sundome hosts a symphony of Sun Citians plus visiting celebrities. So calm and safe is the environment that circulation is largely by bicycle and golf cart. With a long waiting list for potential residents, Sun City has spawned such kinsmen as Sun City West, Green Valley, and the euphemistically named Youngtown. Arizona's hyper-planned communities offer a bewildering range of activities, yet on streets where nearly identical houses are tinted complementary pastels, and graveled yards are sprayed minutely divergent shades of green,

one can't help feeling that individuality is being held onto only lightly.

Uniformity hardly threatens those with money. Aging jet-setters have discovered the charming adobes of Santa Fe, where they can dabble in the arts, entertain and unwind from trips to Europe. Less sophisticated is Carefree, in the Sonoran Desert north of Scottsdale, where architecturally flamboyant homes pose between giant granite boulders. Zoning defends the surrounding cacti, green fees are a major investment, and addresses include East Street, Landuid Lane, and Ho Street – named to cross with Hum Street, where candle shops flourish.

**Left**, a farmer's wife offers a handful of fresh squash, the fruits of her labor at Lovina farm, New Mexico. **Right**, even a working cowboy gets to sit on the fence occasionally.

**Coffee and cocktails:** Far more numerous are the mobile-home communities found outside El Paso and Albuquerque, along the Colorado River from Boulder City, Nevada, to Yuma, Arizona, and in diminishing perspectives from Tempe through Mesa to Apache Junction, east of Phoenix. Owing to population density, social life is intense, with evenings of bingo and cards, community meals and dances, and the floating coffee klatsch that slides into a cocktail party as the day matures. Forays outside the community are often by recreational vehicle: dune buggies for the hills, motorboats on the reservoir. To give each residence a personal stamp, care is lavished on gardening and

decor, but the turnover is far greater than in communities like Sun City or Carefree. Strangers overcome the sense of impermanence by immediate exchanges of life stories and watch over each others' comings and goings.

Most evanescent and fascinating of all retirement groups are those who converge on the Southwest each winter in campers, trailers, even trucks with homemade cabins, to improvise life wherever they pull up. Some retain roots where they spend the summer, but many are too nomadic even for the tax collector. They range throughout southern New Mexico and the Sonoran Desert but can be found in greatest concentration at

Quartzsite, a two-café desert crossroads in Arizona, near the California border. During the winter Quartzsite swells from a few hundred residents to tens of thousands of Snow-Belt refugees. A few hook up to utilities in compounds, but most just stake out a spot in the surrounding hard sand.

The town's one thoroughfare is lined with acres of open space waiting for their winter-long flea market. Up go the tables of glassware, antiques, tools, old bottles and campaign buttons collected the previous summer, or jewelry, ceramics, leatherwork, wood carvings, and clothing the retirees have made themselves. The season climaxes with February's Powwow – a "rock festival" that features minerals raw and tumbled, gems rough and set. The event draws more than a million visitors annually.

If the Southwest's more settled retirement meccas tend toward conformity, here the opposite trait is dominant. Individuality is flaunted, with the men often bearded and creaking with leather, the women resplendent in homemade clothing, and both genders flashing with silver, feathers and turquoise. For all their independence, the Quartzsite transients have banded together, raised a $200,000 civic center and a medical center, held dances and dinners open to the public, and, without a single local policeman, maintained order through sheer mutual respect.

**Art real and romantic:** Almost the first Anglo-European artists to depict the land and people of the American Southwest were the expeditionary artists. But the earliest images of the Southwest are found in *The Conquest of America,* a pictorial fantasy of the land and inhabitants of New Mexico painted around 1545 by Jan Mostaert, a Dutch painter. Based on reports of the Coronado expedition to Zuni Pueblo, this painting includes images of mountains, hills, forests, animals and naked aboriginals.

John Mix Stanley, the official recorder of the W.H. Emory Survey Expedition of 1846-1847, was among the earliest painters to actually see the area. Stanley's 1855 painting, *Chain of Spires Along the Hila River*, is one of the first heroic landscapes of Arizona.

During the next three decades, many of America's most distinguished artists travelled to the Southwest. In 1872, Thomas Moran, after completing his monumental series of watercolors of the Yellowstone, visited the Grand Canyon and painted a wide range of watercolor sketches which served as preliminary studies for a series of heroic landscapes. *The Chasm of the Colorado* was purchased by the United States Congress (for $10,000) for display in the center of the lobby. Throughout the rest of his life, Moran often returned to paint the geological wonders in the landscapes of the Southwest.

By the last quarter of the 19th century, only the Apache offered even a limited resistance to the American reservation system, and artists began chronicling what they perceived as the last days of a defeated race. The white man took their lands and devastated their culture, then white artists depicted a noble, primitive world destined for extinction. They wanted to record for posterity a world they believed they were among the last to witness.

During the early years of the 20th century, Frederic Remington and Charles M. Russell won world renown as master painters and sculptors of the romantic West. Remington's work extols the beauty of the land, dramatizes the heroic lives of the first white settlers and soldiers, and glorifies the superhero of the West, the American cowboy. The work of Remington and Russell became the primary model for narrative paintings of the West, their choice of subject and style setting the standards for traditional Western art.

In the course of the 20th century, the artist colonies of Taos and Santa Fe have become a major feature of the Southwest, attracting both conservative and avant-garde artists. In 1898, Bert Phillips' decision to establish permanent residence in Taos marked its beginning as an artists' colony. In 1915, Taos painters founded the famous Taos Society of Artists. Although the primary function of the organization was to encourage excellence in the arts and to provide marketing and exhibition opportunities for its members, by the time the society dissolved in 1927, the members had achieved critical and financial success and Taos had become the established art center it is today.

The artists' colony in Santa Fe developed later than in Taos and followed a different direction. Santa Fe was a more cosmopolitan area and the keystone of the colony was the Museum of New Mexico, which opened in 1917 and offered visitors and newcomers community studio facilities, exhibition space and financial assistance. The arrival of Robert Henri in the summer of 1914 marked the beginning of a new direction for art in the community. His insistence that art must be a record of life, focusing on the daily doings of average people, set the focus of the realist vision in America. Henri spent three summers in Santa Fe, painted an outstanding series of portraits of Indian people and encouraged many of his friends, disciples and students to travel to the Southwest to experience it for themselves.

**Old arts die hard:** Although the new realist and abstract art is gaining acceptance in the Southwest, representational narrative paintings are favored by most dealers and collectors – paintings that illustrate incidents in history, traditional ranch life, the heroic feats of the rodeo and vignettes of an Indian world untouched by time. Traditional sculpture is characterized by a similar fusion of idealism and realism, a romantic subject accurately depicted, particularly in the costumes, weapons and artifacts. The Southwest is the center of traditional art that confirms basic American values and celebrates heroes of the West – past and present.

Left, a hard-working water tender of Avalon Dam near Carlsbad, New Mexico. Right, a potash miner near Carlsbad.

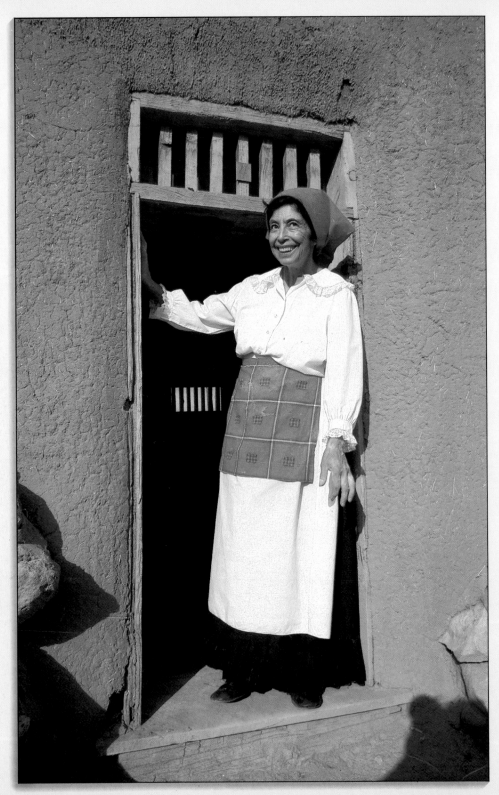

In 1598 Governor Don Juan de Oñate led 130 families and 270 single men, the first colonists, from Mexico to settle just north of present-day Santa Fe. The Pueblo Indian world which existed along the Rio Grande was forever linked from that time to the destiny of the new colonists.

For over a century the Hispanic villages, surrounded by towering green and enchanting mountains, clung to the Rio Grande. To the first Hispanic colonists making their living from the fields and their flocks, Mexico and its urban centers were far away. The settlers were Hispanos and Mexicanos who had come in search of a new life, the Catholic friars had come for souls to convert . El Paso was the resting point, the link between Old Mexico and New Mexico, as it and Júarez are today. Heading north from El Paso through the stretch of desert called *La Jornada del Muerto* (The Journey of Death), the colonists were rewarded with the high plateaus and mountains of the *Sangre de Cristo* (Blood of Christ), a land which reminded some of southern Spain and others of Mexico.

From these first villages the settlers began to extend their influence. Groups of families petitioned the Spanish authorities in Mexico for land grants, and communities spread along the river and into the mountains. When Mexico broke from Spain in 1821 the land grant system continued; Anglo-Americans coming to the Southwest found a communal system it did not entirely understand.

The land grants system played a crucial part in the formation of the culture. The original grants provided space for homes, fields, irrigation water, firewood and the grazing of animals, and communal land helped shape the character of the Hispanos. But in 1846 the Anglo-Americans brought a new system of land ownership, and many land grants were lost or greatly diminished. Those that still remain struggle for survival, and as the Hispanic people move away from their villages into the larger urban centers, a cultural transformation is underway. For

Hispanic culture in the Southwest today, the dominant theme is rapid transformation brought about by assimilation into mainstream Anglo culture.

For centuries the neighbors of the Hispanos of the Southwest were the Native American Pueblo. A sharing of the cultures continued until 1680, when the Pueblo Indians of New Mexico, enraged because Hispanic colonists got preferential treatment and Catholic friars insisted they give up their native religion, took up arms and drove the Hispanos out of New Mexico in a bloody revolution. But in 1692 the Spanish returned, led by Don Diego Vargas. They reconquered Santa Fe and re-established Spanish rule. Thereafter the cultures survived side by side, not always in harmony, but certainly historically linked.

**Earth, water and sky:** Three elements seem to characterize individuals and communities in the Southwest: earth, water and sky. The Hispanos discovered that Pueblo Indians had a sacred partnership with the earth. They understood the earth and her creatures nurtured the community, and that the relationship was fragile and needed tending. In Spanish the earth is *la tierra*, and the land which belongs to the community of the land grant or village is to be guarded for the well-being of all. Hispanics love their village; their sense of place is strong. They are honorbound and loyal to family and community, and this long history of attachment to the lands of the village evolved into a close relationship with *la sagrada tierra*, the sacred earth. Like the Pueblo Indians before them, the Hispanos learned to live in close harmony with their native land. Now that the Hispanic population is primarily an urban population, the attachment takes new forms. A garden, a few trees, a flower patch or just the geraniums in an old coffee tin express this love for the land.

Two rivers dominate the Hispanic Southwest. The Colorado cuts down from Colorado to form the Grand Canyon in Arizona and empties into the Gulf of Baja California. The Rio Grande originates in southern Colorado and flows through New Mexico on its way to the Gulf of Mexico. Historically, the Hispanic population clung to the life-giving

**Left**, a Hispanic woman takes a break at El Rancho de las Golondrinas, an 18th-century Spanish working ranch.

Rio Grande. The river is not only an important source of water, it is a corridor of Hispanic culture which strides the border between Mexico and the United States. The Rio Grande is to Southwestern Hispanics what the Mississippi is to the Midwesterner.

The third element in the fragile desert completes the picture: the sky delivers the light and determines the tone, the color, the mood. The sky is clear, the air is crisp and the colors sharp. Sunrise and sunset are definite times, and the cloud formations of summer are unrivaled in beauty.

Hispanics have lent their unique character and industry to the land. They gave rise to the first mining industry in the Southwest. They were the original horsemen, the *vaqueros* who introduced the lore and trappings of the cowboy. They learned from the Pueblo Indians how to build humble mansions of *adobe*, the sun-dried mud bricks, and how to use the system of *acequia* to water their fields.

Spanish is spoken all over the Southwest, and the place names attest to centuries of Hispanic influence. From San Francisco to San Antonio, the corridor of the border region bears a real Hispanic stamp. Santa Fe, Española, Albuquerque, Belen, Socorro, Las Cruces, El Paso, they all sit along the Rio Grande, all were Hispanic settlements.

Hispanic culture was nurtured by Catholic faith, family and community ceremonies, oral storytelling and other folk arts. The Spanish language is still at the core of the culture, but as more activities take place in an English-speaking world, the loss of the language is inevitable. However, ethnic consciousness and pride are rallying to make the language more available in schools and the marketplace.

Family and home are at the center of the value system, as is strong identification with family name. Family relationships are extended by the *compadrazco* network. *Compadres* and *comadres,* godfathers and godmothers, extend the family ties. Godparents are selected for baptisms, confirmation in the Catholic Church, and weddings. This cultural tradition helps to extend the nuclear family into the larger community. A New Mexican family may have *compadres* as far away as California, Texas or the Midwest, and they are all included in the family. This vast network of communication also helps keep the cultural ways alive.

Likewise, the migrations of Mexican northward into the United States reinforce the culture. As the workers move north, so does their music, life-style, social needs and language. There are millions of Hispanics in the United States, with a considerable proportion living along the border.

**Chicano pride:** Of all the border states, the Hispano has been most actively involved in the development of the Southwest. The contemporary social and political movement began in the 1960s with the Chicano Movement. Like the Black Civil Rights movement, it demanded equality in schooling and health care and acceptable working and living conditions for Mexican-Americans. The

movement was a resurgence of ethnic pride, and the word *Chicano* reflected that pride.

To find their roots, Mexican-American leaders and artists returned to the mother country, Mexico. By asserting their heritage, they reinforced their pride. Political leaders, folk heroes, the role of Chicanos in mining, ranching and the railroad industry revealed an active community. Folk arts, oral storytelling, religious music and the presentation of morality plays during the Christmas season all display a creative imagination which has been kept alive and well by the elders.

The Southwest today is not so much a melting pot as a sharing pot. The various cultural groups try to give and take, share and learn to grow with each other. For Christmas, native people and world travelers attend the festive lighting of the *luminarias*, the lights which illuminate churches and homes. These candles, burning in brown bags, have become a staple item for Christmas, as have the foods. Everyone eats *posole*, *chili*, *carne adovada*, *natillas*, *biscochitos* and *enpanaditas* – all traditional Christmas foods. The rest of the year, beans, *chili*, *enchiladas*, *burritos* and *tacos* are the fare for those who like Mexican food. For Chicanos, the kitchen is still the heart of the house.

The Chicano Movement inspired a renaissance of artistic expression. Art groups sprang

up in every community. A resurgence of ethnic pride and creativity carried the Chicano into new fields: cinema, mural artworks and innovations in music.

**An expression of tradition:** Traditional art and ritual are at the root of this renaissance. Picture, for instance, a solemn procession winding its way down the *arroyo*, meandering like a long, colorful ribbon through fields and chaparral, finally coming to a halt on top

**Left**, chili harvest in New Mexico – a variety of these devilishly hot peppers are used in traditional Southwestern cooking. **Above**, Mexican-style dress can also be found north of the border.

of a hill crowned by an ancient adobe chapel. There is a ringing of bells, the sound of fiddles, of voices singing. At the head of the procession stands a man holding aloft a gilded cross, by his side the village priest. Behind them four men carry a wooden image representing San Isidro, patron saint of all who till the soil, with his yoke and oxen, his plow and his helper, a diminutive angel – a fine example of traditional wood carving. Behind them follow the worshippers – men in old costumes, devout women in black shawls beneath black umbrellas shading them from the bright the sun, children, tourists.

The procession blesses the fields in spring and gives thanks for a plentiful harvest in the fall. It takes place at El Rancho De Las Golondrinas, a working 18th-century Spanish ranch and living museum. The procession heralds a two-day fiesta of music and dance and a gathering of Hispanic craftsmen – *santeros* (carvers of holy images), painters of religious *retablos*, smiths handcrafting beautiful objects, women weaving colorful Chimayo blankets, basket makers, women embroidering or ladling out devilishly hot chilli dishes. All this is set against ancient chapels and buildings which underscore the historical roots of today's traditional artists and *artesanos*.

Traditional Hispanic art was, and is, homemade, rustic and original, fashioned by simple farmers who, by necessity, became artists. This art was created with little outside influence, because for centuries the Southwest was all but cut off from the rest of the world. The populous cities of Mexico were more than a thousand inhospitable desert miles away. Maybe two or three times a year a mule train, or a caravan of *carretas*, clumsy, lumbering oxcarts, prone to breakdowns and agonizingly slow, made their way to Santa Fe. And when the Apache were on the warpath no caravans arrived at all. From the 1820s onward, Yankee goods arrived via the long and perilous Santa Fe Trail, but until the railway, the country remained isolated. Artworks that might have influenced local craftsmen were rarely seen.

Hispanic artists were thrown upon their own resources, making do with the materials their environment offered. Even the homes of the *ricos*, the *gente fina* (fine folks, or well-to-do), were simple with only essential furnishings. Finery belonged to the rich.

The main piece of furniture in the Hispanic house was the *trastero*, or cupboard, often richly carved and painted. Chests, in which a family's possessions were kept, also served as tables or benches. Fancy chests and boxes had elaborate hand-forged locks and were richly decorated with carved lions and scalloped wheels, less often with designs of Moorish origin. Chairs were sturdy, rough-hewn and thick-legged. Hanging in the corners of rooms were ornate painted *nichos*, to hold the images of saints and other religious objects. Lithographs of saints or biblical figures were displayed in punched tin frames. There were also usually a number of *retablos*, pictures of saints painted on wooden boards. Many churches held naive paintings on tin, showing the person who ordered them on his or her knees, giving thanks to some saint for having cured them of an illness. Other such *retablos* might show a fire or fall from a horse which someone had survived, thanks to the intercession of a patron saint.

**Santos – religious art:** *Santeros* were the men who carved *santos* – figures of the Savior, the Virgin, saints and angels. The images were not anatomically correct, they were works of faith rather than art. Angels were short-legged; saints were elongated, narrow-waisted and big-footed. Anglos, used to the realistic, formal art of white America, first said *santos* were "fearful artistic abominations." Today, these abominations are highly prized works of art eagerly sought by museums and serious collectors who value them for their peculiar charm. One also often encounters tragic figures of the suffering Christ, hollow-cheeked and emaciated, the body chalk-white, hair and beard coal-black, the bright blood trickling from many wounds.

Death and suffering have traditionally played a large part in Hispanic art, possibly as a reminder of centuries of oppression of Spanish Christians by the Moors. They are uppermost in the mind of the mysterious sect called *Penitentes* who will scourge themselves until the blood flows and whose prayer is, "Lord, give us a good death." This preoccupation with the inevitability of dying, with damnation and salvation, shows itself in the most impressive of Southwestern sculpture, the large death cart with its skeleton which admonishes the viewer, "As I am now, so you will be. Repent!" Typical also are statues of *La Conquista*, patroness of Santa Fe;

of *Nuestra Senora de Guadalupe*, the Indian Virgin; and of the Holy Trinity. More ambitious sculptures are known as *bultos*.

Material used for *santos* is usually cottonwood and plaster made from locally found gypsum. Colors came out of the native earth – the red and orange from pulverized iron ocher; white and yellow from the abundant clay; black from finely ground charcoal; green from boiled herbs. Blue had to be imported and was not much used before the 1850s. *Santos* are an integral part of every household, particularly patron saints after whom family members have been named.

Women excel in embroidering coverlets – *colchas* – using designs of humans, birds and flowers, usually on a white background. Sheep had been brought to New Mexico by the earliest Spanish settlers and provided cheap and superabundant wool. Women wove, and still weave, their richly colored thick blankets described as "made in the pattern of a maze of concentric diamonds." Chimayo and Truchas weavers also create strikingly modern blankets, woolen carrying bags and pillowcases or miniature rugs.

**Silver and clay:** Silversmithing is done by the *platero* who sometimes still fashions his wares with the help of a homemade mud oven, charcoal, bellows of goatskin and a blow pipe. Often also doubling as blacksmith, the *platero* melted down silver pesos to make crosses, necklaces of hollow beads, rosaries, bracelets, earrings, tobacco and powder flasks, silver buttons, head stalls for horses and spurs for the rider. It was the Spanish *plateros* who taught the craft to Navajo Indians in the 1850s.

Pottery was simple, made for everyday use, though nowadays some ceramicists make charmingly painted and fired clay figures of Mary, Joseph and the Holy Child in his manger, the three wise kings and praying shepherds, all of them typical Hispanic farmers surrounded by their animals – burros and lambs, oxen and goats. These things may be admired and bought in museums and antique shops throughout the Southwest, particularly in Taos and Santa Fe. In spite of a flood of plastic saints made in Taiwan, the ancient crafts are still practiced.

**Right**, woman in Truchas, a village in northern New Mexico, where the Hispanic way of life is still in evidence.

Whether they are called "American Indians" or "Native Americans" seems to matter less to most individuals than their tribal identity. Native American people tend to think of themselves first as members of a particular tribe, and many tribes further differentiate according to specific locales. Even tribal names such as Navajo, Ute or Pueblo are mere labels attached to the tribes by Europeans who were unable to pronounce, or did not bother to discover, the name each tribe has to identify itself.

The myth that all "Indians" are alike still persists, but nowhere is this falsehood easier to disprove than in the Southwest. For here, often within a few miles, are Native American communities whose cultural and linguistic differences are as pronounced as those between England and Turkey.

**Climate and land:** Whatever the tribe, the determining factors in the life-patterns that were followed, and still practiced, have always been the weather and the terrain. The Native-American people of the Southwest, no matter what their linguistic or philosophical differences, have always seen themselves in relation to the landscape around them. Survival, until very recently, has always depended upon powers of adaptation, not change, and upon intimate knowledge of weather patterns, clouds, animals and plants.

In places where annual rainfall and drainage patterns allowed farming, and where nearby hills and mountains offered small game or deer, groups like the Pueblo people of New Mexico and the Hopi of northern Arizona established permanent villages with massive stone-and-mortar walls to ward off the rigors of winter. The Pima and Tohono O'odham of southern Arizona settled in villages near desert springs since water was of primary concern in their locale. Their villages, while permanent, did not require elaborate masonry walls but, rather, cool, airy thatching woven from local cane to provide protection from the sun and to allow the wind to circulate throughout. Although vast cultural and linguistic differences existed between them, these communities, which

farmed and supplemented crops with hunting and gathering, shared similar concerns with clouds and rainfall. In religious ceremonies, the focus was always, and continues to be, on adequate rain throughout the year. Prayers for rain and careful surveillance of the sky are activities understood by all cultures engaged in farming without benefit of modern technology.

Because the terrain and climate of the Southwest are so unpredictable and the consequences of long droughts irreparable, all Native American tribes of the Southwest have survived here, as one Hopi elder put it, "By prayer... we live by our prayers." Thus, the figure of the Rainbow Woman arching over the Great Seal of the Navajo Tribe (displayed prominently on tribal motor-pool vehicles) symbolizes, literally, the sustenance that the Rainbow Woman is believed to provide the Navajo people.

**Creation or migration?:** All tribes in the Southwest have religious beliefs connecting their creation and the creation of the Universe with a higher force or being. Each tribe has its own particular story of Creation, and anthropological theories about origins in Asia or the South Seas are firmly rejected by many Native American people.

Regardless of how the Native Americans came to the Southwest, when the Spanish arrived in 1540, Native American people had already been living there for some 10,000 years. It is within this immense span of time that the tribes of the Southwest have come to understand their intimate relationship with Earth, the Mother Creator for many Pueblo tribes. Mountains, hills, streams and springs are sacred.

It is difficult to gauge the impact of the arrival of the Spaniards and later European settlers upon the tribal cultures of the Southwest. The difficulty lies in the fact that any attempt to evaluate or compare the "before" of Native American cultures with the "after" is impossible. Furthermore, implicit in such an assessment are Western assumptions about "change" or "loss of cultural purity," which are appropriate only when applied to Western cultures. Western views of life and culture tend to place an inordinate emphasis on

**Left**, handsome Navajo elder and teacher.

material evidence, while the Native American cultures of the Southwest tend to assert the spiritual dimension. No outsider, no matter how "expert," can truly comprehend what lies at the heart of the Navajo or Pueblo or Apache cultures.

What is visible is evidence that deep within these Native American cultures is the profound philosophical belief in coexistence with all living things, including human beings of other races and cultures. The Native American cultures of the Southwest have continually demonstrated their belief in and respect for many alternative ways and beliefs. This adaptability and intellectual breadth enabled these cultures to survive and even thrive in the harsh Southwestern climate. Within the world view of these Southwestern Indian cultures, the fact that a medicine man has a color television in his house does not necessarily mean that he has rejected ancient beliefs and traditions; what it means is that his curiosity and belief in knowledge about all humanity have prompted him to include within his world this peculiar artifact of high-tech culture. His view is that what he might see, or learn by seeing, can strengthen his traditional healing powers.

While many of the sacred dances and ceremonies are closed to outside visitors (as a result of 150 years of onlookers often displaying boorish behavior), a great many are performed for the renewal of all human beings and all the world, and these ceremonies do include outside visitors. In fact, the Zuni Pueblo people of western New Mexico believe that, if they were to bar outsiders from their impressive Winter Solstice Shalako Ceremony, the ritual would have no effect and the world would not be renewed. So the giant carved wooden masks of Shalako Dancers who appear at sundown and cross the Zuni river are witnessed every year by many hundreds of people.

**No-nonsense patriotism:** At the same time, it is important to remember that nearly all Native American people, no matter which tribe they come from, are intensely conscious of being Americans, of being not only the original Americans but Americans who have fought and died for this land in every major war. The overwhelming richness and intensity of tribal identity may occasionally obscure the plain patriotism, also a key ingredient in the identity of a White Mountain

Apache or an Isleta Pueblo. The "trusteeship" of the US Government over tribal lands is not a Native American scheme. The Founding Fathers conferred this unique (and, as some Indians see it, paternalistic) legal status upon Indian Tribes in the Commerce Clause of the US Constitution.

The unusual legal status of communities located on federal Indian reservations often brings strange or interesting results. For example, in Arizona, the New Pascua Tribe of Yaqui Indians can conduct million-dollar bingo games 10 miles (16 km) west of Tucson because Arizona state laws limiting the size of bingo jackpots do not apply to the Pascua Yaqui Reservation, which lies under

the federal jurisdiction of the United States Department of the Interior. The special legal status means that the Jicarilla Apache Tribe in northern New Mexico may manage their trophy-size elk and mule deer as they see fit, without state intervention. The result is a paradise for big-game hunters and for trout fishermen at the Jicarilla's Stone Lake Resort.

On the negative side, Native-American communities do not have direct control over the leasing or development of their tribal lands. Before tribes can do *anything* on their land, they must secure the approval of the Secretary of the Department of the Interior and the Commissioner of the Bureau of Indian Affairs. The results of this 200-year-old policy toward Indian tribes is readily apparent: Native American communities are notoriously lacking in many of the modern amenities other American communities take for granted. Because neither individual tribal members nor the tribe itself has "ownership" of the land, financing for housing, sewage treatment and solid-waste disposal were in past years impossible for Native American communities to obtain.

Very few of the businesses located on reservations are controlled by Native Americans. Again, until recently, it has been extremely difficult for enterprising Native American businessmen to obtain bank fi-

nancing since reservation lands cannot be used as collateral. Because of these complexities, in past years tribes in the Southwest had little control over land use and development of natural resources on tribal lands. Large mining corporations, aided by apathetic bureaucrats in the Department of the Interior, obtained vast mineral and petroleum leases on tribal lands without paying more than token sums for these lease privi-

**The Indian way of life is a rhythmic one: left, a cloud dancer at San Juan could well be dancing to the beat of drums by, above, musicians at San Ildefonso Pueblo.**

leges. Although these unfortunate leases were made in the mid-1950s, many have a duration of 40 or 50 years. Equally unfortunate was the policy of the Department of the Interior allowing mining operations to strip-mine coal and uranium without requiring reclamation of the land. Evidence of these past abuses is visible on many reservations.

For people who trace their origins to Mother Earth, the natural-resource policies of the Department of the Interior have been particularly painful. But in the past 10 years a gradual shift has been taking place, in which young Indian lawyers and PhDs have helped their tribes assert more control over their lands and natural resources. But always there remains a deep conflict between the traditional reverence for Mother Earth and the critical need for jobs and money and housing in communities where unemployment may run as high as 75 percent, and woefully scarce housing is often without electricity or indoor plumbing.

Because the tribes of the Southwest remained relatively untouched by Western influences for so long after the arrival of the first Spaniards, the appearance of the modern technological age is quite a shock to the eye. High-tech sewage plants are juxtaposed with sandstone walls built in AD 1000.

This juxtaposition of ancient non-European culture with a high-tech world disturbs because it raises many questions and provides no answers about the multiplicity of cultural identities. Clearly, tribal people living in the Southwest are very much part of the present and its attendant material culture.

But time and again, outsiders have seriously misjudged the visible and superficial evidence. In 1900, Franz Boas, a towering figure in cultural anthropology, announced that the Pueblo tribes faced cultural extinction within a decade. A century later, cultural anthropologists are just beginning to realize that, as outsiders to Native American cultures, they are unable to understand that ineffable core of tribal identity which lies well intact beneath layers and layers of debris left behind by successive waves of explorers and invaders.

But as one old Pueblo woman said, "How much could you expect Franz Boas to know? The United States of America hasn't even existed 250 years yet. But we have been around 9 or 10 thousand years at least."

There are more than 50 Native-American reservations in the Southwest, each the modern tribal lands of a more or less separate group. The largest and most culturally intact of these groups are the Pueblo, the Navajo, the Hopi, the Apache, the Tohono O'odham, and the Pima. These tribes are described below. Smaller tribes include the Havasupai of the Grand Canyon, the Ute of southern Utah, and the Paiute of northern Arizona. The Walapai, Hualapai, Mohave, Yavapai, Chemehuevi, Yuma, Cocopa, Maricopa, and Yaqui live in western Arizona, but many have friends or family in Mexico. The border created by modern states was not theirs.

**THE PUEBLO:** Details may vary from village to village, but the story of the Creation begins with a single Mind which "thought" the entire Universe into existence. Once the Creation had been completed, the people and animals found themselves in a dimness full of running water which was the First World, the Blue World. They journeyed upward, into the Red World, then the Yellow World or Third World where they rested before climbing upward into the White World, which was full of flowers and grass and beautiful running water. Many wanted to remain because it was a paradise, but had been told that theirs must be the Fifth World, and a certain way of life that could be accomplished only by traveling there.

The animals, insects and plants decided they must accompany their brethren, the human beings, into the Fifth World. But when the people and creatures arrived at the opening into the Fifth World, they found the hole was blocked by a large stone. The people tried but were unable to move the stone. The Badger People began digging with their long claws and managed to loosen the stone. But it was one of the Antelope People who decided to butt the stone. The fourth time he struck it with his head, the stone flew out of the hole and Antelope led all the people and the creatures into the Present World.

The Present World of the Pueblo Indian people is comprised of around 20 separate

**Left, Jose Toledo, the most famous artist of Jemez Pueblo.**

Pueblo tribes in New Mexico and the Hopi Pueblo tribe in northeastern Arizona. Although the Pueblo people share similar religious beliefs which reveal a common world view, linguistic differences distinguish each group from the other.

From the beginning, the Present World was filled with a great many challenges and difficulties for the people. But it is by these struggles that the people realize their spirituality and humanity and, most important, their place with all other living beings in the Universe. Thus the Pueblo view of the world emphasizes the interdependence of human beings and animals, the lowliest insects, and the plants and trees. Pueblo clans further recognize this familial relationship by calling themselves, say, the Badger Clan or the Corn Clan. Each animal, each plant, each tree that the people might take to satisfy human needs has always been prayed to and asked to give itself to the people.

**Voluntary sacrifices:** Among the Keresan-speaking Pueblo, for instance, a deer brought home by the hunter is placed in the center of the home and treated as a guest of honor. Turquoise is draped on the dead animal's neck and antlers, and family and guests approach the deer to "feed" it ceremonially by placing pinches of blessed corn meal on its nose. No part of the deer's body is wasted or in any way dishonored. The hunter must participate in the Deer Dance rituals, and "dance" the soul of the deer back to the mountains where the people believe the soul will be reborn into another deer, who will remember the love and respect of the humans and thus choose to once again give its life.

The Southwest land the Pueblo people call "Mother" is beautiful but unpredictable, and extremes of drought or winter cold have made human survival a great challenge. For thousands of years the Pueblo people have met this challenge, but only with the grace of the spirits of all living beings and the love of Mother Earth. The Pueblo people are by necessity among the greatest skywatchers. In ancient Pueblo observatories throughout the Southwest, winter sun symbols were inscribed on sandstone and special windows allowed the sun to illuminate the petroglyphs only on the winter solstice. In a land where the sky determines the fortunes of farming, religious devotion to cloud formations, winds, the positions of the sun and the moon and the tracking of Venus, Jupiter and Mars gave the Pueblo people the intricate information necessary for successful agriculture.

When the Spanish invaders arrived at Zuni Pueblo in 1540, they found neat, prosperous fields full of corn, beans, squash, melons and cotton, which was woven into cloth. The Spaniards taxed the agriculture and, gradually, the Pueblo people got fed up. The agricultural output was barely enough to feed the people of each pueblo. So, in 1680, the people organized a military maneuver which

What you may see at a pueblo is not nearly so important as what you will never see. Outsiders may attend a Pueblo dance, but it is only part of a longer religious ritual, and certain ritual dances are now off-limits to visitors owing to years of bad manners. Dances which are accessible to visitors are important religious acts, regardless of the apparent informality of the Pueblo crowd around them: tape recorders and cameras are in extremely bad taste.

Among the ceremonies open to the public is Taos Pueblo's San Geronimo Festival (on September 29 and 30 each fall). For centuries, this event has included an intertribal trade fair. On display are cottonwood drums,

is still marveled at because of the great distances between the pueblos. The Pueblo staged a great revolt, in which Spanish priests, soldiers and settlers were slaughtered and the survivors driven out of Pueblo country to El Paso del Norte. The Pueblo again enjoyed life without the invaders. But in 1692 the Spanish returned and, although the Pueblo couldn't manage another military victory, the Spaniards were more cautious.

Eventually, even the King of Spain realized he was dealing with governmental entities, and Pueblo leaders were acknowledged as sovereign powers by the gift of a silver-headed cane and grants of land.

undecorated micaceous pottery (a gleaming pinkish ware with occasional smoke spots), and beadwork on moccasins.

In Santa Clara Canyon each July, the Puye Cliff Ceremonial takes place high atop the mesa. A modest craft show accompanies traditional dances performed against a backdrop of stone and adobe ruins. Puye, which is part of the Pajarito Plateau, is a majestic place to see a pair of eagle dancers, wearing white feathered headdresses.

Indian dances are requests to the spirit world for blessings, and they often are combined with Christian feast days. On Christmas Eve in the Catholic church of San Felipe

Pueblo, the spirits of the animal kingdom pay homage to the Christ Child as dancers representing deer or buffalo, and elaborately dressed women dancers enter the church after midnight Mass. In hushed closeness, onlookers await the arrival of the procession. No one is supposed to see the dancers come from their *kiva*. Buffalo dancers, wearing the dark fur and horned headdress of the buffalo, with their exposed skin darkened, stomp on the floor. Deer dancers, who are bent over their sticks and whose headdresses are decked with antlers, move more lightly.

The Corn Dance is held at various times at the different pueblos. Santo Domingo holds it on August 4, the feast of Saint Dominic, in

In late November or early December, the Zuni Pueblo hold the Shalako Ceremonial, among the most spectacular Indian celebrations. The all-night event centers on the coming of 12-ft (3.5-meter) Shalakos and their retinues who bless new or renovated homes. In part-completed houses, pits are dug to enable the tall Shalako to enter and dance. The costly costumes are draped over a wooden framework, which includes pulleys to move parts like a puppeteer.

Complex social relationships grow out of the Pueblo world view in which the well-being of all creatures is tied to the well-being of every individual. In this way, the day-to-day comings and goings between neighbors

an open-air extravaganza involving 500 dancers aged two to 80. Barefoot women have blue stepped tablita painted on their glossy black hair to symbolize a mountain with an indication of rain. They each wear a one-shouldered manta (woven sash), the best family jewelry, and hold a pine bough in each hand. The men wear short white embroidered kilts, long bold sashes, armbands and moccasins. They too carry pine boughs.

**Left: a Navajo checks the condition of his horse by looking at its teeth and gums. Above: eagle dancers: their mimicry of the bird goes beyond the external, and they become eagles in spirit.**

and families are part of a greater spiritual and religious whole. Pueblo silverwork, pottery, baskets or Hopi "kachina dolls" invariably gain the most attention, but the most powerful manifestation of the Pueblo is still their vision of Wholeness.

**THE NAVAJO:** White men called them Navajo, but they call themselves *Dine* – the People, and they came a long way to settle in the American Southwest. Of Athabascan stock, they came from the forests of northwest Canada, drifting into the Four Corners area as small groups of skin-clad hunters. By 1400 they were well-established in their new homeland, a land of ever-changing colors, of yellow deserts, blood-red mesas and canyons, green fir and aspen-covered highlands and silvery expanses of sage overspread by a turquoise sky. This beautiful land was sacred to them because it had been created by the Holy Ones for the People to live in.

They came as hunters, bringing lances, sinew-backed bows and hide shields. Nomadic and warlike, at first they raided the villages of the Pueblo who had lived on the land long before them. They took from the peaceful Pueblo many useful things, including women who taught them how to plant corn and squash, weave and make pottery. The Navajo were good learners. In time, their weavers even outstripped their Pueblo

Winter came and many Indians, cooped up in their canyons, starved and froze to death. At last, they surrendered.

They were made to go on the Long Walk to Bosque Redondo, 350 miles (563 km) away. Their destination was worse than the march itself. They had been moved to a flat, inhospitable land with alkali water which made them sick. They had no materials to build shelters and lived like gophers in earthen holes. They never had enough to eat as their crops withered in the hostile soil. Out of 8,000 Navajo, 1,500 died. After four years, the government relented and let the survivors go back to their homeland. They set out again on the punishing five-week trek.

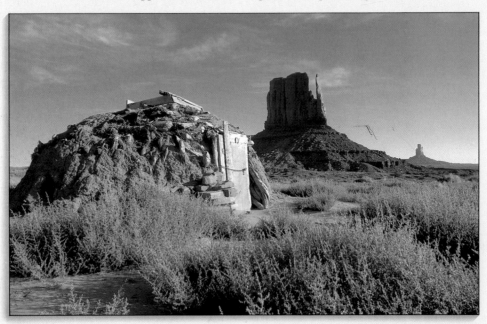

teachers. Much later, they learned from the Spaniards how to ride horses, raise sheep and, still later, become silversmiths.

**Nomads no more:** Planting and shepherding turned the roving nomads into sedentary herdsmen with a settled home at whose core was the beautiful Canyon de Chelly. Then, in 1851, the US Army built Fort Defiance to "defy" and control the Navajo, and in 1863 Kit Carson was sent to subdue and remove the People. Carson waged a cruel war. He did not hunt down the small groups of Navajo hidden in the depths of their canyons. He made war instead upon their crops and sheep. Livestock was killed, corn supplies burned.

The People made a new start under the most unfavorable conditions. The Navajo is now the largest of all Native-American tribes, but this speaks only of Navajo hardiness and resilience. More than a hundred years on, the Long Walk still haunts tribal memories.

Navajo home life revolves around the *hogan* (dwelling). The earliest type was the "forked stick" hogan made of three crotched poles interlaced at the top, covered with sticks and plastered over with earth. In the center of the sunken floor was a firepit below a smoke hole. The hogan was well-suited to the country – cool in summer and snug in winter. People slept with their feet toward the fire like spokes in a wheel. Modern hogans are octagonal log cabins with a domed roof through which the stovepipe rises. Many have electric lights, refrigerators and a color TV set. They are roomier than the old-style hogan, but preserve its original design.

In the oldest of traditions, if a Navajo dies in the hogan, an opening is made in the back of the dwelling through which the body is removed. The hogan and its contents are then burned. The place is then considered the haunt of *chindi*, the ghosts of the dead.

Not observing taboos can arouse the anger of powerful spirits, and traditional Navajo life is so regulated that people inevitably do break a few. However, they tend to honor

trembling. His whole body shakes, and his trembling hands hover over a patch of corn-meal. Finally, the finger traces an ancient design that indicates the cause of the disease and the appropriate ritual to exorcise it.

This tracing of an ancient design, called sand painting, can last several days. If the Sing is right, the song chanted beautifully, and the sand painting as it should be, then all will be well. Some sand paintings are small and can be finished by one man in an hour or two. Others may be 20 feet long, requiring several assistants. The patient who is sung over sits in the center of the painting, and their living body is part of the sacred altar. When the ritual is over, patient and painting

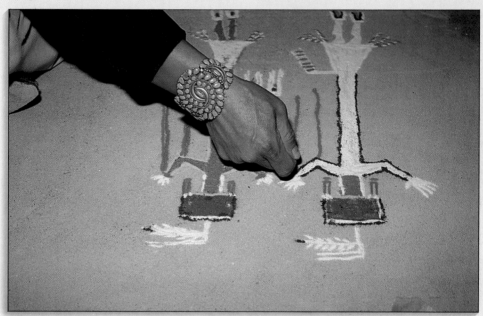

strictly the most serious taboos and, in time of misfortune, try to determine how they have erred and seek to propitiate the spirits.

Communicating with the spirits needs song and a medicine man, the *hatathli* or chanter, who can bring evil under ritual control. His knowledge is not gained easily. Before a Sing, he fasts for days, taking sweat baths and communing with the powers. He searches for the cause of evil through listening or

**Navajo culture is as intriguing as it is old. <u>Left</u>, a *hogan* at Monument Valley preserves the original design of such dwellings. <u>Above</u>, sand painting is a time-honored art form.**

are symbolically united when the medicine man dips his wet fingers into the sand paint-ing and transfers some of it (and its power) to the patient. Finally the painting is destroyed, the sand scattered in all the sacred directions. The "sand paintings" on plywood or certain rugs sold as curios have their roots in this Navajo religious symbolism.

**The Holy People's family tree:** Navajo reli-gion is complex, its teachings, legends, songs and rituals beautifully haunting and poetic. Navajo believe in the Holy People, powerful and mysterious, who travel on the wind, a sunbeam or a thunderbolt. At the head of these supernaturals stands Changing Woman,

the Earth Mother, beautiful, gift-giving, watching over the people's well-being. Changing Woman was found by First Man and First Woman as a baby, lying in a supernaturally created cradleboard on top of a sacred mountain. Within four days, Changing Woman grew to maturity. It was She who taught humans how to live in harmony with the forces of nature. She built the first hogan out of turquoise and shell. The Navajo's chief ritual, Blessing Way, came to them from Changing Woman and other Holy People. Changing Woman was impregnated by the rays of the Sun and gave birth to the Hero Twins, who killed many evil monsters and enemies of mankind, but she allowed Old Age and Death to exist because they have their part in the human scheme.

Religion was an integral part of daily life and, for many traditional Navajo, still is today. Men go into the fields singing corn-growing songs, weavers make a spirit path thread in their rugs, and hide-curers put a turquoise bead on their tanning poles to keep their joints limber. When a woman has a difficult birth, her female relatives and friends loosen their hair to "untie" the baby. A chanter might be summoned to coax the baby along with an eagle-feather fan. Twins are a cause for great joy because they are a sign of the Holy People's blessing. The father makes the cradleboard. When the baby is placed in it, a special song is chanted:

*I have made a baby board for you, my child.*
*May you grow to a great old age.*
*Of the sun's rays have I made the back.*
*Of clouds have I made the blanket.*
*Of the rainbow have I made the head bow.*

Coming of age is the occasion for many rituals, which in the case of girls are very elaborate. The time of a girl's "first bleed" is a proud moment for her, and she hurries to tell her parents, who joyfully spread the news. The event is celebrated by a ceremony called *Kinaalda*.

The girl has her hair washed in yucca suds. For three days, wearing her best jewelry, she grinds corn on the old family metate. Each day, she undergoes a "molding" rite. Lying on a blanket, she is kneaded and "shaped" by

a favorite friend or relative to make her as beautiful as Changing Woman. Every dawn, the girl races toward the east, each time a little faster. Others are allowed to run with her but are careful not to pass her so that they do not grow old before she does. On the fourth day, older women make a big cake from the corn which the girl has ground, sometimes as big as 6 feet across. When the cake is ready, after racing for the last time, the girl distributes it to all the guests. After that she is considered a woman, ready to marry and to start a family of her own.

Religious symbolism has influenced Navajo art, which is rich, beautiful and economically important. Wherever there is a Navajo woman, there is a loom. Originally only blankets were woven. The famous Navajo rug was an invention of white traders after the coming of the railroads and tourists. The traders didn't take long to find out that travelers from the East had little use for blankets worn like ponchos. So they called them rugs and gave birth to a new industry.

Different regions of the Navajo reservation developed their own characteristic styles – Ganado Reds, geometric Two Gray Hills, figural Shiprock, to name a few. Fine Navajo rugs are a good investment, provided one does not fall for cheap Mexican imitations. Women also weave fine baskets, while men excel in creating some of the best silver and turquoise work to be found in the Southwest. At the tribal capital of Window Rock, one may visit the Navajo Arts and Crafts Center, but rugs, baskets and jewelry are also sold in shops throughout the area.

**The giant bulldozer:** The modern Navajo, who does not choose to live the traditional life in the hogan, might be a lawyer, an electrician, a policewoman, a telephone operator. He might operate one of the giant cranes at the nearby strip mine or operate one of the complicated Japanese-built machines at the huge tribal sawmill. He might be a newspaper editor on the *Navajo Times* or a professor at the Navajo Community College – all glass and steel but built in the shape of a traditional hogan. The modern Navajo man or woman shares some of the advantages and all of the frustrations, problems and anxieties of their fellow Americans.

With a population in excess of 200,000, the Navajo are one of the largest tribes in the US. The Navajo reservation is bigger than

**Left**, a modern youth who chooses to live far away from his parents faces the danger of cultural alienation.

New Hampshire, Connecticut, Vermont and Rhode Island combined. It has oil, coal, uranium and timber. These resources bring in money but also wrenching changes: pollution, dependency on outside forces, a certain amount of industrialization, and the relocation of people whose homes happen to be in the way of development.

In spite of all the natural resources, poverty is still pervasive, housing and health care substandard. Schools do not prepare students for the problems they will face in a technological world dominated by Anglos. Religion and language fight for survival against the inroads of an alien culture which is not better but more powerful. But the

hospitable and helpful. Tradition and custom mandate such attitudes and behavior. Today these qualities are very much in evidence among those of earlier generations raised and taught in a simpler cultural milieu. Modern influences tend to neutralize this natural elan with a wariness and sophistication which is most evident among the young.

Hopi country can be loosely described as high desert supporting little else beside the tenacious Hopi. They manage to coax the most wondrous yield of cultivated farm products out of it, notably an infinite variety of corn. Hopi country is comprised of 11 distinct villages situated along the 35-mile (56-km) perimeter of Black Mesa in northeastern

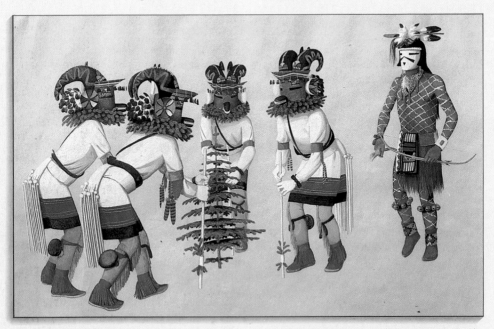

young people are not discouraged. They are proud to be Indians, to be Navajo.

One said: "We have survived the Spaniards, the missionaries and the Long Walk. We still walk in beauty. We will still be here, still be Navajo, a hundred years from now."

**THE HOPI:** Approaching Hopi country from any direction may be a bleak or nondescript experience for some travelers, but once they meet and mingle with its inhabitants, a visitor generally comes away from the experience with anything but bleak or nondescript impressions. If Hopi people were inclined to describe themselves, which they are not, they would say they aspire to be industrious,

Arizona. These villages, some settled for centuries some founded as recently as 1910, are home to 10,000 people closely knit by tradition, blood and custom, but distinctively separate linguistically and politically.

Speech patterns and vocabulary differ from village to village within the same general language structure, providing natural boundaries. These differences also provide a great deal of chauvinistic interplay with words among residents of each village. The traditional governing system also encourages a political distance between villages. However, the differences are not easily discernible to those unfamiliar with Hopi society.

The kinship system, which is still intact, provides the unity which allows free intercourse between villages in all the important functions of communal living: family relationships, rites and ceremonies. It may be overstressing the point, but only a little, to say that most Hopi growing up and living on the reservation know, if they know nothing else, who they are and where they came from. Hopi will first give you the name of their village home, and if prodded further, they will most likely tell you clan affiliation and Hopi name.

The kinship system, in which lineage passes through the female line, is crucial in keeping familial and spiritual unity. All children of

Superimposed on biological kinship is the clan system, which sees people within a single relational universe, that of brother and sister. The clan line is also matrilineal.

Legendary tales, closely guarded by hereditary caretakers within each clan unit, recount the extensive prehistoric migrations of one ancestral group after another over a vast area of the southwestern United States, southern California and Mexico. Storytellers can identify landmarks as far away as central New Mexico, southern Colorado and Utah. Mythic tales of creation provide the basis for a system of beliefs and practices so complex as to mesmerize generations of scholars throughout the world.

maternal sisters and paternal brothers, for instance, become brothers and sisters, enjoying common parent-figures, although in lesser degrees of intimacy beyond the immediate family. Paternal sisters and maternal brothers are aunts and uncles, but within the second generation only the uncle's children are named nephews and nieces. The aunt's children fall into relationship patterns dictated by clan formulas.

**Ceremonial dances may be the most distinctive aspect of Hopi culture. <u>Left</u>, painting shows the Bighorn Dance, *circa* 1930. <u>Above</u>, 19th-century Hopi girls, each with a butterfly hairdo.**

**Ritual and ceremony:** The traveler will find Hopi people naturally open and friendly in the privacy of their home, though somewhat distant at public, social and ceremonial gatherings – unless of course the traveler has "Hopi friends." It is not uncommon to find at least one *Pahaana* (white man) among the participants at wedding, natal and kachina ceremonial preparation parties.

Hopi are particularly sensitive to the aesthetic tastes of the traveling public, whether these tastes be for art, services or showmanship such as the dancing kachinas, which have become such a magnetic attraction for countless outsiders. Ritual and ceremony may be the most distinctive aspects of Hopi culture today. A serious issue among them today is how best to preserve Hopi ways which are rapidly changing because of pressures, both within and without, created by modern living and technology. There is no doubt that Hopi do not want to let go of all the "old" ways of doing things. The specter of losing tradition and custom to modern technology and life-styles hovers constantly over the activities which serve to perpetuate those very traditions.

The modern Hopi wedding was being discussed around the breakfast table recently in a Hopi home. One man remarked at the marshaling of a caravan of automobiles to

Young people sitting around the table in that modern house were quite surprised and fascinated to hear this; no one had really explained these things to them. Their only experience with weddings consisted of the mixture of Western and Hopi ceremonial activities which has become the modern Hopi wedding: at most, a two-day affair replete with an abundance of foods from the traditional pantry as well as the supermarket, wrapped gifts mingling with the native foodstuffs customarily given to the bride's and groom's families, table decor contrasting with makeshift outdoor open fires for cooking. So it goes. And so it goes in other rites which are still vital, such as natal rites and

escort the new bride home at the culmination of wedding festivities. He counted 20-odd trucks, each loaded down with gifts to be distributed among the bride's relatives. He was obviously saddened at the blatant ignorance displayed by the relatives about the original significance of the bridal homecoming. "The bride goes back to her mother's house alone to await her new husband's pleasure. When he decides to accept her as a bride he will follow her, bearing appropriate gifts," he said. (Even second-generation Hopi born this century might be hard put to know that the right gift for him to bring is a load of wood, symbol of hearth and home.)

initiation into ceremonial societies. It is this innovative mixing of the old and new that separates one generation from the other, because, if the truth be told, these hybrids have an ambience of their own, and an appealing vitality not to be dismissed.

This attractive mixture of the old and new can also be seen during one of the many summer weekends on which kachina or other dances are sponsored. Less than a generation ago, kachinas were first introduced to the Hopi child as spiritual beings who come to this world from the Spirit Home, which may refer to either an opening in the floor of a ceremonial room called the *kiva* or to a shrine on the San Francisco Peaks near Flagstaff, Arizona, which is a "secret opening."

**Kachina dances:** Kachinas are commonly presented in the dances held indoors, in *kivas*, and outdoors, in village plazas, depending on the time of year. These colorful masked beings represent elements, qualities and inhabitants of the universe; they may be cast, in their spiritual state, in roles for various purposes, some didactic and others inspirational.

Kachina dances are very much taken as a matter of course; there is at least one in each village each year. The kachina and kachina dancing act as a magnet to a new breed of Hopi urban dwellers a generation or two removed from reservation upbringing who return as spectators and participants.

An upcoming dance mobilizes, as nothing else can, all the combined resources of a village. It is not unusual for Hopi to travel from Los Angeles, San Francisco, Denver or Oklahoma City for these events; coming in from Tucson, Phoenix and even Salt Lake City can be a weekly or monthly habit with some families. When all the relatives have gathered, there may be a fleet of five to 10 vehicles, mostly trucks, in front of each house in that village. Even though these autos may have come loaded with provisions from the supermarkets of the urban centers, the preparation of traditional feast foods is not abandoned. It is within this backdrop to the drama of the dance where many a *pahaana* has found a fascinating niche.

The atmosphere in a village during dance day is a fascinating mixture of old and new ways, appreciated most by those who have experienced the speed with which time changes everything. Corn, the symbolic Mother to the Hopi, is the most visible traditional food, secular and sacred, for this occasion as it is for most ceremonial observances. Visitors are well-warned to expect to see and eat corn in some form all day.

The ceremony is a series of dances, usually seven or eight, performed every two hours during the day, with 30-minute intermissions, beginning about mid-morning and ending at sundown. The staging of a kachina dance is an example of the refined sense of the dramatic which is another trademark of

**Left** and **right**, the Puberty Ceremony is performed at Apache reservations by masked Mountain Spirit dancers.

Hopi and the other Pueblo peoples of the Southwest. Aside from being a colorful spectacle, the kachinas represent the most visible evidence of the Hopi's creative talents.

**THE APACHE:** Like most other Southwest Native Americans, the Apache dispute the anthropological theory that they migrated to North America across the Bering Strait. An elderly San Carlos Apache tells the story handed down for centuries: "Our ancestors tell us that we were created in the area where we now live. In the beginning, there was no living person upon Mother Earth, only supernatural beings. When our people were created, there were wicked creatures who killed them. During this time, the White

Painted Lady gave birth to twin sons. One of these sons went to his father, Sun, and returned to Mother Earth dressed in proper Apache clothing, carrying a bow and arrows and leading several horses. After he taught our people how to use these things, he helped kill the evil creatures. Mother Earth then became a good place to live for our people." All Apache have a Creation story with ideas similar to this one.

Before contact with the Spaniards during the middle to late 1500s, the Apache intermingled freely among themselves and the Navajo. The Apache, like the Navajo, are of the Athabascan-speaking family and have

no written history or language. The Apache called themselves the People, but to others they were the "Enemy."

The land the Apache roamed, hunting and gathering for their livelihood, encompassed present-day Arizona, New Mexico and northern Mexico. While they were, in essence, one family, each group had its own hunting territory and did not encroach on that of its neighbors. The relatively peaceful, nomadic life the Apache led was one day drastically altered by the intrusion of outsiders into the Apache domain: Spaniards, Mexicans and finally Anglos.

**Anglo and Spanish colonization:** When Coronado made his expedition into the Southwest, he unwittingly introduced a new mode of travel to the Apache, which they would adopt and use more than any other Southwestern tribe. The horse became a beast of burden, a source of food and a reliable form of transportation that enabled the Apache to expand their geographical range far beyond their original territories.

Apache reaction to Spanish and Anglo colonization was raiding and warfare, which was so effective that twice the intruders were driven out for as long as a decade. Southern Arizona was one of the last areas of the Southwest to be settled by the Spanish and Americans. Contrary to popular belief, Apache raiding did not include wanton destruction; its aim was to steal livestock.

When the Gadsden Purchase was made in 1853, all of Arizona came under the control of the United States of America. This, and the discovery of gold in western Apache territory 10 years later, brought an influx of Anglo settlers and prospectors. The Arizona Territory Legislature officially decided that the only way to control the Apache was to exterminate them. The Department of the Interior in Washington disagreed with this policy, and the Territory lacked the means to carry out the extermination. This fact, together with the slaughter of 75 unarmed Apache women and children near Tucson by a mob of outraged citizens and a group of Tohono O'odham Indians, led to the implementation of the so-called Peace Policy.

This policy called for rounding up Apache and confining them to reservations, where

**Left**, elder of the Elmer Campus Papago tribe in San Xavier, Arizona.

they would have to make a living by growing crops and raising livestock. This plan required the removal of some tribes from their homelands. The removals were met with surprisingly mixed feelings by the Apache. Some had become weary of the hardships of war and preferred to settle down in peace. Others, however, waited for a chance to escape. Two of those who bolted were Geronimo and Victorio. But by 1890, the Apache wars were over.

Today, the remaining Apache tribes of Arizona and New Mexico have been significantly anglicized. Many of the old tribal ways are gone. Present-day Apache are struggling to become economically self-sufficient by using modern technologies, and in the past decade there has been a shift from a livestock to a wage economy. Some very important aspects of Apache culture are intact, however, and they pertain to religion, mythology and craftsmanship.

**Ceremony and crafts:** The Apache Puberty Ceremony can be seen several times a year on the San Carlos, White Mountain and Jicarilla reservations. The Mescalero Apache ceremonies are all performed in summer.

The awesome and colorful masked Mountain Spirit dancers, or *gans*, still perform at the puberty rites of the San Carlos, White Mountain and Mescalero tribes. The Jicarilla Apache have not used the dancers as part of their ceremonies since the introduction of the vaccination program on their reservation. The Jicarilla leaders decreed that anyone who had been vaccinated could not participate as a Mountain Spirit dancer, and the result was the disqualification of nearly all Jicarilla youth.

The ceremony for a girl – the Mountain Spirit Dance – if she and her family want and can afford it, is usually held after she has had her first menstruation. The girl, who enters womanhood upon completion of the ceremony, needs four general qualities – strength, patience, good luck and wisdom – to help her during her lifetime. These qualities are possessed by the White Painted Lady and are acquired by the girl during the four-day ceremony when the White Painted Lady resides in her body. Interestingly, this four-day rite is the most important ceremony for the Apache. Girls are believed to possess curative powers at puberty and treat the ill by touching and massaging them.

**THE TOHONO O'ODHAM and PIMA:** A Tohono O'odham may come from any number of small villages dotting the Sonoran Desert. The reservation is comprised of over 2.5 million acres (1 million hectares) for a population of fewer than 18,000 people.

A person can be from any one of these villages, or he might be from Sells, which has, in the past decade, become the melting-pot village. Tohono O'odham who make up the community of Sells (named after an Indian Commissioner) are from someplace else. Most of them have come for a specific reason. Some have come for job opportunities with the Bureau of Indian Affairs; others for government housing, which has become prevalent on all reservation communities.

Sells is a quasi-urbanized sprawl nestled below the sacred mountain, *Waw Giwulk* or *Baboquivari*, the home of the Protector of the Tohono O'odham people. Despite the non-traditional housing, many Tohono O'odham call this place home, the place where one is from. But the entire reservation is home as well, since all of it was the aboriginal land of the tribe. To the east of the reservation lies the metropolis of Tucson, whose name is a bastardization of *Cuk Son* (Black base mountain). To the west, there is the mining town of Ajo (the Spanish name given because of the abundance of wild garlic in the area); the Tohono O'odham called this area *Moik Wahia* (Soft Well) for the nice wells there. To the south (on the American-Mexican border) there is Sonoita, called *Son Oidag* (Spring Field), and inside Mexico, where a majority of the aboriginal land became a part of Mexico, there is Poso Verde, called *Cerdagi Wahia* (Green Well).

Approximately 50 miles north of the Tohono O'odham home lies the Pima reservation. Fewer than 11,000 Pima Indians live on a little over 3,000 acres (1,214 hectares). The main reservation is called the Gila River Indian Reservation, a reserve shared with a few hundred Maricopa Indians. (The Maricopa Indians belong to the linguistic family called Yuman and are not related to the Pima in any way.)

From all evidence, archaeological and anthropological, the Pima and Tohono O'odham Indians were, at one time, the same. They are said to be descendants of Hohokam, or as they are called by the people, the *Hukukam*, "the ones that have gone now."

Linguistically the two groups are closely related. Their languages are mutually intelligible, and socially the two tribes resemble one another. Many of their rituals, stories and songs are similar. The only distinction that separates them, again, is place, the area where one is from.

The Pima and Tohono O'odham distinguish one another by placing in front of their tribal name the geographic feature that refers to the place they are from. Tohono O'odham *means* "Desert People." The Pima, who have traditionally lived along the banks of rivers in the valley of south-central Arizona call themselves, *Akimel O'odham* or "River People" even though the river which winds through their reservation no longer carries water. The floor of the river is now cracked and dusty, a home only to lizards, horned toads and rattlesnakes. There is no traditional farming, only that which uses water brought from other places in concrete canals or pumped from deep within the ground. But this place along the dry river is home. The other lands that make up the reservation, like the one along the Salt River, are only a small part of what was once the aboriginal land of the Pima. The Salt River Reservation butts against the condominiums of Scottsdale. Another tiny segment (shared with the Tohono O'odham) is called, ironically, *Aki Cin* (River Mouth).

The Pima, and to a lesser extent the Tohono O'odham, are the most acculturated Native American tribes in the Southwest. Since the time of their earliest recorded contacts with whites, the Pima especially have been looked upon as friendly Indians. During the mid-19th century Gold Rush in California, the Pima sold provisions to white gold diggers and escorted them through Apache territory. At the time of the Apache wars (1861-86), a large number of the Pima served as scouts for the US Army. Such close contacts with white culture resulted in disintegration of aboriginal culture. Both tribes have retained their language and a few ceremonies, and Tohono O'odham woven baskets are still believed to be among the finest made, but their lifestyles and beliefs do not differ greatly from their Anglo and Hispanic neighbors.

**Right**, smiling Pima woman exemplifies her tribe whom the white men have regarded as "friendly Indians" since the mid-19th century.

OVERLAND STAGE LINE & DEPOT.

In John Ford's *The Man Who Shot Liberty Valance,* a senator played by James Stewart confesses to a newspaper editor that for decades he has lived a lie. The senator admits that 30 years earlier he did not actually gun down the sadistic outlaw, an act that launched his political career. Having heard the whole story, the editor tosses away his notes and declares, "This is the West, sir. When the legend becomes fact, print the legend."

**Duels in the sun:** By the time *Liberty Valance* came out in 1962, the makers of Westerns had instinctively followed that creed for nearly 70 years. They portrayed a West of duels in the sun, cavalry charges across desert dreamscapes and savage Indians lined up on ruddy buttes. These films offer little sense of everyday life, just an idealized world where things usually go according to plan: the bad guy embodies evil, while the hero upholds all that is good, reluctantly resorting to violence to right a world gone wrong. It's a simple scheme, one that prevailed in countless B Westerns, the second-billed feature at old-time movie houses. Wildly popular, B movies both influenced the public's image of the West and cemented a perception of the Western as light entertainment.

That perspective disregards the artistry of leading filmmakers from silent-movie star William S. Hart to John Ford and Clint Eastwood. Traditional elements run through their work, but all three take the Western beyond simple formula, an achievement long ignored: Ford won six Academy Awards but none for his Westerns. Only recently, during a minor Western revival, has the genre earned greater respect, especially Kevin Costner's *Dances with Wolves* and Eastwood's *Unforgiven*. Both won Academy Awards for best film – the first Western winners since *Cimarron* 60 years earlier.

Western mythologizing was well under way by the time movies flickered into the public consciousness. Even before the Old

West rode off into the sunset for good, 19th-century novels, stage plays and Wild West shows had reshaped it. Film just offered a new medium for an already popular genre.

One of the first movies filmed in Hollywood was also a Western, Cecil B. DeMille's *The Squaw Man* (1913). Originally produced for the stage, *The Squaw Man* played another pivotal role in film history. It launched the film career of actor-director William S. Hart, who won Broadway acclaim in the play as a cowboy named Cash Hawkins.

Hart knew and loved the West. Born in New York State in 1865, his family took him to the Midwest, and he grew up playing with Sioux children in the frontier towns where his father set up gristmills. He traveled with his father deep into Sioux Country before the family returned east.

After *The Squaw Man*, Hart began getting more Western roles, such as the lead in *The Virginian*, enhancing his cowboy reputation. None other than Bat Masterson touted Hart's portrayal as "a true type of that reckless nomad who flourished on the border when the six-shooter was the final arbiter of all disputes between man and man."

**Preceding pages:** stunning Monument Valley in *Stagecoach*, 1939. **Left**, John Wayne, James Stewart and director John Ford on the set of *The Man Who Shot Liberty Valance*, 1962. **Right**, Henry Fonda in *My Darling Clementine*, 1946.

Committed to an honest depiction (and chronically in need of money), Hart had a revelation while watching a Western movie in 1913. Horrified at its inaccuracies, he likened the film to burlesque. But he also recognized that if this movie succeeded, then his truer vision of the West would surely capture movie audiences.

By the time Hart arrived in Hollywood, producers were sounding a death knell for Westerns, one of several times the genre seemed to be on its way to the last roundup. Under film pioneer Thomas Ince's guidance, he began his career, and many credit Hart with reviving the Western. His sober face and hunched, two-gun stance (like Richard

Nixon with six-shooters) became as famous as Charlie Chaplin's Little Tramp.

Unlike the glossy Tom Mix movies, Hart didn't depict a rhinestone West. His had dust and grit. Wild West shows had popularized flashy western duds, more Liberace than Laramie. Hart righted that image with a plaid shirt, simple kerchief and a vest. He prided himself on his vision and in his autobiography wrote, "My pictures of the West in the early days will make that colorful period of American life live forever."

Western expert William K. Everson agreed with Hart and wrote, "His films were raw, unglamorous, and gutsy... the ramshackle

Western towns and their inhabitants like unretouched Matthew Brady photographs, the sense of dry heat ever present (panchromatic film stock, developed in the 1920s, softened and glamorized the landscapes in later Westerns), and the clouds of dust everywhere." Other directors had wetted the ground for a cleaner look. Considered Hart's masterpiece, *Tumbleweeds* (1925) has a documentary feel, especially the scenes of Oklahoma's Cherokee Strip Land Rush. Pioneers race across the screen with a sense of urgency and danger, on horseback, in wagons, even on bicycles. Filmed by a semi-buried camera, ground-level shots of thundering hooves and wagon wheels mesmerized audiences and became Western classics.

Hart's character declares, "Boys, it's the last of the West," and indeed *Tumbleweeds* proved to be Hart's final film. Hart pioneered the Western hero as a loner, the austere good-bad man who finds purpose and redemption in riding to the rescue. That strict moralistic quality appealed to World War I audiences but seemed heavy-handed by the Roaring Twenties.

Clashing with the studios, Hart retired to his ranch north of Los Angeles. Over the years, a steady stream of notables, including Charles Russell and Will Rogers, visited him at his Spanish-style home. Hart died in 1946 and gave the Newhall estate to Los Angeles County for a museum. In typical Two-Gun Bill fashion, he explained, "While I was making pictures, the people gave me their nickels, dimes, and quarters. When I am gone, I want them to have my home."

**Ford Country:** There are statues of John Wayne in California; they even named an airport after him. To the public, John Wayne is the Western. But no man dominated the genre like director John Ford. Within the film community, Ford's legend is as big as Wayne's. Ingmar Bergman called him the world's greatest film maker. Orson Welles watched Ford's 1939 *Stagecoach* 40 times and declared his three great influences "John Ford, John Ford, and John Ford."

Born in Maine of Irish immigrants, Ford headed west following the Hollywood acting success of his brother Francis. As he explained in an interview with Peter Bogdanovich, he got his chance when a director failed to show for a big scene the same morning that Universal Studios chief

Carl Laemmle visited the lot. Someone needed to look in charge, so Ford took control of the action, ultimately burning down the street in a scene he described as "more pogrom than Western." Later, when a new film needed a director, Laemmle said, "Give Jack Ford the job. He yells good."

Yelling good and using his sharp eye for composition, Ford first directed silent two-reelers, then moved on to some of the earliest Western epics, most notably *The Iron Horse* (1924). Like Hart, Ford sought authenticity. He often consulted old-timers and eschewed quick-draw duels and showy costumes. Ford met Wyatt Earp on the back lot a few times and based his 1946 O.K. Corral tale *My*

grown into a kind of holy trinity of the classic Western. But the West they portrayed was one of considerable complexity. The early Wayne is as different from the icon Duke of later years as Hound Dog Elvis is from Vegas Elvis. Jane Tompkins in *West of Everything* writes, "The expression of the young John Wayne is tender… Pure and sweet…"

Ford cast Wayne in the roles of men with clashing emotions and loyalties, such as the cavalry officer who is torn between obedience to his commanding officer and his better judgment in *Fort Apache*. And the classic Monument Valley films often ended ambiguously, allowing audiences to reach conflicting conclusions, something that never

Will Rogers ~

*Darling Clementine* on Earp's accounts, although by that time the old gunfighter was definitely printing the legend, not the facts.

Ford rode out to locations and slept under the stars during shooting. In 1938, he headed out to a more distant location, Monument Valley, to film his first sound Western, *Stagecoach*, starring John Wayne. Dubbed "Ford Country," the valley and its towering red rock formations evolved into a trademark.

Ford, Wayne and Monument Valley have

**"When the legend becomes fact, print the legend." Left, silent-film star Tom Mix. Above, cowboy philosopher and film star Will Rogers.**

happened in good guy-bad guy Westerns.

In *Fort Apache*, Henry Fonda plays the commanding officer, a martinet who leads his troops on a suicidal charge against Apaches. Based on Custer's last stand, the film feels almost like a Vietnam-vintage attack on military incompetence. But as the movie closes, Wayne, whose advice Fonda disastrously ignored, tells myth-seeking reporters of the officer's heroism and eulogizes, "No man died more gallantly."

Critics chastise Ford for his depictions of Indians as bloodthirsty marauders. Certainly in *Stagecoach* they appear as anonymous killers, while in *The Searchers* (1956), the white women captured by Indians have gone insane. Wayne's character is even ready to shoot his captive niece, the one he spent seven years searching for, declaring, "Living with Comanches ain't being alive." Yet in *Fort Apache*, Cochise appears as the man of reason, and it is Fonda who displays the bloodlust and bigotry that draw the Indians into reluctant battle.

"Let's face it," Ford told Bogdanovich, "we've treated them very badly – it's a blot on our shield; we've cheated and robbed, killed, murdered, massacred and everything else, but they kill one white man and, God, out come the troops."

Certainly, if you've seen one Ford film,

the social pressures of the 1960s, Westerns underwent major changes. The lilting cavalry song that accompanied an Indian surrender in *The Searchers* was used to ironic effect behind a scene of slaughter in *Little Big Man* (1969). And the new Western man had as much Liberty Valance in him as he did John Wayne.

He smoked a foul little Italian cigar, wore a poncho, sported stubble and a scowl. He was Clint Eastwood as The Man With No Name in a trilogy of mid-1960s Westerns shot in Spain by Italian director Sergio Leone.

The low-budget Spaghetti Westerns helped revive the genre at a time when big-money American epics had bombed. Eastwood told

you haven't seen them all. Ford's West was one of shadings, not unlike the changing play of natural light and shadow found in his movies. It reflects the man himself, who could charm his actors or, as he did to Wayne, reduce them to tears. As James Stewart said of the director, "Take everything you've heard, everything you've ever heard and multiply it about a hundred times – and you still won't have a picture of John Ford."

**The Man With No Name:** Ford filmed his final Western in 1964. John Wayne continued making Westerns until 1976 and won an Oscar for his portrayal of Marshal Rooster Cogburn in *True Grit* (1969). But reflecting

Kenneth Turan of the *Los Angeles Times*, "When I first went and did *A Fistful of Dollars*, there were a lot of predictions in the trade papers that Westerns were through. And I said, 'Swell, now that I'm doing one they're through,' but that film turned out to have its place in the world."

Eastwood is not exclusively a Western actor, but his career follows some of the genre's trends. His break came in the modern equivalent of a B picture, the television show *Rawhide,* where he played the amicable Rowdy Yates. His appearance in the musical *Paint Your Wagon* evoked the heyday of Roy Rogers and the singing cowboys.

But The Man With No Name had no Hollywood precedent. He subscribed to no moral code like William S. Hart's characters. He and his cohorts did what they had to do in order to survive in a moral and physical desert. In *The Good, The Bad, and The Ugly*, the Eastwood character kills three men before the audience even sees his face – then takes the man he saved captive so he can collect the bounty.

**Cynical loner:** In an essay on Eastwood the actor, writer Jim Miller describes the character as "a cynical loner at a time when the mood of the country was shaped in much the same line of thought… he brought a whole new look at the Western hero as a lone wolf,

*Wolves*, a kind of New Age eco-Western, stunned Hollywood with its success and launched a revival that had everyone from rapper Tone Loc to party girl Drew Barrymore back in the saddle again. And after years of waiting, Eastwood decided that he had aged enough to portray reformed killer William Munny in *Unforgiven.*

Now a widower and hog farmer, Munny tries to convince himself that he is truly a changed man, even as he heads out again as a bounty hunter. He struggles with almost everything – his past, his horse and his shooting – and looks as weary as The Man With No Name looked invincible. When his young partner asks him about what the Old West

anti-hero that was totally different than characters John Wayne played."

Westerns declined steadily during the 1970s and 1980s; Eastwood went nearly 10 years without making one after he directed and starred in the modern classic *The Outlaw Josey Wales* (1976). In 1980, one of the biggest movie bombs of all time, *Heaven's Gate*, convinced Hollywood that, finally, Westerns were truly dead.

In the early 1990s, Costner's *Dances with*

days were like, Munny replies, "I can't remember. I was drunk most of the time."

Every murder has its consequences, and Eastwood demythologizes killers and sheriffs alike by exposing the fictions of a reporter who would twist their exploits into the kind of dime novels that inspired Westerns in the first place. As in *Liberty Valance*, the genre has turned in on itself, exposing its own false origins. In 1992, Eastwood told a *Los Angeles Times* reporter that *Unforgiven* would be his final Western. "Maybe that's why I didn't do it right away. I was kind of savoring it as the last of that genre, maybe the last film of that type for me."

**Left**, a Colt Peacemaker, perhaps the most ironic name for a handgun ever. **Above**, Clint Eastwood as The Man With No Name.

The vast and varied world of outdoor recreation awaiting visitors to the Southwest cannot be easily described. You'll find a unique blend of enticing, year-round activities, many of which are unavailable in other regions of the continental United States. Where else, for example, can you ski two miles high in the morning, then play afternoon tennis or golf in 75°F (24°C) sunshine? Where else can you, wearing only shorts and a T-shirt, cast streamer flies for huge rainbow trout in January? Where else can you drive a herd of longhorn cattle across an open prairie, accompanied by a chuckwagon (circa 1870) complete with banging pots and a cowgirl cook? Where else can you ride a bucking raft through the white water thundering down an isolated desert canyon and then later that evening dine on *steak tartare* in the comfort of an urban restaurant?

These questions have a simple answer: only in the Southwest! From biking to bass-fishing, hiking to hot-air ballooning, trail-riding to turkey-hunting, whatever your particular craving in outdoor fun, you'll find this heterogeneous land to be an eager and willing host. "When your spirit cries for peace," wrote August Frugé, "come to a world of canyons deep in an old land; feel the exultation of high plateaus, the strength of moving waters, the simplicity of sand and grass, the silence of growth." Take a single sojourn into the great outdoors of the American Southwest, and you'll know exactly what Frugé meant.

To help you along, a selected potpourri of outdoor adventures appears in the following pages. There are many more, hundreds more.

**Ride the Big Water:** *We have an unknown distance yet to run; an unknown river yet to explore. What falls there are, we know not; what rocks beset the channel, we know not; what walls rise over the river, we know not.*

Amateur naturalist John Wesley Powell scribbled that diary notation on August 13, 1869, and a few hours later set forth with nine companions in three flimsy wooden boats to explore the Grand Canyon on the Colorado River in Arizona. Sixteen days later, half starved and totally exhausted, Powell and his party emerged from the chasm's lower end, the first men in history to negotiate the full 277 river miles (462 km) of the Grand Canyon successfully.

The termination of Powell's historic voyage marked the beginning of an era. Within a century, white-water boating – as sport, not transportation – would be one of America's

favorite pastimes. And not surprisingly, thousands of participants have discovered in recent years that nowhere is the scenery more breathtaking or the rapids more exciting than where it all began.

The prevailing monarch of all desert streams is the Colorado River, a 1,600-mile (2,576-km) ribbon of watery turmoil that heads in the Rocky Mountains and terminates in the silty waters of the Gulf of California in Mexico. You can float this magnificent river along most of its length, but a raft or dory trip through Arizona's Grand Canyon is by far the most visually overwhelming. Float trip adventures on the Grand begin

**Preceding pages:** a camper winds down Zion National Park. **Left,** backpacker contemplates Petrified Forest National Monument. **Right,** skiing near Durango, southern Colorado.

at Lees Ferry, a tiny desert community a few miles below Glen Canyon Dam on Lake Powell. Depending on whether your boats are oar- or motor-powered, you'll need anything between 8 to 15 days to run all 277 miles (462 km) of the canyon, but you can arrange to float to the halfway point at Phantom Ranch and then catch a helicopter to the rim. Reservations far in advance of your trip are necessary.

The upper Colorado River in southern Utah offers a couple of fine white-water escapades as well. Float trips through 26-mile (42-km) Westwater Canyon and 47-mile (76-km) Cataract Canyon begin in the town of Moab, Utah, just east of Canyonlands

of Dinosaur National Monument on the Colorado-Utah border, via the Yampa River, a wide, turbulent stream that tumbles, like its cousin the Colorado, from the Rockies.

If you're looking for something short but sassy, take a kayak or paddle-boat tour of the Rio Grande Gorge west of Taos, New Mexico. Fifty miles (81 km) long, 800 ft (244 meters) deep and generally less than a mile in width, this slab-sided gouge in the earth's crust is known locally as "The Box."

Only the lower 25 miles are navigable, but nowhere will you find a more exciting one-day trip. Rapids like Powerline Falls and Ski-Jump give plenty of white-water thrills, but long quiet eddies and meandering

National Park on US Highway 163. Here, numerous expedition companies offer full-length excursions through both of these canyons as well as single-day junkets on less demanding sections of the Colorado. Most river companies furnish everything you'll need for your trip except sleeping bags and personal clothing.

Plenty of other Southwest waterways exist to carry you into the wilderness. You may want to float the mighty Green River through Desolation Canyon or The Canyon of Lodore, both extraordinarily beautiful chasms carved from the Utah red rock north of Moab. You can also explore the inscrutable back-country

currents allow time to enjoy the spectacle of vertical, lava-rock walls that seem to grow literally from the water's edge. The most favorable season in which to float the Rio Grande and other Southwestern rivers is from early May to late June when streams are gorged with spring runoff.

**The Wild West revisited:** Less than a century ago, horseback travel was the only available transportation on the Western frontier. A man's horse was precious; horse thieves were summarily hanged while murderers, bank robbers, cattle rustlers and other "owlhoots" often went unpunished for their crimes. "Pity the scoundrel who pilfers a horse," said one judge, passing sentence, "his boots will kick air before sundown."

The era of inflexible, Wild West justice is gone, but horseback travel is not. Recently this ancient mode of transportation has undergone a rebirth of sorts as more "dudes" seek adventurous vacations away from the madding crowd.

If you don't mind thornbush, cactus and wide-open vistas, try a horseback camping trip into Arizona's 125,000-acre (51,250-hectare) Superstition Mountain Wilderness, which lies 30 miles (48 km) northeast of Phoenix. Of all America's mountain ranges, the Superstitions are the most legendary – steeped in mystery, surrounded by tales of

Roger's Canyon Cliff Ruin and Weaver's Needle, a shark's-tooth desert peak that for two centuries has been a landmark for westbound travelers.

In the evenings, chances are you'll camp beneath towering saguaro cactus, eat such desert delicacies as fried rattlesnake (not mandatory) and watch glorious sunsets. Most pack trips vary in length from two to seven days. Outfitters usually furnish everything but riding clothes and toothbrushes.

Another memorable desert trail ride is a 25-mile (42-km) trip from Navajo Mountain Trading Post, Arizona, to Rainbow Bridge National Monument on the eastern shore of Utah's Lake Powell, along the old Rainbow

misplaced treasure and miscreant men. The most famous tale is that of the Lost Dutchman Mine, an enormously rich vein of gold worked for years by prospector Jacob Waltz (known to his friends as The Dutchman), its secret location lost from knowledge in 1892 when Waltz died.

Today, astride surefooted horses, you can visit Dutchman's Valley, supposedly the site of the old mine, and view breathtaking sights like the ancient Sinagua Indian dwellings at

**Left**, motorcyclists at Winter Park, Colorado. **Above**, almost ready for dinner – a cattle drive in New Mexico.

Trail. Rainbow Bridge is one of the seven natural wonders of the world. A Native American legend claims that it is a rainbow turned to stone. Used probably from the time of Christ by nomadic Indians, this ancient pathway winds its way through a land of giant sandstone monoliths and deep, sandstone canyons, both carved by eons of unhindered erosion.

You'll generally spend one full day exploring the Indian ruins of Surprise Valley, a remote box canyon made famous by novelist Zane Grey in *Riders of the Purple Sage*. At the end of the trip, you can leave your horse with the guides and for the next few days leisurely investigate the magical slickrock canyons of Lake Powell, living aboard a fully-equipped houseboat.

If you prefer pine-covered ridges and murmuring brooks to cactus gardens, you'll find plenty of both on a pack trip into one of New Mexico's sprawling wilderness areas. Near Taos, for instance, lies Wheeler Peak Wilderness, 21,000 acres (8,610 hectares) of alpine landscape girdled by half a dozen of the state's loftiest peaks.

Here you may see bighorn sheep, black bear and even mountain lions, but more impressive are the unbelievable panoramas viewable from the higher ridges; some of them encompass 11,000 sq. miles (28,490

cattle drive. Simulating as closely as possible the strenuous Texas trail drives of the 1870s, these modern-day junkets offer guests an opportunity to relive a bit of Western history. You'll work alongside real cowhands, branding, herding cattle and shoeing horses. Sleeping on the ground and eating traditional cowboy grub like mountain oysters (fried calf testicles), beans and beef, sourdough biscuits and spotted-pup pudding are part of the experience.

Several of these cattle drives are on offer in the Southwest, and most of them are run by working cattle ranches and last from three days up to a full week. Previous riding experience is not necessary, and most of the

sq. km) of terrain. Two hours' drive south near Santa Fe is the 220,000-acre (90,200-hectare) Pecos Wilderness, once a favorite beaver-trapping area for 17th-century mountain men. Take your fishing rod if you make a trail ride here; most lakes and streams in the high country abound with hungry brook and cut-throat trout. In the southern part of the state near Silver City are the Gila and Aldo Leopold Wilderness areas, two adjacent hinterlands that together offer 800,000 acres (328,000 hectares) of virtually unexplored high-desert terrain to trail-riders.

If you want to try America's most unique horseback adventure, sign up for an old-time

organizations furnish everything you'll need for the trip except your personal gear.

Spring and early winter are the best times to go exploring on the desert trails of the Southwest. By mid-October the merciless heat of summer has abated, desert springs are usually brimming, and wildlife is more active. The most favorable season for mountain trips is late June through September. You'll experience warm, pleasant days, crisp nights, few biting insects and the wildest and most colorful selection of wildflowers in the Rocky Mountains.

Have you ever dreamed of going on safari in Africa? You could safari in New Mexico instead, where sportsmen stalk exotic species of African and Asian game animals through terrain closely resembling the veldt of Kenya. Two decades ago, selected breeding pairs of kudu and oryx (both large examples of African antelope) and Barbary sheep were imported and released in protected reserves in New Mexico.

The programs were so successful that limited hunting seasons are held annually on the White Sands Missile Range near Alamogordo and in the Canadian River Canyon near Wagon Mound.

If you have no desire to emulate Frank Buck or Jungle Jim but still enjoy the shooting sports, conventional big-game hunting

are coaxed from the central fly-way to rest and feed in quiet river sloughs.

In these same areas, you'll find healthy populations of upland game birds like quail, dove and chukar grouse.

Trout fishing in the Southwest boasts many aficionados because of year-round seasons and countless miles of uncrowded shorelines. You'll find rainbow and German brown trout inhabiting most mountain streams, while high lakes usually contain cutthroat and brook trout. Two noteworthy areas that for decades have drawn anglers from all over the world are New Mexico's San Juan River east of Farmington, New Mexico and the Colorado River below Glen Canyon Dam in Arizona.

opportunities in the Southwest are numerous. Mule deer, elk, black bear and wild-turkey seasons run from November to Christmas. Permits for mountain lion and javelina – a pig-like member of the hippopotamus family that is native to South America – are also available in limited quantity.

For waterfowl hunters, the golden days of autumn bring with them enormous flights of ducks and geese into the Rio Grande and Colorado basins. Skies turn black as flocks of mallards, pintails, Canada and snow geese

**Left**, making waves. **Above**, duck hunters at Caballo Lake, New Mexico.

Both of these streams contain rainbow trout that reach weights of 15 lbs (7 kg).

Warm-water angling on man-made reservoirs has become popular with rod-and-reel addicts, and Arizona's Lake Mead, Lake Roosevelt and Lake Powell and New Mexico's Navajo Lake and Elephant Butte Lake draw their share of anglers. Large-mouth bass fishing is particularly superb in these lakes, but you'll find crappie, small-mouth bass, channel, and blue and yellow catfish, too. The striped bass, a rangy battler native to the Atlantic Ocean, has found a new home here, too. Quite often, Southwest stripers attain weights of 70 lbs (32 kg).

Surprise! Snow is no stranger to the Southwest. More than 50 percent of the region, in fact, lies above 7,000 ft (2,134 meters) in elevation, and winter sports of all kinds are in good supply from mid-November right through to Easter.

Alpine skiers find New Mexico best equipped to satiate their downhill desires. The state contains 12 major ski areas, most of them within easy reach of Albuquerque. The most famous names in Southwest skiing are Taos Ski Valley, located northeast of the town of Taos, and Santa Fe Ski Basin, "up mountain" from the capital city. Reasonable prices, short lift lines and magnificent winter scenery make both of these resorts a must if you like a Swiss Alps environment.

On the outskirts of Albuquerque, atop 10,447-ft (3,166-meter) Sandia Crest, lies Sandia Peak Winter Recreation Area. You can, if you wish, drive to this ski area, but most visitors load their equipment aboard the Sandia Peak Tramway and take an 18-minute "skyride" to the top. The slopes are within a snowball's throw of the tram's upper terminal. Because Albuquerque's winter climate is so moderate, many visitors ski in the morning, then enjoy a sunny afternoon of tennis or golf in the city.

Arizona has only two major downhill ski areas, the Snow Bowl, north of Flagstaff, and Mount Lemmon, 40 miles (64 km) northeast of Tucson in the Catalina Mountains. Cross-country skiing is superb, however, in the state's numerous national forests. Two unique cross-country areas are along the rims of the Grand Canyon and atop the famed Mogollon Rim near the town of Payson.

Southern Colorado's best-known ski resort is Purgatory, north of Durango. Hellish in name only, this large, well-groomed basin offers fine views of the southern Rocky Mountains and an average snowpack of 100 inches (254 cm) at the base. Reasonably priced accommodation is available in nearby Durango.

Another noteworthy resort is Wolf Creek Ski Basin, northeast of Pagosa Springs, atop 10,850-ft (3,307-meter) Wolf Creek Pass. This ski area boasts the longest season of all Southwest resorts. If you don't mind toting your gear uphill, you can ski here into July.

The Southwest offers several unusual outdoor activities that are available in few other regions in the United States. If, for instance,

you find yourself in Albuquerque during the first weeks of October, you'll notice lots of hot air in the atmosphere, and it won't be coming from a boastful companion. The International Hot Air Balloon Festival comes to town in October, and for nine days the Albuquerque skies are filled with these lighter-than-air craft, drifting where they will on the desert breezes. On the first and last weekends of the festival, pilots take part in a mass ascension. The sight of more than 400 balloons lifting as one in the crisp morning light is unforgettable.

Not as death-defying as ballooning, llama trekking is a relatively new outdoor activity in the Southwest. If you're a backpacker but hate to carry all that weight up the mountain, then this sport is for you. Long-eared, bulbous-nosed cud-chewers with the front end of a camel and the caboose of an ostrich, llamas will patiently haul your camping equipment into the wilderness.

Llama treks are available in both the Pecos and Gila Wilderness areas of New Mexico and in the San Juan National Forest of southern Colorado. More and more outfitters are using them instead of horses or mules on pack trips because llamas eat very little, drink almost no water and have an almost negligible effect on forest trails and meadows. If you're on a tight budget, you'll find llama trekking cheaper than standard horse and mule pack trips.

Ever had a hankering to captain your own yacht? The opportunity awaits on Utah's Lake Powell and Arizona's Lake Mead. Here, you can rent a fully equipped houseboat for two or 20 people, then spend up to two weeks exploring the thousands of remote backwaters that few speedboaters or fishermen ever reach. Most rental boats are large – 30–70 ft (9–21 meters) in length, but you'll need no previous boating experience.

All hands are given a crash course in navigation, marine mechanics and the rules of the watery road before leaving the marina dock. Each craft comes equipped with a complete set of navigational charts, plus linens and kitchen utensils. All you need to bring along are food, clothing and, of course, an appetite for adventure.

**Right**, advertisers go to great lengths to create unusual balloons to fly at the International Balloon Festival in Albuquerque.

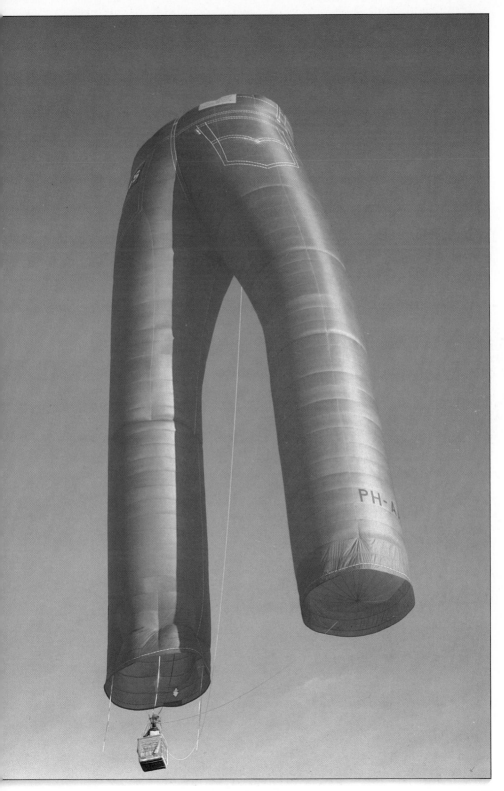

PH-A

After spending time in the American Southwest, most other places will seem cramped. This is a land of endless horizons and big skies. At the same time, usually hidden in the landscape and discovered off the beaten track, are lush green canyons and valleys that rest the eye and provide shelter from the sun. These unexpected pleasures are as much a part of the Southwest as the great masses of red rock and open stretches of desert, but ones which a traveler rushing from national monument to natural spectacle can easily miss.

The Southwest has been defined geographically in dozens of ways, sometimes to include areas as far east as Oklahoma, as far west as Southern California, and as far north as Salt Lake City, Utah, and Reno, Nevada. This book defines the Southwest on the basis of cultural and geographical similarities, and so the area can be reasonably explored by car without long detours.

This tour of the Southwest includes the Grand Canyon – one of the most frequently visited natural spots in the world. Also Southern Utah, as spectacular in many ways as the Grand Canyon but less accessible, less crowded and on a more human scale. Near Utah is "Indian Country," which spills over from Arizona into New Mexico and Utah, and as the home of the Navajo and Hopi Indians, is an entity unto itself. Next comes Pueblo Country, which includes Albuquerque, Santa Fe and Taos, all in New Mexico. This area represents a mixture of Indian Pueblo and Hispanic villages existing side by side with the cities. It is culturally and geographically so rich that a traveler could literally spend years exploring it. Here is the place to satisfy a fascination for old Spanish churches and adobe architecture; to look for Native American and Hispanic arts and crafts in the plazas, pueblos and villages; and the place with the best red chilis to be had anywhere. Eastern and southern New Mexico are more spread out, but the deserts, mountains and plains offer equal rewards of a different quality for those who stop and explore. Southern Arizona is border country – the line between the United States and Mexico creating almost a separate country, offering the most interesting desert flora and fauna, as well as the laid-back ambience of Tucson.

Phoenix dominates central Arizona on the map, but the mountains surrounding it to the south, east and north are an outdoorsman's paradise as well as the home of the largest Apache Indian tribes.

Las Vegas is an anomaly in the Southwest – a big, garish nonstop neon city dedicated to entertainment of every imaginable variety. Try it out and you'll probably end up going back for more.

The writers of this section have lived in and written about the Southwest for most or all of their adult lives. Rather than trying to do the impossible and cover everything, they have concentrated on their favorite spots.

**Preceding pages:** Bryce Canyon National Park, Utah; rich and varied cactus growth at Saguaro National Monument; yellow blossoms in a Flagstaff field, Arizona. **Left,** gunman performs a shoot-out on cue at Old Tucson, Arizona.

# American Southwest

100 miles / 160 km

**East Tavaputs Plateau**

○ Green River

6

○ Salina

15

**Mt. Marvine**
▲ **11,610**

70

Arches
Nat'l. Park

Milford ○

**Delano Pk.**
▲
**12,173**

Capitol Reef
Nat'l. Park

Colorad

Mt. Pea
12,7

○ Warm Springs

93

89

**Mt. Ellen**
▲ **11,615**

Canyon

**UTAH**

Canyonlands

○ Caliente

Nat'l. Park

Monticello

○ Cedar City

Bryce Canyon
Nat'l. Park

Natural Bridge
■ Nat'l. Mo

**NEVADA**

■

Cedar Breaks
Nat'l. Mon.

Zion Nat'l.
Park

*Lake
Powell*

Hove
Nat'

St. George

Glen Canyon
Nat'l. Rec. Area

**10,388**
▲ **Navajo Mtn.**

**Monument
Valley**

95

Indian Springs

Moapa ○

15

Littlefield

*Virgin*

Kaibob
Ind. Res.

C o l o r a
Page

Navajo
Nat'l. Mon.

N a v a j

**Charleston
Peak** ▲
**11,918**

**Las Vegas**

*Lake
Mead*

Colorado R.

160

Hopi

I n

**Nat'l. Rec. Area**

Grand

Canyon

89

Canyon de Chelly
Nat'l. Mon.

Black Mountains

Coconino
Plateau

*Little Colorado*

Indian Res.

R e

93

Hualapai Ind. Res.

Wupatki
Nat'l. Mon.

P l a t e

○ Kingman

**Humphreys Peak** ▲
Williams **12,633** **Flagstaff**

40

Needles ○

Sedona

Winslow

**ARIZONA**

Holbrook

Petrified F
Nat'l. Park

40

Lake Havasu
City

93

Prescott ○

Ind. Res.

Show Low ○

Parker
Dam

17

Springerville

○ Wickenburg

60

**Fort Apache**

Joshua Tree
Nat'l. Park

Colorado River
Ind. Res.

Ind. Res.

Alp
Ind. Res.

10

○ Ehrenberg

Ind. Res.

*Salton
Sea*

Glendale ○

**Phoenix**

Globe ○

San Carlos

Ind.
Res.

★

Salt

70

Ind. Res.

○ El Centro ○ Brawley

80

Mesa

**Mexicali**

Laguna
Ind. Res.

Gila Blend ○

Casa Grande ○

Safford ○

**Mt. Graham**
▲
**10,120**

*Laguna
Salada*

8

○ Yuma

San Manuel ○

10

○ El Mayor

San Luis

*Gran Desierto*

Organ Pipe
Cactus
Nat'l. Mon.

**P a p a g o  I n d i a n
R e s.**

Ind.
Res.

**Tucson**

Willcox ○

Saguaro Nat'l. Mon.

Chiri
Nat'l

5

Vamori ○

19

Tombstone ○

*Gulf of California*

Puerto Peñasco ○

2

Nogales

Coronado
Nat'l. Mon.

De

○ San Felipe

**M E X I C O**

126

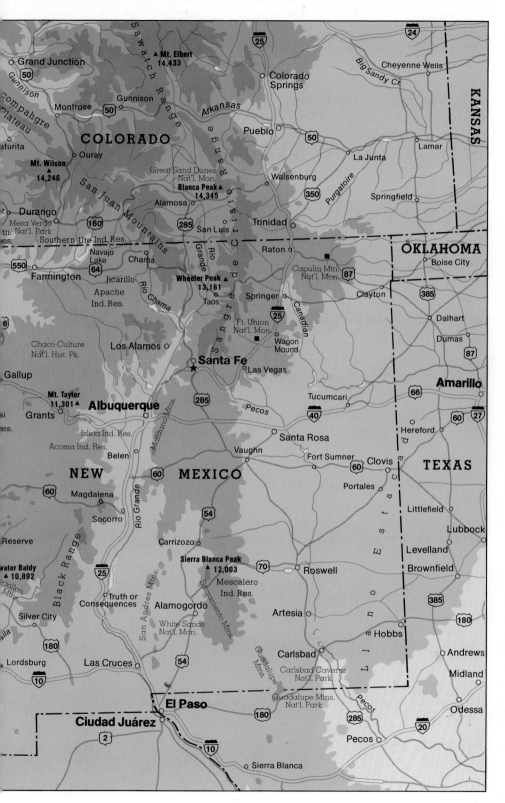

Mt. Elbert
14,433

Grand Junction
50

Gunnison

Gunnison

Montrose
50

Sawatch Range

COLORADO

Colorado Springs

25

24

Cheyenne Wells

Big Sandy Cr

KANSAS

Arkansas

Uncompahgre Plateau

Naturita

Ouray

Pueblo

50

La Junta

Lamar

Mt. Wilson
14,246

Great Sand Dunes
Nat'l. Mon.

Blanca Peak ▲
14,345

Walsenburg

350

Purgatoire

Springfield

Durango

Mesa Verde
Nat'l. Park

Alamosa

San Luis

285

350

Southern Ute Ind. Res.

San Juan Mountains

Rio Grande

San Luis

Trinidad

Raton

OKLAHOMA

Boise City

550

Navajo Lake

Chama

64

Capulin Mtn.
Nat'l. Mon.

87

Clayton

385

Farmington

Jicarillo
Apache
Ind. Res.

Rio Chama

Wheeler Peak ▲
13,161

Taos

Springer

Dalhart

Sangre de Cristo Range

Canadian

25

Ft. Union
Nat'l. Mon.

Dumas

87

Chaco Culture
Nat'l. Hist. Pk.

Los Alamos

Wagon Mound

Gallup

Santa Fe
★

Las Vegas

Mt. Taylor
11,301 ▲

Albuquerque

285

Pecos

Tucumcari

66

Amarillo

Grants

40

Hereford

60

27

Isleta Ind. Res.

Acoma Ind. Res.

Belen

Santa Rosa

Vaughn

Fort Sumner

Clovis

TEXAS

NEW

MEXICO

60

Portales

Manzano Mtns.

60

Magdalena

Rio Grande

54

Littlefield

Socorro

Lubbock

Reserve

Carrizozo

Levelland

Water Baldy
▲ 10,892

Black Range

25

Sierra Blanca Peak
▲ 12,003

70

Roswell

Brownfield

Gollin
Mtns.

Mescalero
Ind. Res.

Silver City

Truth or
Consequences

Alamogordo

Artesia

385

White Sands
Nat'l. Mon.

Hobbs

180

180

Lordsburg

Las Cruces

54

Carlsbad

Andrews

10

San Andres Mtns.

Sacramento Mtns.

Guadalupe Mtns.

Carlsbad Caverns
Nat'l. Park

Midland

El Paso

Guadalupe Mtns.
Nat'l. Park

Pecos

Odessa

Ciudad Juárez

2

180

285

20

10

Pecos

Sierra Blanca

# PHOENIX AND ENVIRONS

When Frank Lloyd Wright first saw the Salt River Valley in the late 1920s, it struck him as a "vast battleground of Titanic natural forces." Like a revelation were its "leopard spotted mountains... its great striated and stratified masses, noble and quiet," its patterns modeled on the "realism of the rattlesnake," its "nature masonry rising from the desert floor." Here, thought Wright with the zeal of someone moving in, if Arizonans could avoid the "candy-makers and cactus-hunters," a proper civilization could be created that would "allow man to become a godlike native part of Arizona."

Even today, when candy-makers and cactus-hunters in the form of land developers have won out over Wright's visions, the setting of Phoenix is impressive. To the east soar the massive Four Peaks and the formal flank of the Superstition Mountains, while the Sierra Estrella rides the southeast horizon in *dorsales* of blue silk. Hemming in the city north and south are lower ranges of Precambrian gneiss and schist, framing the Phoenix trademark, Camelback Mountain – a freestanding, rosy, recumbent dromedary with a sedimentary head and granitic hump.

Many of the mountains within the town are pocked with exclusive homes, and some of the smaller formations, separating business areas from bedroom communities from tourist playgrounds, have come to function as the urban version of room dividers. Still, geological immediacy is what gives Phoenix its own look. And by acquiring the two major mountain ranges within its borders, the city of Phoenix, for all its commerce, has amassed more square footage of parkland than any other town in the world.

A civilization that adapted man to the Salt River Valley preceded Wright's visions by some 2,500 years. As early as 500 BC the Hohokam Indians developed an intricate system of canals for irrigating fields of corn, beans, squash and cotton. Remains of that system were taken over and expanded in 1868 by the Swilling Irrigation Canal Co., the first organized Anglos to stake claims in the long-deserted valley. The following year their settlement was named Phoenix by an Englishman who saw a new civilization rising like the mythical bird from the ashes of the vanished Hohokam.

**A "dry" river:** What rose from the ashes was an aggressive ranching community that catered to miners and military outposts. Canals were extended through the alluvial valley, watering fields of cotton and alfalfa, pasturage for cattle and rows of citrus to the horizon's edge. Water storage commenced on a grand scale with the construction, in 1911, of **Roosevelt Dam**, still the world's largest masonry dam, on the Salt River some 90 miles (145 km) upstream from Phoenix.

Three more dams on the Salt, and two on its major tributary, the Verde, allowed agriculturalists to send water where they liked. The riverbed of the Salt became the driest place in Phoenix, while all available water was diverted through the stems of plants and the gullets of mammals, including the thirsty human being.

Because of its dry air and temperate winter climate, asthmatic and tubercular patients came to Phoenix as soon as ranchers had made enough of a community to receive visitors. Medical centers for pulmonary diseases sprang up soon after the turn of the century to treat what locals referred to as "Arizona tenors."

Now that the Southwest seemed safe as well as glamorous, the outskirts of Phoenix also bloomed with that Arizona specialty, the desert dude ranch. What became the Santa Fe Railroad already reached Phoenix in the 1880s, and air service began in the late 1920s. It was discovered that eastern dudes, usually arriving by train, would pay handsomely for the chance to ride horses, eat T-bones grilled over mesquite fires, dance Put-Your-Little-Foot to guitars and accordions and wear those exotic pants called blue jeans. Dude ranches from rustic to lavish numbered in the hundreds and succumbed only recently to urbanization and more extravagant tastes in entertainment.

The extremes of dude-ranch living still survive in obscure corners. **The Wigwam** in Litchfield Park west of Phoenix, begun as a corporate retreat by the Goodyear Corporation in the late 1920s and now a quiet contemporary resort, retains its plush leather and copper-flecked adobe interiors. Perpetuating the actual way of life is **Saguaro Lake Ranch**, just south of Stewart Mountain Dam, where Arizona's oldest continually operating dude ranch preserves the mission furniture and cactus skeleton decor of the 1930s as if under a bell jar.

**The Phoenician Golden Age:** With a slack economy to begin with, Phoenix hardly noticed the Depression, living off its own agriculture and catering to those tourists who had kept their money. The great monument to that period is the **Arizona Biltmore** hotel. Built just before the financial crash of 1929, it sailed in splendor through the bleakest of times.

It is to the Biltmore that Phoenix owes the arrival of Frank Lloyd Wright. The hotel was originally designed by a former student of Wright who found himself in trouble and summoned the master for help. Wright probably gave more help than required, for the result was a masterpiece of textile block construction from Wright's middle period.

Gutted by fire in 1973, the interior was refurnished with furniture and textile designs from all periods of Wright's career. The visitor who enters no other building in Phoenix should make it to 24th Street and Missouri to inspect the Arizona Biltmore. It was through working on the hotel, that Wright was moved to establish **Taliesin West**, the winter quarters of his architectural school, in the desert west of Phoenix.

Residents with long memories recall the 1930s as a Phoenician golden age. Those who couldn't afford the Biltmore found it too snobbish anyway and frequented a lively downtown that still retained a Spanish-American flavor. In summer, when temperatures climbed

**Rawhide, a stagecoach stop town during the 1880s.**

over 120°F (50°C) and daytime highs did not dip below the hundreds for months, locals complained less of the heat than they boasted of trick ways to stay cool. It was common sport to be pulled on an aquaplane along the canals, holding a rope from a car.

Phoenix was transformed forever by World War II. The open desert was ideal for aviation training, and all Phoenix became a kind of extension of Luke Air Force Base. Aviation equipment companies moved into the valley, and even the cotton fields turned out silk for parachutes. It is less known that Phoenix had concentration camps for German prisoners of war, and many of the prisoners, as susceptible to the desert as anyone else, remained in the area after the war to become a part of the community.

**Arrival of the air conditioner:** Besides popularizing the area with young people who otherwise would never have seen it, the military revolutionized Phoenician life with a device called air-conditioning. The city had previously seen minor use of the evaporative or "swamp"

cooler, but what it now discovered was genuine refrigeration. Suddenly Phoenix was a year-round possibility for those who couldn't stand the heat. The great migration was on.

Camelback Mountain, at whose feet lay the most elegant dude ranches, was swamped by suburbia. To the east, greater Phoenix swallowed up the once isolated communities of Scottsdale, Tempe, Mesa and Apache Junction, sitting at the base of the Superstition Mountains some 25 miles (40 km) from Phoenix city limits.

Development leapt to the southwest when **Sun City**, America's first fully planned retirement community, was pitched by the Del Webb Corporation in 1960. More recently, cactus forest to the north of Phoenix has been bulldozed for a realtors' bonanza, and Phoenix and **Scottsdale** have competed in annexing the area under the pretext that they are trying only to control development. Expansion has taken such forms as trailer parks to the east, tract housing to the west and walled-in mazes of simulated

All Arabian Horse Show, Scottsdale.

adobe ranchettes in the newly populated areas to the northeast.

Another civic problem is the classic decline in health. With the advent of peripheral shopping malls, downtown businesses collapsed, prosperity dropped and the crime rate soared. Small-scale buildings with Spanish tracery were felled for slab-style office buildings, many of which have stood half-empty years after construction. Lateral growth doomed the trolley system, and the automobile took over. The city's mountains, lovely as they are, trap pollutants, and at the height of the tourist season its redeeming backdrop recedes disappointingly through a scrim of particulates. Phoenix is now one of America's largest cities, and when the mountains disappear it may well be one of its ugliest.

**The Valley of the Sun:** Many Phoenicians, particularly those who predate the end of World War II, lament the urbanization of the Salt River Valley. But it is important to remember that the forces that transformed Phoenix were,

like the mythical bird, self-generated. Whatever freedom and individualism may have meant to the authors of the Constitution, they have been interpreted locally as the right to do whatever one wants with any property one can get one's hands on.

Zoning, pollution control, and even a minimal sign ordinance, have been seen as socialism rather than social responsibility; a symbol of the conservative viewpoint for many years was the hilltop mansion of high-profile politician Barry Goldwater, from which the apostle of free enterprise observed the prosperity through binoculars kept on his desk.

The migration of Snowbelt retirees, ironically living in rule-bound planned communities, only fueled a conservatism already entrenched. The more recent influx of career-oriented young people to the microchip industry has so altered the population that the average resident within city limits, astonishingly, is *younger* than the national average, and the ideological balance may even tip. But the brakes are being applied a little too late. The Salt River Valley is now known to the outside world by its Chamber of Commerce nickname, the Valley of the Sun, while jaded locals call it the Valley of the Schmun, Phoenicia, the Valley of Celestial Heat, or just the Valley.

Still, Phoenix draws millions of visitors annually, and the past is their least concern. They even overlook the most interesting historical remnants – the canals that were first plotted two and a half millennia ago by the Hohokam and today are lined by smooth-topped banks some 10 ft (3 meters) wide.

Slicing the city at rakish angles, the canals provide a welcome refuge from city traffic for strollers, joggers and bicyclists, acting as a hidden system of transportation for those making their way without combustion. Though alfalfa fields and orange groves have given way to residential areas, irrigation near the canals is still accomplished by opening the floodgates once a month and letting water soak into the lawns overnight. Periodically the canals are drained for repairs, revealing modern artefacts

**Paradise Valley golf course; the Phoenix area appeals to those seeking a relaxed lifestyle.**

such as shopping carts and bicycles, and the occasional missing person.

Those interested in the original canal diggers may visit several excavation sites near the Salt River, as well as those in the path of the Papago Freeway, a long-planned crosstown expressway held up, in part, by frantic archaeologists. The area's most impressive survivor is the freestanding four-story pueblo at **Casa Grande Ruins National Monument**, 50 miles (80 km) south of Phoenix near Coolidge. A permanent collection of traditional Indian art plus changing shows of contemporary work are displayed at the **Heard Museum**, a mission-style building just east of Central Avenue on Monte Vista. Other sites include the **Desert Botanical Garden** in Papago Park and the nearby **Phoenix Zoo**. Across from the zoo is the **Hall of Flame Firefighting Museum** containing a history of this occupation and its courageous crews.

**Desert mountains:** Of the desert drives outside Phoenix, the most spectacular is the **Apache Trail**. One must endure the drive 25 miles (40 km) eastward through trailer parks and roadside businesses to **Apache Junction**, where the western flank of the Superstition Mountains rises like a crumbling mansard roof. The road from there to Roosevelt Dam weaves through 50 miles (80 km) of volcanic ash spewed millions of years ago and settled into rhyolite and tuff swirling like brains. Here and there, lakes of the dammed Salt River form blue calms in the riot of cactus and disordered stone. The Superstition Mountains themselves are protected by wilderness status and offer labyrinthine trails for hiking, horse riding and backpacking.

Another fine drive, with fewer maddening turns and less preliminary clutter, is west on Shea Boulevard to State Highway 87, then north toward **Payson**, leading one through saguaro forest, past the majestic **Four Peaks**, through slopes of granite boulders, into uplands of chaparral. Those preferring to sample the desert without fighting traffic may take the trails up **Camelback Mountain** and **Squaw Peak** from parks at their base or

**Washington Street, Phoenix, in days gone by.**

the network of easier hiking trails in **South Mountain Park**.

And for those preferring man untrammeled by nature, there are the sumptuous new resorts north of Scottsdale and the three mountainside **Pointe** resorts on the north and south edges of Phoenix. Gone is any pretense of dude ranch culture, and the only reference to cactus may be worked into the macrame in the lobby. Offering golf, tennis, saunas, pools with underwater bar stools, French restaurants, nightclubs, discos, refrigerated suites and a clientele armored in credit cards, these are not desert hideaways but total-concept luxury resort complexes. One has to admire that the creators have thought of everything, but the traveler could be anywhere. Those with the means and the wish to remember they are in Phoenix, not Cancun, are advised to stick to the older places that have survived – **Camelback Inn**, **The Royal Palms**, **The Arizona Biltmore**, the **Wigwam** in Litchfield Park – or to seek modest digs and save their money for more local vices.

Chief among these is shopping, a Phoenician specialty ever since **Scottsdale** grew from a ranching crossroad to a gift shop maelstrom in the late 1950s. Jammed side by side are card shops, candle shops, brass shops, leather shops, gem shops, kitchen shops and optical shops, plus the tightest phalanx of art galleries between Santa Fe and Carmel. Some are stocked with desert sunsets and weeping clowns, but several are noted for quality: **O'Brien's Art Emporium** for good desert realism, **Gallery 10** for ancient and current Native American art, the **Horwich-Newman** and **Marilyn Butler galleries** for contemporary art, and the **Suzanne Brown Gallery** for the trendiest in hip and hype. Giving Scottsdale stiff competition is the **Borgata,** a shopping center on Scottsdale Road south of Lincoln Drive, built to resemble an Italian walled city. The Disneyesque exterior gives way inside to gracious courtyards of splashing fountains.

**The cultural scene:** With a population explosion on top of a ranching tradition, Phoenix cannot be called culturally mature. Phoenix did build a glittering **Symphony Hall** at its downtown convention plaza, and Scottsdale has a **Center for the Arts** in an impressively planned park. The Phoenix Symphony Orchestra is improving in quality, but adventurous conductors collide with recalcitrant audiences and conservative board members. Community theater is lively, if uneven, and Phoenix seems a last stand for national touring companies. The **Phoenix Art Museum**, at Central Avenue and McDowell Road, supplements an obscure permanent collection with splendid visiting shows and owns a choice group of recent Mexican works. Phoenix's cultural community despairs, conceding that Tucson, with the help of the University of Arizona, is the state's cultural capital.

Golf, tennis and swimming are available all year, while spectators have the Phoenix Suns in basketball, the Cardinals in Football and such national events as the **Phoenix Open** in golf.

It seems unproductive to seek in Phoenix what other cities offer more lavishly, but in one area Phoenix is unmatched. Architecture buffs are in luck, for works from the middle and late periods of Frank Lloyd Wright, America's most protean architect, are spread joyously through the valley. Besides a half-dozen homes, unlisted as a service to the inhabitants, must viewing are the Arizona Biltmore, **First Christian Church** on North Seventh Avenue, **Grady Gammage Auditorium** in Tempe, and **Taliesin West**, Wright's architectural school on Shea Boulevard, where students conduct guided tours hourly on workdays. For contrast one can visit the studio of **Paolo Soleri** on Double-tree Road in Paradise Valley. A student of Wright, Soleri broke away to design futuristic cities that pack residents into monumental hives, leaving the landscape intact. Scale models of his visions are sure to provide you with visions of your own, either of allure or of fright.

Surrounded by volcanism, Phoenix itself is spreading like lava. Still dramatic in its setting, it is a classically American disharmony of the scenic, the vulgar and the hidden treasure.

**Right, Sun City is closing in on farmlands.**

# TUCSON AND THE BORDER COUNTRY

Arizona's lower third lies almost entirely within the Sonoran Desert, a land mass respected by all, with the possible exception of real estate developers. The classic image of a desert – blowing sand, scorching sun and flat, waterless terrain – is found in only part of the region. The desert also includes lush mountain saddlebacks, highland firs and canyon streams. Rainfall is seasonal – toward summer's end and again at the beginning of winter – and entirely disruptive. On occasion the rain alters its schedule and dumps more water in a few days than it usually does in a year. In 1983, for example, an unexpected torrential downpour filled every gully and *arroyo* for four days, flooding streets and highways, eroding riverbanks, washing out bridges and causing untold damages to homes and crops.

**New kids in town:** Tucson is the major city in southern Arizona. Its first known settlement, about 1,200 years ago, included living quarters near present-day Church Avenue and Washington Street downtown; the site is now marked, rather unceremoniously, by a parking lot. Those first Tucsonans are today called *Hohokam*, "those who have disappeared" in the language of the Tohono O'odham Indians, whose settlement at the base of a small mountain on Tucson's west side gave the city its name. It was called "Tu-uk-so-on", meaning, more or less, "settlement near a black-based mountain." Spanish-speaking newcomers in the 16th century corrupted the O'odham name to "Tuquison," which English-speaking latecomers further changed to "Tucson."

Spanish-speaking settlers established a *presidio*, whose walls protected them from Apache and others who didn't like the new kids in town. This neighborhood is now Tucson's oldest continually inhabited community; a walk around **El Presidio** reveals generations of life and work. The **Tucson Museum of Art**, El Presidio's showpiece, exhibits holdings ranging from pre-Columbian to modern cowboy. Architecture in El Presidio varies from Mexican-style homes with cactus-ribbed ceilings and patios out back to broad Midwestern-style houses with wide porches and roomy interiors. As in other downtown neighborhoods, lawyers and other young aesthetes have gentrified the more established residents out of the area. The result is a comfortable and attractive white-collar *barrio*. Diagonally placed to the museum is **Old Town Artisans**, which carries goods crafted by Southwestern and Latin American artists.

The original walled *presidio* area now serves as the backyard for downtown government buildings. One weekend every October it vibrates with the Tucson Heritage Experience Festival, also known by the acronym THE, a potpourri of music, dance and food from every cultural and ethnic group living in southern Arizona. Scottish highland dancers follow oldtime fiddlers; Burmese performers are sandwiched between a *mariachi* band and Polish singers. Food

**Preceding pages:** riding at sunset, New Mexico. **Left**, the country is big, so everyone needs wheels. **Right**, Tucson is cactus country.

booths offer delicacies. It's a chance for locals to flash their heritage. Most Tucsonans never knew that a Swedish sailor who can still hand-tie nets lives in their midst.

**Controversy at Congress Street:** The major east-west thoroughfare south of the government complex is **Congress Street**. In the middle of a median strip in front of the Pima County office buildings, Pancho Villa sits astride a horse. This statue – Villa riding south, knowing and confident – has been the source of a highly vocal controversy since it was given to the state by some Mexicans in 1981. Villa was a hero of the Mexican Revolution of 1910, a guerrilla bandit of the highest order. His rallying cry throughout Mexico's northwest gave hope to tens of thousands of impoverished and illiterate *campesinos*, many of whose descendants now live in the American Southwest. Villa's savagery, however, sometimes got the best of him, and survivors of his bloody raids upon innocent victims bore witness to his brutality. Their descendants also live in the Southwest, and they tried to block Villa's appearance. But the Mexican enigma remains, cocky and spirited, the pride of like-minded Tucsonans. Not even impromptu paint jobs, usually yellow and down the back, daunt him.

Another downtown landmark is Ronstadt's Hardware Store, founded by Frederico Ronstadt, who, in 1882, at the age of 14, moved from Mexico to Tucson to learn blacksmithing and the wheelwright trade. Two of his sons eventually took over the store, and starting in 1983, the next generation assumed operation. Although best known to the world for singer Linda, the Ronstadts are locally prominent as community leaders – one as head of city parks, another as the former chief of police, and others scattered throughout civic and cultural groups. They still have family ties to Mexico, a situation common to many in the Southwest borderlands. Ranchers and farmers from Arizona and Mexico come to their store for horseshoes, windmills and everything in between – including Linda's records.

**Night falls on Tucson.**

Two institutions, neither having much to do with the other, give the city distinct character – the **University of Arizona** (UA) and **Davis-Monthan Air Force Base**. On almost any given day, the university will have some low-cost or free event open to travelers – a poetry reading, football practice, a political demonstration or a movie. **The Loft** cinema south of the campus shows fare from Woody Allen to artsy foreign films. A block west of the university is the **Arizona Heritage Center**, where the state's history is on exhibit, and the **Center for Creative Photography**, a world-renowned repository for collections of the most acclaimed artistic and journalistic photographers. The photography center's library serves researchers, both casual and scholarly, and its public gallery offers a view of some striking works.

The Air Force decided to place its airplane graveyard at Davis-Monthan Air Force Base, where the desert atmosphere keeps corrosion to a minimum. Tours of the metallic cemetery are given twice weekly. Training for support teams for the cruise missile system is also carried out at the base.

**Hi Corbett Field**, where the Cleveland Indians practice every spring against other "cactus-league" teams, is also the home field for the minor league Tucson Toros. The Toros squaring off against Pacific Coast League opponents on hot summer evenings never fails to attract crowds.

A sign advertising the ARIZONA MOTEL wins Tucson's "best neon" competition; cruising past it on South Sixth Avenue between 28th and 29th streets on a weekend night will also expose you to youthful low riders, whose cars are low, slow and customized to the hilt.

One last sight you may find interesting is Tucson's largest tree, a eucalyptus on West Congress Street in front of a supermarket next to the usually dry Santa Cruz River. Its circumference measures more than 19.5 ft (6 meters).

**White dove of the desert:** Driving south from Tucson on I-19 – the only interstate highway in the country which

The San Xavier Mission.

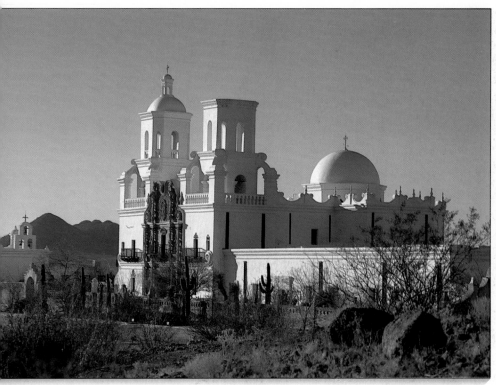

measures distance solely in kilometers – a white dove appears out the right window. This is the **San Xavier de Bac Mission**, a magnificent 18th-century structure which serves the spiritual needs of many Tohono O'odham living on the surrounding reservation. The outer church is maintained remarkably well, as if whitewashed daily at dawn. Public tours point out the Moorish and Byzantine features of this bedrock of Catholicism in the desert.

Most of the 8,000 Tohono O'odham live further west of town on a reservation covering 3 million acres (1.2 million hectares) of cactus, mesquite and scrub. The US government recognizes their reservation as far as Arizona's southern border, but **Papaguería** – the land of the Tohono O'odham, formerly known as the Papago – stretches into Mexico, and many of the tribe cross freely back and forth at convenient breaks in the international fence. The tribe is understandably sensitive to outsiders who approach their 75 miles (120 km) of the line for the same purpose.

**Kitt Peak National Observatory**, at 6,875 ft (2,095 meters) in the Quinlan Mountains 52 miles (83 km) west of Tucson on land leased from the tribe, carries out solar and stellar research. Its visitors center sells high-quality O'odham handicrafts at fair prices.

Yaqui Indians also have their tribal headquarters southwest of Tucson at the **Pascua Yaqui Reservation**. A tribe lacking solid economic footing, the Pascua Yaqui were among the first to take advantage of court decisions permitting on-reservation gambling. The result is a high-stakes bingo game which nightly draws a full house to a huge hall. These Indians, known in literature for incredible powers of perception, are now masters of a Yaqui way of bingo.

Outsiders are allowed to watch spiritual plays, ceremonial dances and other Yaqui activities leading up to Easter Sunday with the strict proviso that no cameras, tape recorders or even paper and pencil record the proceedings. The Tucson Festival Society gives directions to interested visitors.

**Country entertainers out to play.**

142

**Nogales**, Mexico, booms and busts simultaneously. Generally, the worse off the Mexican economy, the better the shopping for tourists. Take advantage of this – good kitsch is hard to find these days. But, as in **Agua Prieta**, seek out the qualities which have attracted and repulsed so many for so long. Buy some white cheese and a fruit you've never seen before at **Futería Chihuahua**, the open-air *mercado* on the right side of Calle Obregón. Climb the stairs on the east side and look down into the city. But exercise caution with the drinking water. Nogales is crowded, and urban poverty is very visible. Lack of public sanitation is an ongoing problem.

Walking through town is the best way to experience Nogales. Notice the shanty towns that sprawl across the mountainsides. These are the homes of factory workers who make about $4 a day. In the center of town is the **Santuario de Guadalupe**, church of the Mexican priest who was arrested and brought to trial in Tucson in 1986 for his assistance to Central American refugees.

**Cactus chatter:** What distinguishes southern Arizona from other parts of the Southwest is its abundance and variety of cacti and all the critters which use their branches, shade and roots for homes. A cursory understanding of the desert and its mysterious life cycles makes the traveler more aware of and comfortable with the region's subtleties. At first glance a cactus is little more than a thick, thorny, green plant with its arms waving at the sky. Look closer: the root system may tell you about water storage, the direction the cactus points can serve as a compass, flowers may indicate the month, the ash-like holes may be seasonal homes to birds. Insects parading up and down its crevices are a strong link in the food chain of nearby animals, and scrub brush near the bottom may hide the entrance to cottontail rabbit or iguana lizard homes.

This information can be absorbed from any of dozens of primers about the desert, or at the **Arizona-Sonora Desert Museum** (ASDM) in **Tucson Mountain Park** west of the city. "Museum" is

gleaming
46 Chevy.

a benign misnomer, though, for the exhibits are changing every second of the day and night. Entertaining and educational, the ASDM displays almost all Sonoran Desert living plants and animals, from plants barely visible to the naked eye such as blue-green algae, to giant cottonwood trees, from tiny doodle bugs to the overpowering black bear. Every effort is made to duplicate the natural surroundings of each life form. A desert trek of any length from an hour to a week or longer should begin with a visit to the Desert Museum. While you may not encounter a bobcat, rattler, javelina or otter on your journey – yes, otters live in the Sonoran Desert in the Sea of Cortez – it is good to learn about their habits and habitats.

ASDM's special events are scheduled to coincide with bursts of flowers, depth of snow, heat of day and clearness of night. When flowers blossom suddenly in mid-March, ASDM guides lead day trips to see the new life and explain the surrounding natural history which has shaped the desert area for eons. The

ASDM tells us how the Boojum – a funny-looking tree in Mexico's northwest – got its name. It seems that during a 1922 expedition near Puerto Libertad in Mexico, Godfrey Sykes was looking at distant wildlife through a telescope when a tree he'd never seen before came into view. "He gazed intently for a few minutes," his son later wrote, "and then said, "Ho ho – a Boojum, definitely a Boojum." Although called *Fougueria columnaris* by botanists, the tree will forever be known to the rest of us as a Boojum, Lewis Carroll's creature of fantasy from his 1876 tale *The Hunting of the Snark*.

Changing plant and animal life become startlingly clear during the "one hour to Canada" drive from the base of **Mount Lemmon** northeast of Tucson to firs and aspens near the 9,100-ft (2,800-meter) top. To ride up Mount Lemmon is to travel through as many eco-zones as there are between Mexico and Canada. More wilderness adventures await at nearby **Saguaro National Park**. The park is divided into two units

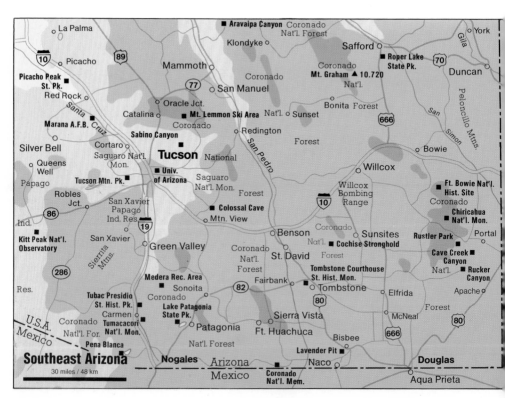

on either side of Tucson: Saguaro East sprawls across 67,000 acres (27,114 hectares) including much of the rocky Rincon Mountains, which peak at an elevation of 8,400 feet (2,560 meters). Saguaro West takes in 24,000 acres (9,713 hectares) and is bordered on the south by the lower, gentler Tucson Mountains. Scenic drives and a network of trails at both units are designed to acquaint visitors with the park's geology and wildlife. Special attention is paid to the saguaro cactus itself, found mainly on rocky slopes *(bajadas)* at the base of desert mountains.

**Covering Cochise County:** Arizona has many laws for those who choose to abide by them. Heading east from Tucson you enter what some call The Free State of Cochise, a land protected on all sides from conventional standards by splendid mountains, working ranches, old mining towns and the Mexican border. Historically, Cochise County has established its own code of conduct, law and behavior. Take the Benson exit off Interstate 10 50 miles (80 km) east of

Saguaro National Park near Tucson.

Tucson. You'll know you're there by the huge semi in the sky, on the right side of the street, which says MARIE'S TRUCK STOP. (You won't find the cafe, however – it's been razed.) A stop at the **Singing Wind Bookshop** is in order. Located in an old ranch house just north of Benson, it carries about the most comprehensive collection of Southwestern literature assembled anywhere, including guides for birders and hikers, history and biography, Indian detective stories and cowboy picture books.

**Tombstone**, a bit farther down the road, once a mining town of some worth, was the unfortunate site of some minor gunplay in the late 1800s. Between then and now television was invented, and today the town spends most of its weekends recreating a history that never was. Amble down Allen Street – in Tombstone you don't walk, you amble – past the **Bird Cage Theater**, the **O.K. Corral** and other mock tributes to the Earp brothers and their ilk, and you'll likely run into gunslingers performing shootouts on cue. After taking in **Boot Hill**

**Cemetery**, you'll have completed your journey to the heart of the myth of the Old West. **Helldorado Days** in October draw the largest crowds.

Continue east on US80, past the cutoff to Sierra Vista and Fort Huachuca, where the US Army trains spies and Mule Pass Tunnel appears at the crest of a hill. Emerging on the other side you'll begin to understand why it's often referred to as the "Time Tunnel." Toward the bottom of the hill on your left you'll swear a picture postcard town from the turn of the century has been preserved. Gingerbread architecture, homes stacked up on canyon hillsides, a main street that winds past friendly storefronts, and a curious mix of aging hippies, small-town merchants, alcoholic vets, struggling artists, retired miners, single parents and venture capitalists.

This is **Bisbee**, a town for seekers of the quaint. Today the town is known for its artsy community, whose industrious output covers the range from works only a mother could love to impressive art carried out with integrity and skill.

**A pit, a hotel and a gulch:** The biggest tourist attraction around by far is **Lavender Pit**, a 120-yard- (110-meter-) deep hole in the ground, 1½ miles long and ¾-mile wide (2.2 by 1.2 km). Tours of the pit and also of the underground Copper Queen Mine give some idea of what laborers faced daily, and why during World War I the Industrial Workers of the World – the Wobblies – attracted workers to their cause.

An IWW strike in 1917 proved too irksome for the Phelps Dodge mining operation, which one night rounded up all Wobblies, marched them off in boxcars, and let them out in the desert near Columbus, New Mexico. This infamous event in American history became known as the Bisbee Deportation, a subject about which one still speaks politely with local boosters.

The **Copper Queen Hotel**, once host to mining barons, is in good shape today, its bar convivial and its rooms comfortable. **Brewery Gulch** around the corner had it all – fine restaurants, brothels, theaters and gambling halls.

**Church at Tumacacori, Arizona.**

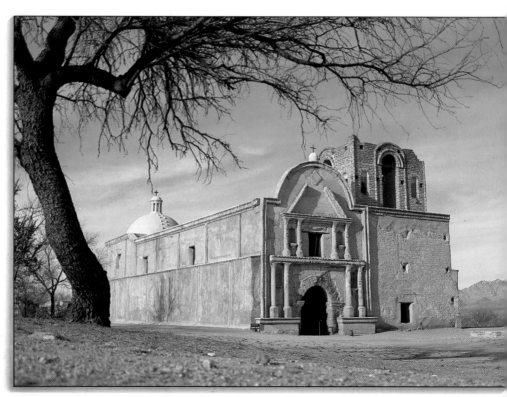

That was in the early 20th century, when copper boomed and miners caroused. Today the street is far tamer. Walk down the Gulch past **St Elmo** – oldest of the local bars, where you can still count on a harmless slow-motion fight late at night near closing time – and on into the residential neighborhood. Restoring old homes has become a fetish among Bisbeeites, and Brewery Gulch, or any of the canyons farther uphill, offer fine examples. Bisbee fairly drips with ambience, at least most of it authentic, and its low-end economy makes for a low-profile populace.

The 1.8 million acre (720,000 hectare) **Coronado National Forest**, 12 different mountain islands rising from the desert floor to elevations of more than 10,000 ft (3,050 meters), dominates southern Arizona's horizon. It includes primitive wilderness areas, fishing, and travel on foot, horse, mountain bike, snowmobile and four-wheel drive as marked throughout the forest. A wide variety of easily identifiable birds has turned the forest, particularly the

Chiricahua and Huachuca mountains, into a birder's paradise. Finally, to reach the spot where Apache leader Geronimo made one of his surrenders to US troops, drive about 10 miles (16 km) southeast on a dirt road from the town of Apache on US80, pass by a ranch and through a gate, and park just inside the Forest Service sign welcoming you to the Peloncillo Mountains. The precise site, determined by photographic accounts, is a ¼-mile (400-meter) walk west at a bench on a mesa.

**More border adventures:** Six miles (10 km) southwest of Bisbee is Naco, Mexico, small enough to get a sense of border towns without feeling overwhelmed. When you drive into Mexico you will have to enter a customs house where an official will look up inquiring either with his eyes or voice where you're going. Tell him, "*aqui no más*" (just here). You should have few problems.

**Naco**'s commercial district is confined to cross streets within three blocks of the border. Stores selling tortillas, groceries, furniture, knick-knacks and

S Border atrol on rizona side.

clothes welcome your business. Pesos are not necessary; border-town merchants know the exchange rate for dollars better than most bankers.

About ½-mile (800 meters) or so down the road, turn left and cruise the quiet residential neighborhood until you find the ruins of the old red-light district. A few former brothels are in splendid decay, with Japanese tile walls, church-like windows and cribs – the tiny rooms where prostitutes entertained – still intact out-back. One of the few still-functioning brothels adjoins a decent all-night cafe, the only place where Bisbeeites and others from north of the border can get a meal after 10pm.

A note about the brothels – they are really quite harmless bars with jarring jukeboxes and male camaraderie. (Women – at least American women – go in on occasion with no ill will.) The prostitutes are friendly, but they will leave you alone unless you want to dance or do more.

Two imposing smelter stacks mark **Douglas**, the US border town opposite

**Agua Prieta**, Mexico. Pancho Villa fought in Agua Prieta, and old-timers retell stories of climbing to the roof of the **Gadsden Hotel** (visit it just for the marble-columned lobby) to watch Villistas battle Mexican government troops. A trench dug along the US side of the border to hide soldiers protecting America from foreign encroachment still exists. In 1990, one of the largest drug busts in US history was made here, largely through the discovery of a highly sophisticated and expensively built tunnel under the border.

**Where two cultures meet:** Spend some time walking in **Agua Prieta**, first along the street leading from the border with its tourist shops. Like most border towns, its culture is an overlay of the United States and Mexico. Look at the faces of *campesinos* from the interior getting off the bus, heading north. Talk with vendors and soldiers on the fringes of the plaza. Browse the sidestreet bookstore, listen to music at the record shop around the corner. Shoot pool and clink beer bottles with the unemployed, order something you can't pronounce at the Café Central. Watch the women leaving their shift at the *maquiladoras* (assembly plants).

Should you find yourself in **Yuma**, a city which inspires nothing more than departure, drive south to **San Luis Río Colorado**, Mexico, for its terrific Chinese restaurants, and, in season, watch the *algodoneros* ("the cotton-pickers") play minor league baseball in the Liga Norte de Sonora. Head east to Sonoita, Mexico, on the **Camino del Diablo**, the "Devil's Highway", a road which slices through 125 miles (200 km) of organ pipe cactus forest, volcanic rock and forbidding desert.

Cross back into the United States at Sonoita, and you'll find yourself in the middle of **Organ Pipe Cactus National Monument**, a 500-sq.-mile (1,295-sq.-km) preserve filled with the unusual plant and its natural friends. The cactus, which grows in clustered "pipes" from the same roots, reaches 20 feet (6 meters) high. Its pinkish-white flower blossoms in early May and lasts eight weeks before yielding to the scorching July sun. **Tuscon sign.**

# GUNFIGHT AT THE O.K. CORRAL

**H**ollywood likes to depict it as an epic confrontation between good and evil, but the famous gunfight at the O.K. Corral was really little more than a small-town grudge match between two factions that wanted things their own way. On one side were the Earp brothers – Virgil, Morgan and Wyatt – and their friend, a tubercular dentist-turned-gambler named John "Doc" Holliday. On the other was a gang of cattle rustlers and thieves including brothers Ike and Billy Clanton, the McLaury brothers and Billy Claiborne.

The Earps came to Tombstone in 1879 and quickly became one of the most powerful families in town. Virgil got himself named town marshal, and his brothers – including Wyatt, a former policeman in Wichita and Dodge City, Kansas – served as deputies. They also invested in several saloons and gambling halls. Doc Holliday befriended Wyatt in Kansas and followed him to Arizona after killing at least one of the 16 men he is credited with shooting. Wyatt later described him as "a long, lean, ash-blond fellow, half-dead of consumption, and all the while, the most skillful gambler and the nerviest, speediest, deadliest man with a six-gun I ever knew."

The Earps and Holliday soon made enemies, and none proved to be more dangerous than the Clantons and McLaurys. After months of bad blood, the grudge finally turned violent on October 26, 1881. The adversaries faced off outside the O.K. Corral. "You sons of bitches," Wyatt yelled, "you've been looking for a fight and now you have it!"

Virgil ordered the cowboys to drop their weapons. What happened next is not exactly certain. Some witnesses testified that the McLaurys and Clantons tried to surrender; others said they reached for their guns.

It is clear, however, that the Earps got off the first shots. Billy Clanton and Frank McLaury went down almost immediately. Unarmed, Ike Clanton grabbed Wyatt and pleaded for him to stop firing. "The fighting has now commenced. Go to fighting or get away," said Wyatt, pushing him away. Ike ran for cover. Tom McLaury tried to escape with his horse but was cut down by Doc Holliday.

In all, the gunfight only lasted for about 30 seconds. When the smoke cleared, Billy Canton and the McLaurys were dead or dying. Virgil and Morgan Earp were severely wounded. Doc Holliday was grazed in the hip, and Wyatt was untouched. Wyatt and Doc stood trial for the killings and were exonerated of any wrongdoing.

But the bloodshed didn't end there. On December 28, 1881 – a little more than two months after the shoot-out – Virgil Earp was gunned down outside the Oriental Saloon. Although he survived the attack, he lost the use of his left arm. About three months later, Morgan Earp was shot and killed by hidden gunmen while he was at Hatch's Billiard Parlor. "This is the last game of pool I'll ever play," he said before taking his last breath.

The cycle of revenge was now to be carried on by Wyatt, his brother Warren and the ever-loyal Doc Holliday. The trio gunned down a suspected assassin – Frank Stilwell – at a Tucson train station and tracked down and killed two other men shortly after.

Now a wanted man, Wyatt fled Arizona. He worked as a boxing referee, con man, gambler and realtor in California and, for a brief cold spell, as a saloonkeeper in the gold fields of Alaska. Doc Holliday died of tuberculosis in a Colorado sanatorium five years after the shoot-out, in 1887. "This is funny," he reportedly said just before expiring.

Both Warren Earp and Ike Clanton were killed in Arizona the same year – Warren in a fight, Ike in a tussle with the law. Only Wyatt grew to be an old man. He died of natural causes in Los Angeles at age 81 in 1929, already enshrined in the mythology of the Wild West. ∎

Wyatt Earp of O.K. Corral fame.

149

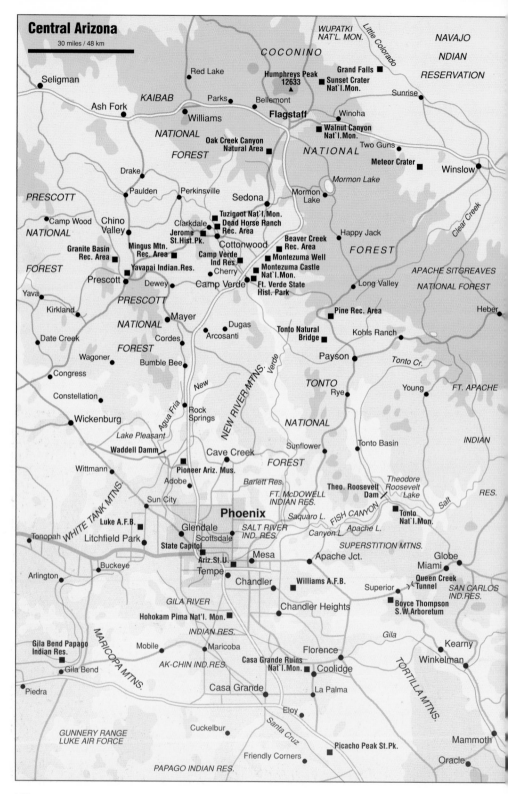

# Central Arizona

30 miles / 48 km

Seligman

Red Lake

*COCONINO*

WUPATKI NAT'L. MON.

Little Colorado

NAVAJO

NDIAN

RESERVATION

Humphreys Peak 12633

Grand Falls

Sunset Crater Nat'l.Mon.

Sunrise

*KAIBAB*

Parks

Bellemont

Ash Fork

Williams

Flagstaff

Winoha

*NATIONAL*

Walnut Canyon Nat'l.Mon.

Two Guns

Drake

Oak Creek Canyon Natural Area

*NATIONAL*

Meteor Crater

Winslow

*FOREST*

*PRESCOTT*

Paulden

Perkinsville

Sedona

Mormon Lake

Mormon Lake

Clear Creek

*NATIONAL*

Camp Wood

Chino Valley

Clarkdale

Tuzigoot Nat'l. Mon.

Dead Horse Ranch Rec. Area

Happy Jack

*FOREST*

Jerome St.Hist.Pk.

Mingus Mtn. Rec. Area

Cottonwood

Beaver Creek Rec. Area

Granite Basin Rec. Area

Camp Verde Ind Res.

Montezuma Well

*APACHE SITGREAVES*

*FOREST*

Yavapai Indian.Res.

Cherry

Montezuma Castle Nat'l.Mon.

*NATIONAL FOREST*

Yava

Prescott

Dewey

Camp Verde

Ft. Verde State Hist. Park

Long Valley

Heber

Kirkland

*PRESCOTT*

Mayer

Dugas

Pine Rec. Area

Kohls Ranch

Date Creek

*NATIONAL*

Cordes

Arcosanti

Tonto Natural Bridge

Wagoner

*FOREST*

Bumble Bee

Payson

Tonto Cr.

Congress

New

*TONTO*

Young

*FT. APACHE*

Constellation

Agua Fria

Rock Springs

*NEW RIVER MTNS.*

Verde

Rye

Wickenburg

*NATIONAL*

*INDIAN*

Lake Pleasant

Sunflower

Tonto Basin

Waddell Damm

Cave Creek

*FOREST*

Theodore Roosevelt Lake

*RES.*

Wittmann

Pioneer Ariz. Mus.

Barlett Res.

Theo. Roosevelt Dam

Salt

Adobe

FT. McDOWELL INDIAN RES.

Tonto Nat'l.Mon.

*WHITE TANK MTNS.*

Sun City

Saquaro L.

FISH CANYON

Tonopah

Luke A.F.B.

Glendale

SALT RIVER IND. RES.

Apache L.

Canyon L.

*SUPERSTITION MTNS.*

Litchfield Park

State Capitol

Scottsdale

Phoenix

Globe

Buckeye

Ariz.St.U.

Mesa

Apache Jct.

Miami

Arlington

Tempe

Chandler

Williams A.F.B.

Superior

Queen Creek Tunnel

*SAN CARLOS IND.RES.*

*GILA RIVER*

Chandler Heights

Boyce Thompson S.W.Arboretum

Hohokam Pima Nat'l. Mon.

*INDIAN RES.*

Gila

Kearny

Gila Bend Papago Indian Res.

Mobile

Maricoba

Florence

Winkelman

Gila Bend

*AK-CHIN IND.RES.*

Casa Grande Ruins Nat'l.Mon.

Coolidge

*TORTILLA MTNS.*

Piedra

*MARICOPA MTNS.*

Casa Grande

La Palma

Eloy

*Santa Cruz*

*GUNNERY RANGE LUKE AIR FORCE*

Cuckelbur

Picacho Peak St.Pk.

Mammoth

Friendly Corners

Oracle

*PAPAGO INDIAN RES.*

# CENTRAL ARIZONA

**Preceding pages:** predawn at the Painted Desert. **Below,** cliff dwellings at Montezuma Castle National Monument.

To understand the scenic richness and variety of human settlement in central Arizona, one must first get a grip on its geology. In the north, one stands on the southern edge of the Colorado Plateau, a mile in the air, surrounded by ponderosa pines and Douglas firs or the prismatic barrens of old seabeds. The plateau ends abruptly to the south, where the Mogollon Rim drops 2,000 ft (600 meters) in an escarpment that runs nearly the width of Arizona and is cut by some of the state's most memorable canyons. From the rim's base rise the central highlands, a band of tight mountains some 80 miles (130 km) wide, enclosing narrow ranching valleys and bristling with a chaparral of small oaks and leathery scrub. More recent volcanic upheavals provide the kind of mining that feeds on geological crack-ups. Southward, the land drops more sanely,

ranges keep their distance, and one enters the rich cactus forest of the Sonoran Desert. Elevations remain high in eastern Arizona, but where the land declines southwest toward the Colorado River delta, there is too little rainfall even for cactus to make much of a showing. The eye, undistracted, is drawn over greasewood and saltbush to mountains that wander the horizon like lost battleships, and one feels on the brink of the surreal.

**Offers of a highway:** The straightest shot through this labyrinth is on Interstate 17 from Flagstaff to Tucson. The road bends through the high forests and follows lava flows down the **Mogollon Rim**. The first interesting exits for travelers driving from Flagstaff take place at **Montezuma Well**, a grand limestone sink, and **Montezuma Castle National Monument**, with well-preserved cliff dwellings from the Sinagua period. After crossing the idyllic Verde Valley, the road climbs toward a cluster of service stations called Cordes Junction. By exiting to the east and following a mile-long dirt road that parallels Interstate 17

northward, one arrives at **Arcosanti**, where futurist architect Paolo Soleri is building a community whose citizens will live in hive-like domes while preserving the surrounding terrain. Arcosanti is open daily for inspection and offers tours by Soleri's students. Beyond Cordes Junction, Interstate 17 crests a yucca-spiked volcanic plateau. The **Sunset Point Rest Area** has shaded picnic tables, educational displays and a panorama of the Bradshaw Mountains.

The highway soon descends toward the **Sonoran Desert**, and the first saguaro cacti burst from the black rock. The horizon flattens and may even disappear as Interstate 17 swings through Phoenix and changes its name to Interstate 10. Cotton and alfalfa fields line the highway for the next 50 miles (80 km). Beyond Eloy, there is a last dramatic movement as Interstate 10 passes between Newman Peak and the spire of **Picacho Peak**. Here the adventurous motorist is encouraged to pause for a two-hour diversion. Picacho Peak looks unclimbable, but a trail leads from a small state park to a saddle, around the back of the mountain, along guardrails and over metallic gangplanks, to deliver the hiker safe and amazed to the summit. On clear days the vistas reach to Mexico. But for all its sideshows, Interstate 17 smothers geology, reduces cactus to a khaki blur and funnels you through mid-Arizona in the dullest, blandest way possible.

A more vivid alternative begins at **Petrified Forest National Park**, 115 miles (185 km) east of Flagstaff. The surrounding **Painted Desert**, a strange landscape of Triassic volcanic ash, spreads in wrinkled undulations of mauve, liver and rust. The same volcanic ash has preserved ancient pines by replacing their cells with silica, so their cross sections shine in blues and reds that glow from a dark mahogany. The Petrified Forest is one of the few natural wonders ideally visited in the rain, which heightens the brilliant colors.

State Highway 77 south from Holbrook leads to **Show Low**, on the edge of the Fort Apache Indian Reservation.

Arcosanti, Paolo Soleri's creation, is open for tours.

The elevation is still high and logging is the principal industry, but the area is rapidly filling with vacation homes for residents of Phoenix and Tucson. **The Sunrise Ski Area** lies nearby, and summer offers fishing, golf and popular relief from desert heat.

**Difficult decision:** From Show Low, one is faced with an agonizing choice, for both routes south are spectacular. State Highway 260 proceeds west along the Mogollon Rim. Near Kohl's Ranch, a small sign indicates a mile-long dirt road to the cabin where Zane Grey wrote many of his novels. Hiking trails lead in both directions along the bottom of the Mogollon Rim. State 260 reaches State 87 at Payson, where you can turn south for an eventful ride into Phoenix.

To the west stretch the **Mazatzal Mountains**, which has wilderness status and an intricate network of hiking trails. The road dives into canyons lined with sycamores, climbs through fields of gigantic granite boulders, descends into saguaro forest against the background of the sawtooth mass of Four Peaks, and crosses the Verde River on the Fort McDowell Indian Reservation.

The alternative from Show Low, US Highway 60, drops off the Mogollon Rim and then dodges and weaves to the brink of the **Salt River Canyon**. For sheer breadth this may be Arizona's most impressive gorge after the Grand Canyon. The **Salt River** itself frays upstream into minor tributaries and dies downstream behind four dams before its dry run through Phoenix.

Beyond the Salt River Canyon, the highway reaches **Globe** and **Miami**, contiguous copper-mining towns surrounded by open pits so deep and tailings so mountainous that one is also stunned by the works of man. Some mines are still worked and offer tours.

Just east of Superior, US 60 passes **Boyce Thompson Southwestern Arboretum**, with 1,500 species of trees and plants from around the world – a near-complete inventory of the world's desert vegetation. The arboretum features seasonal displays and is open daily to the public. US 60 continues along the

A petrified log at the Petrified Forest National Park.

turreted south flank of the Superstition Mountains and on into Phoenix, but a turn southward at Florence Junction allows you to play out your exploration toward Tucson. State 79 is the old road between Phoenix and Tucson, and now that urbanites are speeding back and forth on Interstate 10, it is little-traveled and delightful. It soon leads past the small town of **Florence**, best known as the home of the Arizona State Penitentiary but also distinguished by a number of fine buildings from the Territorial period, including a flamboyant courthouse built in 1891.

One old-timer says that if the Florence city fathers hadn't torn down the old buildings because they were ashamed of them, Florence could have been "another Santa Fe."

**Pinal Pioneer Parkway:** South of Florence, State 79 becomes the Pinal Pioneer Parkway. The road, otherwise unimproved, has sheltered picnic tables, and many of the plants of this dense cactus forest are identified with discreet signs. At one of the rest stops, a cast-iron silhouette of a saddled, riderless horse is dedicated to the Western star Tom Mix, who died nearby in a flash flood while filming. At Oracle Junction, one can continue into Tucson. But to keep avoiding cities, turn east on State 77 to the pleasant town of **Oracle**, under the northern extremity of the Catalina Mountains. Twenty miles (32 km) past Oracle is the turnoff to **Aravaipa Canyon**, with one of the few perennial streams through the desert ranges. Aravaipa can be visited only on foot with the status of wilderness protection.

Those wishing to take the old road from Phoenix to Tucson as an alternative to Interstate 10 may connect with it by taking US 60 east to Florence Junction and turning south, or by taking I-10 as far as the turnoff to Coolidge, then proceeding east to Florence. The latter route takes you past the **Tonto National Monument**, a freestanding four-story adobe building that is one of only a few remnants of the Hohokam Culture.

If one prefers to explore central Arizona on the west side of Interstate 17,

**Meteor Crater, whose rim rises nearly 200 feet above the ground, is near Winslow, Arizona.**

the sights are at least as impressive – and certainly better known. Leaving south from Flagstaff on Alternate 89, the road ambles innocently through ponderosa forest, until suddenly the bottom drops out at the brink of **Oak Creek Canyon**. A set of switchbacks materializes and drops you into a deciduous canyon cut from the same sandstones, limestones and shales that form the upper strata of the Grand Canyon.

At the mouth of the canyon is **Sedona**, once a small western town, now a bustling center of boutiques and galleries popular with the New Age crowd. Unfortunately, its radiant setting has been overtaken by the most thoughtless kind of development; zoning controls are baffled by a county line that runs through the middle of the valley, and the eye that would feast on beauty must look above ground level. A redeeming creation is **Tlaquepaque**, a walled-in shopping area built in true Mexican colonial style, set in a dazzling sycamore grove.

As Alternate 89 proceeds southwest, keep a sharp watch to the north, where new permutations of red keep playing on the Mogollon Rim. At the **Verde River** are the small towns of Cottonwood and Clarkdale, between which lies **Tuzigoot National Monument**, with hilltop ruins dating between AD 1100 and 1450. The Verde Valley is a haven for wildlife, and a walk by the river may lead to heron rookeries and the nesting grounds of great horned owls.

**The town that almost died:** Beyond the Verde River, the road climbs toward **Jerome**, possibly the only American town situated like one of the hill towns of Italy or Spain. But the houses are mostly wooden and are propped up on stilts where the ground drops from beneath them: some on the ridge tops show only one story from the street but reveal two more stories beneath entrance level inside. Jerome was founded in 1876 as a company town for the Phelps Dodge copper mines. When the mines closed in 1953, the town almost died, but, in recent years, has been restored as a center for shops, galleries and museums. Three major fires have

**Early ruins built of caliche in the 14th century.**

run through the wooden structures, yet the architectural style remains coherent – partly because stiff zoning regulations favor patching up old buildings over raising new ones and partly because the town, for all its economic dependence on visitors, is short on overnight accommodation.

From Jerome, the road finishes its trip over **Mingus Mountain**, crosses the ranchlands of **Chino Valley**, and enters **Prescott** through a granite dell. Prescott was proclaimed the first territorial capital of Arizona in 1864 and is full of splendid Victorian houses and historic public buildings. The history buff should visit the **Sharlot Hall Museum**, which recreates the feel of Territorial Arizona in a series of restored buildings, and the tippler should pay homage to **Whiskey Row**, as old and as seasoned a tavern as the Southwest possesses. There is one more town of note on this road, the dude-ranching capital of **Wickenburg**. Also dating from Territorial days, Wickenburg is less fully preserved but is surrounded by horsey resorts that

have stayed alive with the help of battalions of tennis courts. From Wickenburg, one can head on to Phoenix, or veer farther west, below the little-visited **Harquahala Mountains**, toward the Colorado River.

Two further north-to-south crossings of central Arizona are possible along the state's boundaries. In the east, US 666 stays in little-populated high country where forestry is the leading industry. In the west, State 95 parallels the Colorado River from **Davis Dam** to **Parker**, then heads straight south to Yuma. "River" no longer seems an honest word for the succession of reservoirs and wide sluices that this stretch of the Colorado has become.

It is lined with resorts, instant cities and trailer parks, and is converged upon during the summer by thousands of weekend revelers from Phoenix and Los Angeles. Its most famous attraction is the **London Bridge English Village**, the famous bridge bought and shipped over by the developer of **Lake Havasu City** to call attention to his real estate.

That the Colorado River has not just been tamed but Thamed may seem a last absurdity, but those who go to laugh at the bridge may be surprised – for its graceful, solid arches match in integrity the wild volcanic ranges in the background, revealing the essential shabbiness of the developments in between. After leaving the Colorado River, State 95 passes the **Kofa National Wildlife Refuge**. The Kofa Mountains are among the most remote in Arizona. They harbor one of the last stands of desert mountain sheep and offer some of the most adventurous back country for hiking and camping in the state.

If Arizona's Anglo history is brief, its Native American history reaches back into myth, and its visible geology to the Precambrian. A serious exploration presupposes time to follow the whims and arabesques suggested by the road map, rather than the north-south strands arranged for convenience here. Central Arizona is a geological, historical and environmental labyrinth, but you are guaranteed your way out, and you will be bearing gifts.

**Left**, Davis Dam at the Colorado River. **Right**, sunset snowstorm at the Mazatzal Mountains.

# THE GRAND CANYON

Although the Grand Canyon is a 90-minute drive over the horizon, to the locals in Flagstaff it is an elemental part of the landscape. They call it, with a blend of awe, affection and understatement, "the big ditch."

A few miles north of Flagstaff on US Highway 180 is the **Museum of Northern Arizona**, which sponsors much of the scientific research taking place in the Grand Canyon. One popular misconception is that the Canyon is, geologically speaking, an open book. The geologists know better. For more than a century they have carried on their investigations and yet many of the most basic questions about the great abyss still lack definitive answers. For instance, there is a lively debate among geologists over how (and how long ago) the Colorado River came to be established in its current course. It's worth stopping at the museum to inspect its geological exhibits and admire a splendid collection of Indian rugs and pottery.

Then, full of anticipation, continue north through the ponderosa pine forests and broad meadows that cloak the flanks of the **San Francisco Peaks**, the highest mountains in Arizona, sacred to both the Navajo and Hopi Indian tribes. From here to the **South Rim**, the Canyon is hidden from view by a gentle incline. Not until you've entered **Grand Canyon National Park** and driven another 2.5 miles (4 km) is there a glimpse of the abyss from **Mather Point**, which is generally crowded. To savor your first impressions in more seclusion, drive another mile to **Yavapai Point.**

Park your car. Leave **Yavapai Museum** and its explanations of the Canyon's geology for later and walk along the **Rim Trail** to a quiet spot from which to gaze at what 19th-century geologist Clarence Dutton called, "the most sublime of the earthly spectacles."

**Grand Canyon Gestalt:** Having heard so much about the Grand Canyon, most visitors are ready to find it breathtaking.

Another typical response, however, is unanticipated. The inhuman scale of the chasm can be profoundly disconcerting: what should one make of this gulf of space, or the unfathomable span of time that it represents? To put it more graphically, how does a human being, cradling a small black rock from the Inner Gorge, come to grips with the fact that it is 2 billion years old? So old, in fact, that it dates from a time when life, in any of its miraculous forms, had not yet appeared on the planet Earth.

Of course the Canyon's ability to humble us and its ability to amaze us are inextricably intertwined. When we stand on the rim we face a quandary: only by accepting that the Canyon belittles us can we fully appreciate its grandeur. As the Russian poet Yevtushenko writes,

*Into the Canyon*
*with all who are sick with*
*megalomania!*
*As a guest in the abyss*
*the dwarf will quickly*
*understand*
*that he is a dwarf.*

**Preceding pages**: Grand Canyon National Park. **Left**, rafters all ready to take that shot of a lifetime. **Right**, a refreshing sight at the Grand Canyon.

There is nothing new about this quandary. Various Indians who have lived in the canyon for at least 2,000 years must have struggled with it. As did one Lieutenant Joseph Ives in 1857. After reluctantly acknowledging that the landscape promotes a "wondering delight," Ives managed to evade the usual visitor's predicament by protesting: "The region is, of course, altogether valueless. It can be approached only from the south, and after entering it there is nothing to do but leave. Ours has been the first, and will doubtless be the last, party of whites to visit this profitless locality."

He may never have known how wrong he was. Millions of people come each year, a third of them from overseas. The Grand Canyon is America's most universally celebrated natural feature. It is, says a Colorado River boatman, "the first church of the Earth."

**The South Rim:** After a moment's communion at Yavapai Point, walk through the piñon and juniper trees a few hundred yards west to an intersecting trail that leads south to the visitors center.

Take some time to tour the exhibits, see the slide show, browse through the fine selection of books and admire the ancient boats, resting on their laurels after the perilous journey down the rapids of the Colorado.

Across the road from the visitors center are Mather Campground and Babbitt's General Store as well as a gas station, post office, bank, public showers and laundromat. Nearby is **Grand Canyon Village** where most of the lodges and hotels are located, including the **El Tovar Hotel** and the **Bright Angel Lodge**, built at the turn of the century when most visitors arrived by train. But times change, and especially during the summer you may want to avoid the congested traffic by walking between all these places along the Rim trail. (The section between the visitors center and Grand Canyon Village is a self-guided Nature Trail.)

Immediately adjacent to Bright Angel Lodge is **Bright Angel Trailhead**. Since the Bright Angel and the **Kaibab** are the only two maintained trails that

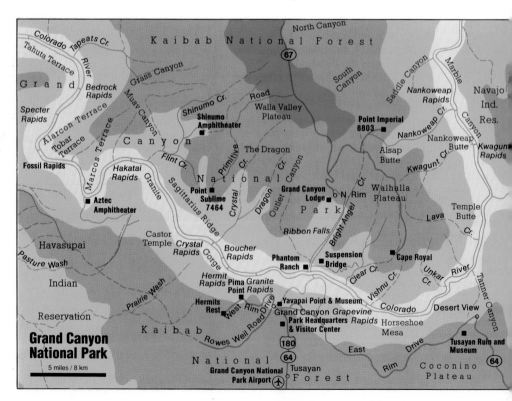

descend into the Canyon, the Park Service recommends hiking one of them before venturing onto any of the unmaintained trails. There is no water on the Kaibab, so most visitors choose to take their introductory hike on the Bright Angel, which has water in three places. Because of the heat – temperatures routinely exceed 105°F (41°C) – hikers should still carry water, at least a gallon per person.

Stepping below the rim of the Grand Canyon changes your experience of it. Suddenly, away from human distractions, you can hear the quiet and measure the grandeur of the landscape against the length of a footstep. You need not go far to sample these pleasures, and everyone should spend at least an hour or two doing so.

A logical destination for an all-day hike is **Indian Gardens**, a verdant oasis 4.5 miles (7 km) and 3,100 vertical feet (945 meters) below the rim. Follow the cue of avid hikers and photographers by rising early; the colors are most radiant and the heat most merciful shortly after

dawn. You can plan on watching the sunrise while eating a leisurely breakfast at the El Tovar.

Day hikes will satisfy most people, but others will want to stay out overnight, perhaps on a hike to the Colorado River and back. Backpacking in the Grand Canyon is hard but rewarding work. If you would rather ride than walk (and are unafraid of heights), consider joining a mule train. To stay overnight below the rim you must have a reservation at either Phantom Ranch or a designated campground. It's sometimes necessary to make arrangements for camping and mule rides several months in advance. For more information, call the visitors center.

**West Rim Drive:** Two roads, one going east and one west, extend along the rim from Grand Canyon Village. During the summer **West Rim Drive** is closed to private vehicles and a free shuttle bus is provided. You can get on or off the bus at a half-dozen viewpoints; this makes it possible to take the 10-minute hike between **Pima Point**, which offers one of

**Sitting on the edge of time at Nankoweap Ruins for a view of the Colorado.**

the best views of the Canyon and the Colorado River, and **Hermit's Rest**, terminus of West Rim Drive.

The hermit was Louis Boucher, one of many prospectors who arrived in the late 1800s and one of the South Rim's first white inhabitants. Deposits of copper, asbestos, lead and silver were found, but the costs of transporting ore by mule train were so astronomical that none of the ventures proved profitable.

We do, however, have the miners to thank for most of the unmaintained trails that enter the canyon, including the **Hermit Trail**, west of Hermit's Rest. There are two good day hikes on the Hermit: a 5-mile (8-km) round-trip to **Santa Maria Springs** and a 6-mile (10-km) round-trip to the less frequently visited **Dripping Springs.**

Although the paved road ends at Hermit's Rest, it is possible, via the **Rowe's Well** road, to venture farther west along the rim. For safety's sake make sure you get a topographic map and a few gallons of water from the visitors center before setting forth. The **Bass Trailhead** is beautifully situated on a narrow peninsula jutting into the canyon and is one possible destination. Backpackers find the Bass one of the most scenic and easy-to-follow of the unmaintained trails, and the trailhead itself makes a fine picnic or camping site for anyone anxious to escape the hustle and bustle of Grand Canyon Village. Even farther west is the **Topocoba Hilltop Trail** that leads to **Havasu Canyon**, home of the Havasupai Indians since 1300 AD.

Until this century the Havasupai, in addition to tilling their fields, spent part of each year roaming widely throughout the canyon in search of game and edible plants. Once a rarely visited Shangri-La, **Havasu Canyon** has recently become a popular vacation spot for boy scouts and college students. The attraction is **Havasu Creek**, a blue-green stream that plunges over three stunning waterfalls, one of which, **Mooney Falls**, is almost 200 ft (60 meters) high.

Havasu is the most stunning of the side canyons that drain into the Colo-

**Havasu Falls Grand Canyon.**

rado, and despite the crowds is still worth visiting – particularly during the off-season, late September through early April. Access is difficult. Most visitors walk or ride horseback along the 8-mile (13-km) trail from **Hualapai Hilltop**, 67 miles (108 km) northeast of **Peach Springs** on US 66.

You can also hike in via the 12-mile (19-km) Topocoba Hilltop Trail or from the Colorado River; most raft trips spend a day doing just this. There is a small lodge in Havasu, but most visitors stay at a campground. Be sure to boil your drinking water and make reservations for accommodations in advance.

**East Rim Drive:** Driving east from Grand Canyon Village through fragrant forests of ponderosa pine on **East Rim Drive**, you pass the Kaibab Trailhead near **Yaki Point** and after 20 miles (32 km) arrive at **Tusayan Ruin and Museum**. Anthropologists believe that the Anasazi Indians who built this small pueblo came to the canyon around 500 AD. The Anasazi were not the ancestors of the Havasupai, but lived a similar life

raising corn, squash and beans on the rim during the summer, moving down to the warmer canyon floor in the winter. The Anasazi abandoned Tusayan and a number of other sites around AD 1150, possibly as a result of a long period of drought.

But the Anasazi were not the first Indians to inhabit the canyon. Anthropologists have discovered split-twig willow figurines pierced by small spears that date to 2000 BC. What, one wonders, did these Indians think of the Grand Canyon? Perhaps Hopi religion offers a clue. Each year, Hopi holy men make a pilgrimage to a sacred site in the canyon where they believe their ancestors emerged from the underworld.

The last viewpoint on East Rim Drive is **Desert View**. Here the **Watchtower**, a beautiful stone tower that rises 67 ft (20 meters) high, offers excellent views of the Colorado River 4,000 ft (1,200 meters) below. There is a campground at Desert View, as well as a little-known road which soon deteriorates to a trail leading to **Comanche Point**. This se-

Towering canyons and the clear Colorado water.

cluded and rarely visited spot with its marvelous views is ideal for lovers, gazers and seekers of solitude.

From Desert View, continue east on State Highway 64 to the **Cameron Trading Post**. Stop for gas and what connoisseurs say is a "respectable Navajo taco," a local dish that is a hybrid of Indian frybread smothered with refried beans, lettuce and cheese.

The road forks south to Flagstaff, north to Page and the North Rim. The Grand Canyon is sandwiched between two immense man-make lakes. **Lake Powell**, upstream of the canyon, is formed by **Glen Canyon Dam**, near Page. Downstream, **Lake Mead** is formed by **Hoover Dam**, near **Boulder City**. Both dams are engineering wonders and are worth exploring on free guided tours.

**Rafting the Colorado:** The departure point for all raft trips, "down the Grand", as the boatmen say, is 15 miles (24 km) below Glen Canyon Dam at **Lees Ferry**. John D. Lee founded the ferry in 1871 while on the lam for his part in the massacre of a wagon train of emigrants bound for California by a band of Mormons and Paiute Indians.

The ferry is just upstream of the mouth of the Paria River. An increasingly popular and spectacular four-day hike goes upstream through the **Paria Canyon Narrows**, where sheer sandstone walls, only 50 ft (15 meters) apart, rise 1,000 ft (300 meters) high. This hike should be avoided during the thunderstorm season because of the danger of flash floods. For more information you should contact the rangers at the ferry or the Bureau of Land Management in Kanab, Utah.

Two years before Lee arrived at the ferry, ten gaunt men in three battered boats drifted out of Glen Canyon. Ten weeks earlier they had left Green River, Wyoming, 500 miles (805 km) away, with four boats and 10 months of supplies. After repeated upsets they were down to rancid bacon, musty flour, dried apples and coffee. The men were getting mutinous, but the man in charge, Major John Wesley Powell, was unperturbed. "If he can only study geology,"

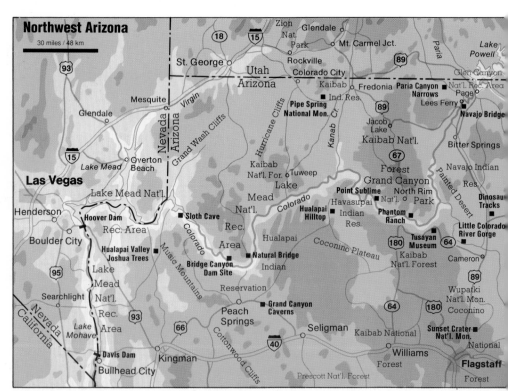

grumbled one of the hands, George Bradley, "he will be happy without food or shelter, but the rest of us are not afflicted with it to an alarming extent."

Years later, as the head of the Geological Survey and the Bureau of Ethnology, Powell would become one of the most influential men in Washington, DC. At the time of the expedition, however, he was unknown, simply a one-armed Civil War veteran, a self-taught amateur scientist who, on the strength of curiosity, intuition and discipline, would make fundamental contributions to the budding sciences of geology and anthropology.

The major was also a gifted writer, as revealed by this passage, often quoted by modern boatmen: "August 13th 1869 – We are now ready to start on our way down the Great Unknown. We are three quarters of a mile in the depths of the earth, and the great river shrinks into insignificance as it dashes its angry waves against the walls and cliffs that rise to the world above; the waves are but puny ripples and we but pigmies running up and down the sands or lost amongst the boulders."

**Rhythms of a river:** Two weeks after writing that passage, Powell and five of his men safely completed the exploration of the Colorado. Another three men, unwilling to risk their lives at an unusually nasty rapid, had abandoned the expedition two days earlier and were killed by Indians while struggling overland toward Mormon settlements in Utah.

Commercial river trips began in 1938 when Norm Nevills shoved off from shore with a boat built of planks scavenged from an outhouse and a horse trough. Nevills' boat was so small that his two passengers were forced to ride through 160 rapids sprawled flat on the deck – sacrificial spread eagles. A decade later the white-water industry was revolutionized by the introduction of Army-surplus rafts. Today, Powell and Nevills would be astonished to learn that more than 10,000 people float through the canyon each year.

A Grand Canyon river trip has its own rhythm that is formed from a series of

**White-water rafters in action.**

small and unexpected delights: the evocative, trilling song of a canyon wren, bighorn sheep grazing at the water's edge, a sudden thunderstorm which runs down the sheer cliffs in hundreds of glistening waterfalls.

Floating downriver you pass through successive layers of rock, each older than the one above, all of them fluted and polished by the river's ceaseless caress. It is the raft as time machine. Three hundred fifty million years of history drift past at arm's length. It is no wonder that one passenger has said, "The river offers a look at the soul of the Canyon." Or that Buzz Holstrom, who made the first solo descent, said, "It seems like I actually lived more in a few hours out there on the river than I have in a year in the city."

**The North Rim:** An hour's drive west of Lees Ferry is **Jacob Lake**, the turnoff point for the **North Rim**. Because the North Rim is 1,000 ft (305 meters) higher than the South Rim, it is closed from late October to late May due to snow. But during the summer and the fall it is open as a cooler and less crowded alternative.

Buy whatever groceries you need in Jacob Lake and then drive south through lush forests of ponderosa pine, spruce, fir and aspen trees, interspersed with wide meadows edged by lingering snow-banks and dotted with duck-filled ponds. After 45 miles (73 km) you arrive at the **North Rim Village**, whose centerpiece is the **Grand Canyon Lodge**. This handsome structure, a masterpiece created in beams and stonework, was built by hand in 1928 and is best appreciated while eating a piece of pie in the lodge restaurant, perched on the edge of the abyss.

During your stay at the North Rim you will want to drive to **Point Imperial,** offering views of the eastern Grand Canyon and the **Painted Desert**, and to **Cape Royal**. Favorite day hikes along the rim include the **Widforss Trail** and the **Ken Patrick Trail**. The only maintained trail into the canyon is the **North Kaibab Trail**.

Allow a full day to hike to **Roaring Springs** and back, a 9-mile (15-km) round-trip. More experienced hikers

**Mules on Kaibab Trail during winter.**

170

might want to backpack the **Thunder River Trail** to **Deer** and **Tapeats creeks**, gorgeous trout streams that plunge full-born from springs at the base of the Redwell Limestone.

West of the North Rim is the least visited section of Grand Canyon National Park – the **Tuweep** area. Tuweep is reached over 60 miles (97 km) of dirt roads from either **Fredonia** or **Colorado City**. Be sure to heed the Park Service's advice: "A trip into this area, one of the most remote in northern Arizona, should not be attempted without ample gasoline, water and food."

**Molten rocks and melted snow:** Despite the difficult access, it's surprising that Tuweep is so rarely visited. "Because what we have there," says Dr Ken Hamblin, "is one of the planet's most spectacular conjunctions of volcanic and erosional phenomena." Hamblin's research suggests that within the last million years the Colorado has been damned 11 times by molten lava. The largest lava dam was 550 ft (165 meters) high, and it backed water 180 miles (290 km) upstream to Lees Ferry. "What a conflict of water and fire there must have been here!" wrote John Wesley Powell on his pioneer voyage. "Just imagine a river of molten rock running down into a river of melted snow. What a seething and boiling of the waters; what clouds of steam rolled into the heavens!"

There are two points of interest at Tuweep: **Toroweap Overlook** offers unexcelled views of the lava flows which cascaded into the canyon. Secondly, there's a short but extraordinary rugged trail to **Lava Falls**, the most violent rapid in the entire canyon and the standard by which boatmen compare other rapids in North America. (Check at the Tuweep Ranger Station for more information on this trail.) If you want to photograph rafts running the rapid, leave the rim at dawn in order to arrive by 10am. Few places testify so convincingly to the sheer power of the river as it courses between bare rock walls. For if the Grand Canyon is a church and we are all pilgrims, there is no better place to get baptized than Lava Falls.

**Antelope Canyon, Arizona.**

# INDIAN COUNTRY

The Hopi are bonded fast to their desert lands, and these ties are sacred and as old as the Hopi people themselves. Two stories demonstrate these facts.

The first story is from the dark night when the Hopi emerged from the underworld in what is now northern Arizona. The people who emerged from the womb of the Earth were greeted by Maasaw, deity of this Fourth World. "You are welcome," Maasaw said. "But know this land offers scant food or water. Living here will not be easy." The Hopi chose to stay.

The second story is set at Bosque Redondo in New Mexico, May 28, 1868, and is taken from the record of the Peace Commission named to establish a reservation for the Navajo. General William Tecumseh Sherman offered the Hopi three options: the tribe could remain at Bosque Redondo where the Army held it, move to fertile river-bottom land in Oklahoma, or return to their homeland – the arid canyon country on the borders between Arizona and New Mexico. Sherman said he doubted that this wasteland could support the tribe, but that since it was worthless the Navajo should be safe there from the greed of white men. It was, General Sherman told President Andrew Johnson, "far from our possible future wants."

It was the same choice the Hopi faced in their myth. The Navajo spokesman that day was Barboncito, a noted fighter, not an orator, who said to Sherman:

"If we are taken back to our own country we will call you our father and mother. If there was only a single goat there, we would all live off of it… I hope to God you will not ask us to go to any other country but our own. When the Navajo were first created, four mountains and four rivers were pointed out to us, outside of which we should not live… Changing Woman gave us this land. Our God created it for us."

The 7,304 Navajo held at Bosque Redondo voted, without a dissent, to turn down the lush Oklahoma reservation and return to their desert. It was, as Barboncito told Sherman, "the very heart of our country."

It is still the very heart of America's Indian country, this high, dry southwestern side of the Colorado Plateau. Thus it seems appropriate when visiting it to follow the advice of Changing Woman, the great teacher of the Navajo Way, who said all things should begin from the East. Thus we begin at Gallup.

**Bureaucrats and sacred places:** The town called **Gallup**, New Mexico, calls itself the "Indian Capital of the World," and is America's most Indian off-reservation town. It's the trading center for the eastern Navajo and the Zuni Reservation, and you're not likely to stroll down Railroad Avenue without meeting Hopi, Laguna, Acoma and possibly Jicarilla Apache. It's a ramshackle, unkempt, lively town, a good place to prowl the pawnshops for Zuni jewelry, Navajo silver, rugs and other artifacts.

From Gallup head into the **Checkerboard Reservation**, so named because

**Preceding pages:** Navajo on horseback watching over her flock. **Left**, heavily bedecked in gems. **Right**, Pueblo Bonito, Chaco Canyon.

the Navajo tribe once owned only alternate square miles – an oddity now partially corrected. Interstate 40 takes you 38 miles (61 km) east to Thoreau. (The great red cliffs to the left were the background for uncounted cowboy movies, and the earthen humps to the right are bunkers of Fort Wingate Ammunition Depot.) A left turn on State Highway 57 leads through Satan Pass 23 miles (27 km) to Crownpoint.

**Crownpoint** has a school, a medical center, a Navajo tribal police station and the offices of the Navajo bureaucrats who administer 3 or 4 million acres (about 1.5 million hectares) of the tribe's eastern territory. Like all Navajo communities, it has a temporary, government-built look as if tomorrow the tumbleweeds will reclaim it. Crownpoint is the site of a rug auction which six times a year attracts scores of Navajo weavers and hundreds of buyers for the sale of the fruit of Navajo looms.

From Crownpoint, State 57 jogs northeast 37 miles (60 km) to the mysteries of **Chaco Culture National Historical Park**. In the shallow canyon a great civilization flourished and fell during the 10th and 12th centuries, leaving the ruins of its multistoried houses and myriad unsolved anthropological puzzles. Satellite photography has confirmed that Chaco Canyon was the center of a network of at least 250 miles (400 km) of improved roads, arousing speculation that the Chaco pueblos housed a religious and administrative base. The visitors center and the ruins offer a rare look into America's past.

Thirty miles (48 km) north, State 57 joins State 44 at Blanco Trading Post. Two miles up the highway toward Farmington is *Dzilth Na O Dith Hle* Navajo Boarding School and beyond it rises **El Huerfano**. This great mesa is the center of an area rich in sacred places for the Navajo. The mesa was the home of First Man and First Woman and other Navajo Holy People. From it you can see other landmarks of Navajo Genesis. The blue shape of **Mount Taylor** looms on the horizon 50 miles (80 km) to the south. It is *Tsoodzil*, the

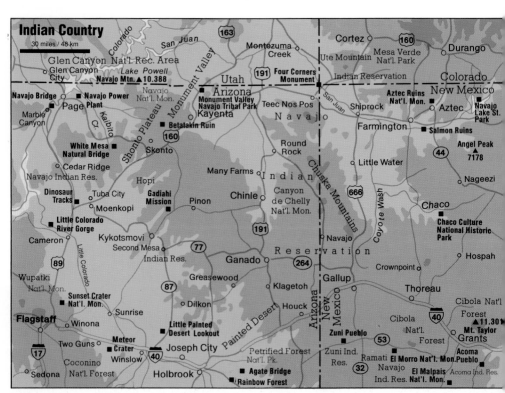

**Indian Country**

30 miles / 48 km

Turquoise Mountain, one of the four sacred peaks that First Man built as corner-posts of the Navajo universe. Northeast of Mount Taylor, the basalt thumb jutting into the sky is Cabezon Knob. In a cloud covering its crest one mythical day, First Man and First Woman found the infant White Shell Girl. According to the traditions of the eastern Navajo clans, it was somewhere on the rolling sagebrush hills north of Huerfano where Talking God, Black God and the other Holy People held the first puberty ceremonial, converting White Shell Girl into Changing Woman.

**The holy birthplace:** Eight miles northeast of El Huerfano, a right turn leads to **Angel Peak Scenic Overlook**, offering a spectacular view across the wilderness formed by the Blanco Wash and Canyon Largo. Here the Holy People hung out the stars, and Changing Woman, made pregnant by sunbeams and mist from the San Juan River, bore Monster Slayer and Born for Water, the Hero Twins who were to purge this "Glittering World" of its monsters.

Just before State 44 drops into the San Juan Valley, it passes one of the West's most spectacular examples of the human power to modify nature. The endless silver-gray of sage and rabbit brush abruptly gives way to the dark green of corn, potatoes and alfalfa – 44,000 acres (18,000 hectares) of the Navajo Irrigation Project. The "capital" of this San Juan River country is **Farmington**. Its economy is based on oil, gas, farming and coal – with tourism and Indian trading secondary.

About 35 miles (56 km) up the river is **Navajo Dam**, which forms a blue-water lake in a network of drowned canyons backed across the Colorado border. The lake is popular with trout and coho salmon fishermen, and on several miles of the river below the dam is the best fly fishing in New Mexico. Aztec, just 13 miles (21 km) east of Farmington, is the site of **Aztec Ruins National Monument**, a wonderfully preserved example of how people lived in the Golden Age of the Pueblo. Visitors can walk into the living quarters of these

Cliff Palace Ruins, Mesa Verde National Park.

ancient people and into a huge *kiva* – the underground "church" of one of the pueblo's religious societies. A 90-minute drive north of Farmington takes you to **Mesa Verde National Park**. The cliff dwellings here are deservedly among the West's most popular tourist attractions. Most visitors tend to focus on Cliff Palace, a 200-room apartment house high on the wall of a cliff, or the Spruce Tree House, a 114-room structure under a massive stone overhang. But you may find yourself staring at the myriad smaller houses in cracks and crevices – wondering at the dangers that motivated the Anasazi to make homes in such dizzying places, and how they raised children where a toddler's misstep meant death.

**A Navajo doughnut:** Farmington is also the gateway to the Navajo Nation or the **"Big Reservation,"** a term which requires explanation. The Navajo Tribe, the nation's largest with more than 200,000 members, controls some 16 million acres (6.5 million hectares) – larger than New England. The biggest chunk is on the borders between New Mexico, Arizona, and Utah in an area the size of West Virginia. Also covered is the "Checkerboard Reservation", the Alamo, the Ramah and the Canoncito. On this Navajo Nation, an elected tribal council operates its own courts, police force and other services. More than 1,100 miles (1,770 km) of paved road, and another thousand which range from quality gravel to tracks impassible in wet weather, tie the reservation together. The lowest Navajo deserts get only a few inches of rainfall annually, while the forested slopes of the Chuska Mountains at 10,416 ft (3,174 meters) gets 25 inches (161 cm). Surrounded by these Navajo lands is the 60,000-acre (250,000-hectare) Hopi Reservation.

It's a huge place, and one of the best ways to visit its interior is by driving west out of Farmington to **Shiprock**, which, like Crownpoint, is a Navajo bureaucrats' town. As you drive west on US Highway 550, you see the sky over the San Juan smudged with plumes of whitish smoke. The pollution (sharply

*Tourists snapping at Shiprock, New Mexico.*

reduced by millions of dollars worth of soot precipitators in the towering stacks) is from the Four Corners Generating Plant. Coal from the adjoining Navajo Mine, the nation's largest open-pit operation, rolls directly into the furnaces, and thence over electrical transmission lines to warm Californian swimming pools. Only the ashes and pollution are left behind. A side trip through the farming town of **Kirtland** gives you a look at this mind-boggling operation.

Take State 504, the **Navajo Trail**, west from Shiprock – but first take US 666 for 16 miles (26 km) south to The Rock With Wings. You have been seeing the ragged blue shape of Shiprock for miles but as you climb the long hill south of town you finally realize its size. It is the core of a volcano, the cinder cone cut away by 15 million years of wind and rain. This core towers 1,450 ft (440 meters) above the grassy prairie – 20 stories taller than the Empire State Building – suggesting an immense black Gothic cathedral. In Navajo mythology, it was the home of the Winged Monster,

slain by the Hero Twins with the help of Spider Woman. Chinese Walls of basalt radiate for miles from its base, 20 or 30 ft (6 to 9 meters) high in places but only 3 or 4 ft (1 meter) thick. They formed when volcanic pressures cracked the earth and molten lava squeezed upward like toothpaste.

West from Shiprock the Navajo Trail takes you past the tiny trading post communities of Teec Nos Pos, Red Mesa, Mexican Water, Tec Nez Iah and Dennehotso to Kayenta, gateway to **Monument Valley Navajo Tribal Park** – that odd vertical landscape made familiar by a million calendar photographs and a hundred Western movies. Erosion is the subject here. All of the Colorado Plateau was ocean bottom in an earlier era and this portion of the Arizona-Utah borderland was repeatedly buried under sediment as the sea rose and receded. What the visitor sees now is the product of millions of years of weather cutting through soft sandstone and shale, leaving wind-sculpted monoliths where harder stone endured. The area north of

Navajos ride through Canyon de Chelly, Arizona.

Kayenta offers the most dramatic of these weird and wonderful forms.

Another not-to-be-missed sight is **Betatakin Ruin**, a drive of about 30 minutes from Kayenta. A mile walk from the visitors center takes you to the 13th-century cliff houses. The **Keet Seel Ruins** are more impressive but reaching them takes half a day. Under the overhanging stone roof which has protected them for 700 years they look as if they were abandoned yesterday.

From Navajo National Monument, a 13-mile (20-km) detour/shortcut down Navajo Route 221 connects with State 98 and a 60-mile (96-km) drive west and north across the dramatic landscape of Kaibito Plateau to Page, Lake Powell and the **Glen Canyon National Recreation Area**. There's a visitors center near the dam, and the lake itself is famous throughout the West as the best possible place to take a vacation on a houseboat. Blue water and a shoreline of carved cliff make the lake a photographer's dream. It also provides access to some of the most spectacular canyon country in Utah, including Rainbow Bridge National Monument.

If you follow US 89 south from Page, a turn on 89A at Bitter Springs takes you to **Marble Canyon** and then under the incredible **Vermilion Cliffs** formation to **Jacob Lake** and the **North Rim of the Grand Canyon**. The drive across the Kaibab Plateau is beautiful and this approach to the Grand Canyon offers a special thrill. When you walk into the lobby of the Grand Canyon Lodge you are confronted with what seems to be an immense mural of the canyon. It takes a moment to realize you are seeing reality through a great glass wall. The effect is unforgettable.

If you decide to skip the North Rim, the route from Page leads south through the narrow Cornfields Valley with the Echo Cliffs towering east of the highway and Limestone Ridge walling off the west. Fifteen miles (25 km) south of the Tuba City turnoff, there's **Cameron**, with a **Navajo Information Center**. From Cameron, it's 53 miles (85 km) west on State 64 to the South Rim of

Two diverse Indian lifestyles: rug weaving...

Grand Canyon National Park. Just 15 miles (24 km) west of Cameron the gorge of the **Little Colorado** bends to within a few hundred yards of the highway. There's a scenic overlook into the incredibly deep and narrow slice which this active river has cut into the crust of the earth.

Somewhere west of this spot, according to Hopi myth, the people who were to occupy the surface of the world emerged from the womb of earth and began this, their fourth existence. From this point, the clans who were to form the Hopi People began the epic migrations to the four corners of the world and returned, eventually, to Black Mesa. The ruins at Mesa Verde, Chaco Canyon, Aztec, Keet Seel and the others are the "footsteps" left by the Hopi ancestors in their travels toward the stone villages on First, Second and Third Mesa, where they now live out their destinies.

At **Wupatki National Monument**, 20 miles (32 km) south of Cameron, more than 800 ruins still exist. Archaeologists say that the eruption of **Sunset Crater** covered the Painted Desert with a fertile black ash. The year was 1065, and the result was a land rush. But about 200 years later a drought lasting 23 years forced evacuation.

The core of Sunset Crater juts a thousand feet above its surrounding lava beds and meadows just 4 miles (6 km) from US 89, which is linked to Wupatki by a 34-mile (55-km) route through the Painted Desert. The crater is interesting and offers a self-guided trail through the blowholes and ice caves of its lava beds.

This entire area is overshadowed by one of America's most sacred landmarks – the **San Francisco Peaks**. They rise to 12,633 ft (3,850 meters) just north of Flagstaff – the highest point in Arizona. For the Navajo, they are Evening Twilight Mountain, First Man's Mountain of the West. For the Hopi, they represent something like Mount Sinai and Islam's Dome of the Rock combined. Here the Kachina spirits live during that half of the year when they are not with their people on the Hopi mesas. Humphreys Peak is the doorway

*..and riding a rodeo special.*

by which these supernaturals pass between the worlds of men and of spirits.

The area around **Flagstaff** is rich in the unusual. Only about 50 miles (80 km) southeast of the volcanic Sunset Crater and just 5 miles (8 km) from Interstate 40 there's **Meteor Crater**, a 570-ft deep, 4150-ft wide (175/1,260 meters) hole punched out by a rock fragment visiting from space. **Walnut Canyon National Monument**, with one of the most beautiful cliff house sites, is even closer to Interstate 40. Don't miss **Grand Falls**, 20 miles (32 km) north of Interstate 40, where a "waterfall" higher than Niagara has formed giant stairsteps into the Little Colorado gorge. The few times each year when runoff water roars down, it stirs up a cloud of red dust. If you continue east on Interstate 40 to New Mexico, the route takes you through the heart of the **Painted Desert** and past **Petrified Forest National Park**, with its fallen forests of broken stone trees. Be sure not to miss the Hopi villages.

Visit **Hopi Country** by turning east on State 264 at **Tuba City**. The road

drops into Moenkopi Wash past the red stone Hopi village of Moenkopi. The little fields of corn, bean and squash you'll see here convey an idea of how people have survived in this desert country for thousands of years. The route takes you through some 50 miles (80 km) of empty country into the oldest continually occupied area of America.

Most of the Hopi villages are built on or near three lofty fingers of stone which jut from Black Mesa. You reach **Third Mesa** first, and the little stone towns of Hotevilla, Bacobi and Oraibi. **Oraibi**, dating back to about 1100, is partly deserted ruins. On **Second Mesa** is the **Hopi Cultural Center**. Besides the museum, the center operates a motel and restaurant. Shungopovi and Mishongnovi on Second Mesa are interesting, but most memorable of all are the **First Mesa** communities of Hano, Sichomovi and Walpi, which perches on its lofty mesa cliff and offers a spectacular view of the desert landscape.

State 264 takes you back to Gallup via the old Hopi government town of Keams Canyon and through Ganado, where John Hubbell, known to the Navajo as "Double Glasses", opened his historic **Hubbell Trading Post** in 1870. It's maintained as a National Historic Site and shouldn't be missed. **Window Rock**, the capital of the Navajo Nation, is also on this route.

But first there's an essential side trip. Thirty miles (50 km) north of Ganado is **Canyon de Chelly National Monument**, where three great gorges have sliced through the plateau under the Chuska Mountains. Generations of cliff dwellers, Hopi and Navajo have lived along the sandy bottoms of these washes, under cliffs which in places tower 1,000 ft (300 meters). There's access by vehicle tours from Thunderbird Lodge, or by a foot trail down the cliff.

In a way these canyons sum up this heartland of America's Indian Country. They offer spectacular sculptured stone. And they offer a sense of the silence, the space and the great beauty which caused Navajo, Hopi and their ancestors to choose this hard, inhospitable land as the heart of their country.

**Views of Canyon de Chelly: left, the Spider Rocks; right, near White House Ruins.**

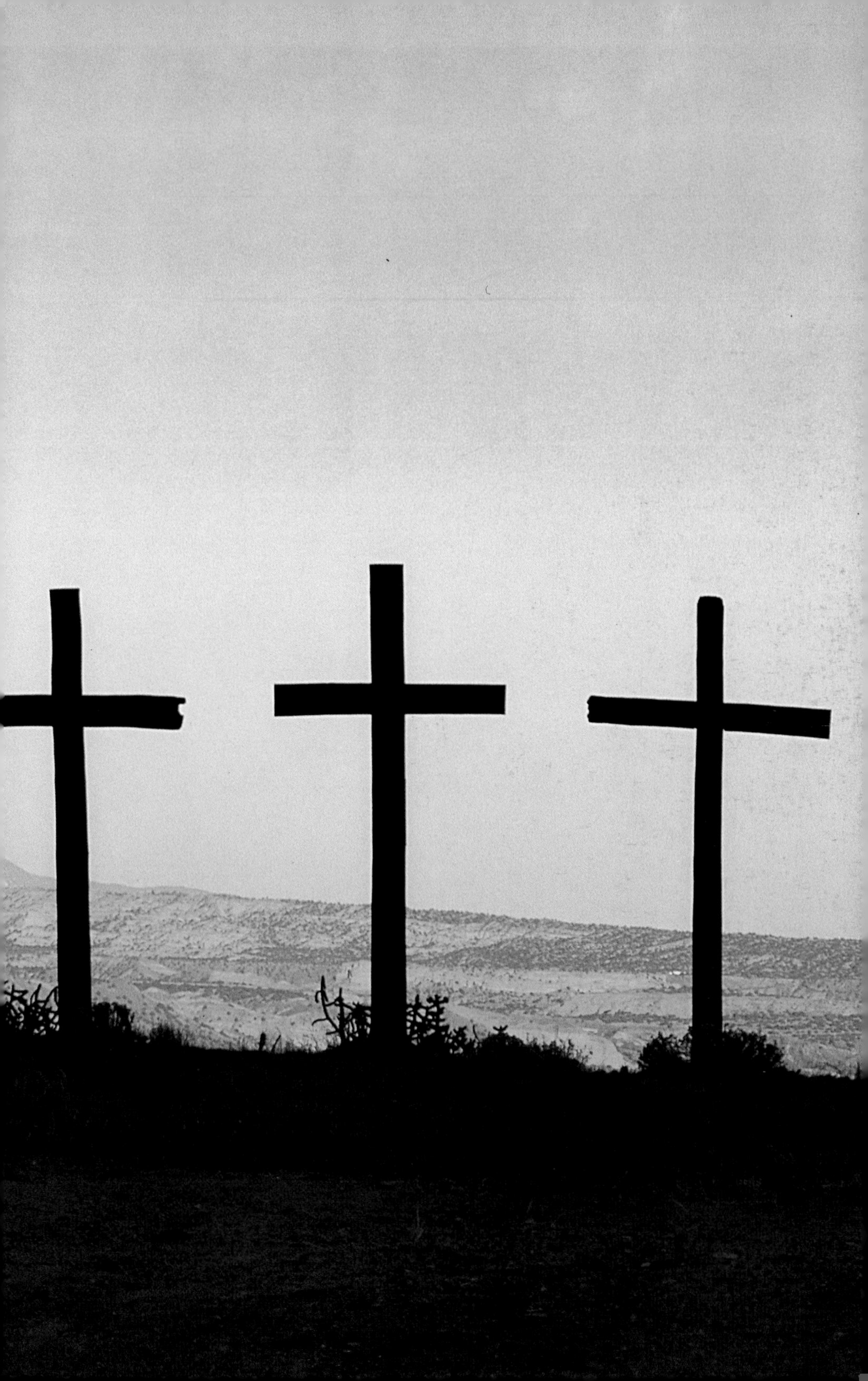

# SOUTHERN UTAH

In 1869, after a two-month journey down the Green River, an expedition led by Major John Wesley Powell reached the confluence of the Green and Colorado rivers, one of the most inaccessible spots on the North American continent. The voyage was not an easy one; there had been more rapids than the men cared to count, and in one of them, Disaster Falls, they had lost not only a boat but also much of their food.

Here at the confluence, in the heart of what Powell called "the Great Unknown," both rivers lay deep within the earth imprisoned by sheer cliffs of their own making. Anxious to determine where, exactly, the confluence was relative to the rest of the world, the Major climbed to the rim. "What a world of grandeur is spread before us!" he wrote. "Wherever we look there is but a wilderness of rocks; deep gorges, where the rivers are lost below cliffs and towers and pinnacles; and ten thousand strangely carved forms in every direction; and beyond them, mountains blending with the clouds."

It is now possible to drive across southern Utah in a couple of days, but to do justice to the geography Powell described, you need more time – anywhere from a week to a year or two. Ironically, part of the area's appeal lies in what it lacks: there are no great cities here, no famous museums or soaring cathedrals. There is simply a landscape whose predominant feature is bare rock sculpted by the ages. On first glance, this slickrock topography may seem desolate, odd or even grotesque. Only later, as one grows more discerning, does it become apparent that the inconceivably bizarre is a transparent mask for the astonishingly beautiful. It is no fluke that so much of the region has been preserved in five national parks, four national monuments, three national forests and three primitive areas.

Every tour must start somewhere, so let's begin in **Moab** in southeastern

Utah. Moab was settled by members of the Church of Jesus Christ of Latter-day Saints, a religious sect founded on the East Coast of the United States during the early 1800s.

In 1847, having endured decades of frequently violent persecution, the Saints (as they called themselves, although they were more commonly known as Mormons) fled across the Great Plains to Utah – at the time an uninhabited wilderness owned by Mexico.

Thereafter, the theocratically organized, methodical and courageous Mormons overcame great obstacles to pioneer **Salt Lake City**, followed by a series of small settlements throughout Utah, including Moab, in 1880. For almost a century, Moab was a sleepy town, 100 miles from nowhere. And it might have stayed that way, if it hadn't been for the Bomb.

As it became clear, following Hiroshima, that the Soviet Union also was building nuclear weapons, the US Atomic Energy Commission (AEC), as part of a nationwide search for uranium, established a generous fixed price for the ore as an incentive to miners. The first big strike was Charlie Steen's. In an area south of Moab that the AEC had deemed "barren of possibilities", Steen discovered his *Mi Vida* (My Life) mine, from which he was able to ship $100 million worth of U235.

Overnight, Moab became the "Uranium Capital of the World." Due to recent difficulties in the US nuclear energy industry, most of the bloom is now off the uranium rose, but Moab remains a sizeable town. It is the departure point for Arches and Canyonlands national parks and is extremely popular among mountain bikers who swarm to the slick rock trails outside of town.

**The truth about Arches:** Superlatives quickly get blisters in southern Utah. Let's stick to the facts: **Arches National Park** has the world's largest cluster of, that's right, arches. The arches – there are more than one hundred – have been carved by wind and water in a 300-ft (90-meter) layer of red sandstone deposited 150 million years ago during the age of dinosaurs. Many arches

**Preceding pages**: a classic scene from the Southwest. **Left**, Delicate Arch at Arches National Park.

are visible along a paved road that begins at the visitors center, 5 miles (8 km) north of Moab, or within easy walking distance along well-maintained trails.

If you're pressed for time, visit the **Windows Section** to view **Double Arch, Parade of the Elephants** and **Balanced Rock**. Then take the short guided hike through the **Fiery Furnace**. This mile-long trail snakes its way through a spectacular maze of rust-colored sandstone cliffs separated by dry streambeds. So many people have gotten lost within the maze that you must accompany a ranger on this hike; check at the visitors center for scheduled departures.

Travelers equipped for camping may spend a night at **Devil's Garden Campground**, 18 miles (29 km) north of the visitors center. From the campground a 6-mile (10-km) loop trail takes you to seven different arches, including **Landscape Arch**. This slender arch, the longest in the world, is nowhere more than a few feet thick yet spans 291 ft (89 meters) or nearly the length of a football field.

Mid-summer temperatures often exceed 105°F (41°C) throughout southern Utah. On this, and any other hike that takes longer than an hour, carry adequate water. A good rule of thumb is a gallon per person per day.

From Arches head back to Moab. Pause here, before visiting **Canyonlands National Park**, to buy gas, groceries and perhaps a meal at one of the lively new cafes that cater to outdoor enthusiasts.

The challenge of Canyonlands is picking and choosing. At more than 500 sq. miles (800 sq. km), this fabulous park is so huge that it's unlikely you'll see more than a portion on any one visit – particularly since the Colorado and Green rivers divide the park into three "districts" which, though adjacent to one another, are isolated by the tortured topography. In Canyonlands, it's generally the case, as the locals say, that "you can't get there from here."

The district closest to Moab is the **Island in the Sky**, 40 miles (67 km) away. The hurried traveler headed north

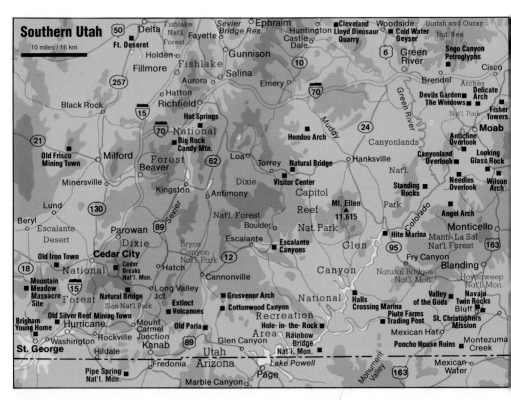

toward Interstate 70 might spend a night at one of the two campgrounds on the Island, perhaps after touring Arches. The Island is a sheer-sided plateau that towers vertically 2,000 ft (600 meters) above the surrounding terrain and consequently offers panoramic views of the rest of Canyonlands from **Grand View Point**, the **Green River Overlook** and **Dead Horse Point State Park**. Below the Island is the best Jeep tour in southern Utah, the **White Rim Trailroad**. (Tours can be arranged in Moab.)

If you have at least a day – preferably two – and are headed south from Moab, visit the **Needles District**. There is a campground within the district at **Squaw Flat**, but no grocery stores, gas stations or motels. These services can only be found 53 miles (85 km) away in **Monticello**. Thus, it is most convenient to buy food in advance and come prepared to camp.

The attractions of the Needles are myriad and include prehistoric Indian ruins and pictographs; a number of arches, one of which, **Angel Arch**, is

perhaps the most sublime in Canyonlands; and the Needles themselves, massive fins of sandstone eroded into buff-red-and-cream-colored pinnacles 500 ft (150 meters) high. For a quick introduction to the Needles, hike the **Peekaboo Springs Trail** that begins at Squaw Flat Campground. After wandering up the floor of a delightful canyon, this trail traverses a long expanse of bare slickrock where the way is marked only by cairns – small piles of rocks for which one must be alert.

A four-wheel-drive vehicle allows quick access to another attraction in the Needles, the downfaulted valleys shaped like shoe boxes that geologists call "grabens" reached via **Elephant Hill**. In surmounting the hill, the driver must at one point turn completely around while perched on a flat rock teetering on the edge of a cliff, negotiate a 30-degree switchback – in reverse! Not surprisingly, passengers often decide to forsake the Jeep in favor of their feet.

On the eastern edge of the Needles, four canyons – **Davis, Lavender, Salt**

**Landscape Arch, the world's longest.**

and **Horse** – contain Indian ruins, arches, intermittent water and splendid scenery. Although the lower sections of these canyons can be explored on day hikes or by Jeep, the magnificent upper reaches are best seen on overnight backpacking trips. Check with the rangers at the visitors center for more information. Finally, to share the view of the Green and Colorado rivers which so inspired Powell, visit the **Confluence Overlook** either by Jeep or by walking a 10-mile (16-km) round-trip trail beginning at **Big Spring Canyon**.

Although the **Maze District** is directly across the Colorado from the Needles, one must have a yearning for adventure to drive the 250 miles (400 km) between the two. To get to the Maze, backtrack to Moab and drive (four-wheel-drive only) north to **Green River**. Since you're going into the "back of beyond", stop here to fill water jugs and the gas tank, and buy three or four days' worth of groceries. (Anyone going through the hassle of getting there will want to stay at least that long.)

Leaving Green River, drive west on Interstate 70, then turn south toward **Hanksville**. After 24 miles (39 km) you'll see a sign warning that you're about to take your life in your hands. Turn left and drive 60 dusty miles (97 km) to **Hans Flat Ranger Station**.

Shortly before you get there you'll pass the **Robber's Roost Ranch**. A century ago, this was the hideout of two of the West's most famous outlaws, Butch Cassidy and the Sundance Kid, along with the rest of their gang, the Wild Bunch.

From Hans Flat, it takes a day to hike or a half day to drive to the **Maze Overlook**, which offers an enticing view of the **Land of Standing Rocks** and the Maze itself, a labyrinthine snarl of six canyons. A trail beginning there takes you into the Maze; there are only a handful of other places in this 30-sq.-mile (49-sq.-km) fortress of stone where one can get in or out. First-time visitors should stop to buy a map from the rangers at Hans Flat and have them mark these routes together with the location

"Courthouse Towers," Arches National Park.

of the scattered Indian ruins and springs.

As an alternative, raft companies in Green River and Moab offer four-to seven-day white-water trips through **Cataract Canyon**; on most trips time is set aside for hiking into the Maze.

**Goin' south:** After Canyonlands, you may want to visit Capitol Reef, Bryce and Zion national parks. If so, you must first head for **Hanksville** – either by driving north through Green River (as if you're going to the Maze) or south via **Blanding**. If you have time, take the southern route – it's twice as long, but three times as interesting.

Driving south from Moab, you reach the small town of **Monticello** on the flanks of the snow-clad **Abajo Mountains**. The Abajos provide a pleasing counterpoint to the slickrock country – and an escape from the summer heat. Between Monticello and Blanding there's a refreshingly cool campground at **Devil's Canyon**.

Backpackers wishing to explore **Grand Gulch Primitive Area** should get hiking permits and information from the Bureau of Land Management (BLM) in Monticello. The Anasazi Indians who once lived in Grand Gulch departed 800 years ago, but hundreds of their buildings, typically built under south-facing overhangs to shield them from the weather, remain in mint condition. So much so that the BLM must patrol Grand Gulch by helicopter to prevent illegal excavation of the ruins by pot hunters dealing in the lucrative black market in pre-Columbian pottery.

A few miles south of Blanding is a highway junction. If you're bound for **Monument Valley** and Arizona or can afford a short detour to see the world-class entrenched meanders of **Goosenecks State Park**, continue south to **Bluff** and **Mexican Hat**. You can double back on scenic State Highway 261 across Cedar Mesa. From Blanding, a right turn on State 95 (which figures so prominently in Ed Abbey's novel, *The Monkey Wrench Gang*) leads directly to **Natural Bridges National Monument**, a logical place to break the journey between Moab and Capitol Reef. There

**Fall colors at Zion National Park, Utah.**

is a campground at the Monument, but no gasoline, groceries or other services.

Bridges is to bridges what Arches is to arches: the world's largest cluster of natural bridges. Although bridges and arches are similar in appearance, only the former have been carved by a stream. Each of the three bridges in the monument can be seen from a paved loop road that departs from the visitors center. But don't just gawk at the bridges from the canyon rim. A 10-minute hike will take you to the base of any of the three.

If you must choose, **Sipapu** is perhaps the most spectacular bridge. For a longer hike, stroll downstream from Sipapu or **Owachomo** to **Kachina Bridge**. A good swimming hole at the base of a waterfall is situated between the latter two. If you're feeling adventurous, go on an overnight hike past Kachina down into **White Canyon** and explore the rarely visited canyons of **Hideout** and **Cheesebox**.

Just west of Natural Bridges is another junction: State 276 goes to **Hall's Crossing Marina** on **Lake Powell**, while State 95 continues north to Hanksville. The 180-mile-long (290-km) **Lake Powell**, named for the explorer, is the second largest and most spectacular man-made lake in the United States. The lake is formed by the 710-ft-high (215-meter) **Glen Canyon Dam**, which generates 1,200 megawatts of hydroelectricity and ample controversy.

When it was begun in 1956, the dam had the blessing of almost everyone concerned. By the time it was finished in 1963, conservationists had belatedly recognized that Glen Canyon, "the place no one knew," was comparable in grandeur to anything – including the Grand Canyon – on the Colorado Plateau. Today, many people believe that the drowning of Glen Canyon was an unspeakable ecological tragedy.

Because so much of southern Utah is a *de facto* wilderness rich in uranium, coal and other natural resources, there have been many such controversies, including a much-debated proposal to store nuclear waste next to Canyonlands National Park. Nevertheless, Lake Powell

**Bryce Canyon National Park, a rose-colored spectacle carved in limestone.**

is a stunning place to waterski, fish or explore. Consider visiting 290-ft-high (188-meter) **Rainbow Bridge**, the tallest natural bridge on the planet. You can buy gas and groceries and rent fishing tackle, powerboats or houseboats at any of the five marinas on the lake. If possible, make reservations in advance.

The mountains to the south of Hanksville are the **Henrys**, the last discovered, named and explored mountain range in the continental United States. Forty miles (64 km) west of Hanksville is **Capitol Reef National Park**, whose central attraction is the **Waterpocket Fold**, a 100-mile-long (160-km) uplifted ridge of rock that was dubbed a "reef" by those who found it a barrier to travel. After it was uplifted, the reef was eroded into narrow canyons interspersed with giant domes of white sandstone that resemble domes found on capitol buildings throughout the US.

Because the reef is nowhere more than 15 miles (25 km) wide, most of the hikes in the park are short; most common are round-trips of 2 to 4 miles (3 to 6 km). For instance, stroll through the **Grand Wash Narrows**, where 500-ft-high (150-meter) canyon walls loom less than 20 ft (6.5 meters) apart. A more difficult hike takes you to the base of the **Golden Throne**, which offers tremendous views of the rest of the park. Another excellent day hike is along the **Chimney Rock Trail**; be sure you walk a mile or two into the upper reaches of marvelous **Spring Canyon**.

**The roads to Bryce Canyon:** Backpackers should be advised that all of Capitol Reef provides rewarding backcountry hiking. However, as the terrain is extremely rugged and water is found in only a few places, it is best to ask at the visitors center for more information on hiking **Spring Canyon**, **Deep Creek**, **Hall's Creek** or **Muley Twist Canyon**.

From Capitol Reef, there are a number of routes you can take to get to **Bryce Canyon National Park**. Some are more civilized than others. If you're in a rush or don't have a spare tire, you'd be advised to keep to Highways 24, 62 and 89. But if you don't mind moseying

*One of the many "goosenecks" of the San Juan River.*

along dirt roads, fill your gas tank and water jugs and drive south to **Boulder** and **Escalante**, either across the **Aquarius Plateau** or along the east side of Capitol Reef to the **Burr Trail**.

Each route has its advantages. During the summer, go the cool way over the top of Aquarius Plateau. In the spring and fall, drive the Burr Trail. On both rounds there are two established campgrounds and any number of other suitable campsites. In either case, you'll be traversing the rugged, lonely heart of the Colorado Plateau. In 1861, the *Desert News* described this area as "measurably valueless, excepting for nomadic purposes, hunting grounds for Indians and to hold the world together."

Clarence Dutton, a member of Powell's Geographical Survey, described the view from the Aquarius Plateau as "a sublime panorama… It is the extreme of desolation, the blandest solitude, a superlative desert." Until 1929, Boulder got its mail by pack mule. Today, the mail comes by what is easily the most beautiful paved road in Utah.

At the BLM office in Escalante, backpackers can get more information on hiking into **Escalante Primitive Area**. Most backpackers enter Escalante by walking past the two stone arches in **Coyote Gulch**. An enjoyable alternative is **Harris Wash**.

From Escalante it's a few hours' drive to Bryce Canyon National Park. The Paiute Indians called Bryce the place where "red rocks stand like men in a bowl-shaped canyon." Mormon settler Ebeneezer Bryce, who gave his name to the canyon, had a more prosaic term. He called it "a hell of a place to lose a cow!"

Bryce is a fantasy land, a colorful fairy tale, a rose-colored palace carved in limestone. Technically, it's not a canyon at all but a series of 12 amphitheaters eroded into an escarpment. The beauty of this gutted badland can be appreciated from overlooks along 20 miles (32 km) of roads, but it's best to take at least one hike below the rim.

Some hikes to consider: a guided walk along the short, easy **Navajo Loop Trail**, the more strenuous **Fairyland Loop Trail** or a horseback trip on the **Peekaboo Loop**. Or walk the **Rim Trail** between any two viewing points and then ride the Inter-park Tram back.

Drive south to **Rainbow Point**. In early summer, the flowers along this road are gorgeous. On a clear day from **Yovimpa Point**, you can gaze over 100 miles (160 km) to the Grand Canyon, where the rocks are 160 million years older than those on which you stand. There are 4,000-year-old bristlecone pines on the **Bristlecone Loop Trail**.

Finally, try one of the classic trails: the thrilling route up **Angel's Landing** in **Zion National Park**. Zion is truly wild, large sections of it accessible only to mountain lions.

Perhaps the most popular trails on the flat floor of the canyon are the **Gateway to the Narrows**, the **Hanging Gardens of Zion**, **Weeping Rock**, and **Emerald Pools**. As is so often the case in southern Utah, it is hard to go wrong in Zion: all of the maintained trails are worth hiking. Since this is a wilderness, explore a bit, perhaps by poking your way up one of the side canyons.

**Left, pretty** *Opuntia phaeacantha* **at Arches National Park. Right, a close-up of "Thor's Hammer," Bryce Canyon.**

# LAS VEGAS

Reputedly Lady Luck's favorite piece of real estate, Las Vegas is a neon valley of round-the-clock risk-taking and endless extravagance. This mecca for schemers, dreamers and pleasure seekers attracts more than 15 million people each year.

The ultimate extrovert, Las Vegas pulls out all the stops to entertain you and to keep you spending your money. The casinos and hotels range from flash to class, the food and entertainment from budget to gourmet. There is something here for the most jaded visitor and much here for the wide-eyed novice. The town's slogan is "No one does it better," and it's true.

Las Vegas is improbably centered in a desert valley ringed by treeless mountains. The sky seems endless, especially to big-city eyes. Gaming and glitter in the middle of nowhere creates a fantasyland atmosphere.

The history of Las Vegas is as colorful as her casinos. The earliest white people in the area were Anglo traders travelling from Santa Fe to California on the old Spanish Trail. They found Las Vegas to be an oasis of refreshing springs and grassy fields. "Las Vegas" means "The Meadows" in Spanish.

Although explorers like Jedediah Smith and Captain John C. Fremont noted this oasis in their travels, the area remained largely uninhabited until 1855, when Brigham Young sent a band of 30 Mormon men to Las Vegas to mine for lead in the mountains and to convert the Indians. They did not stay long, discouraged by their lack of success in converting the Indians and in smelting the ore they found here. They could not have known it then, but the unsatisfactory lead was silver.

When the fabled Comstock Lode, a rich vein of gold and silver, was discovered in 1849, Nevada came into her own. Boom towns sprang up all around Las Vegas. Nevada became a territory in 1861 and as a state in 1864, because

the Union needed the wealth of the Comstock Lode to win the Civil War.

In time, the area around the abandoned Mormon settlement became the property of a succession of ranchers. They provided a way station for California-bound travelers. One of these ranchers, Helen Stewart, is an example of the strong-willed, self-sufficient pioneer women of the Old West.

She remained on the ranch, a lone woman with several children, after her husband was mysteriously shot and killed there. She ran the 1,800-acre (738-hectare) ranch, cooked meals for travelers and offered lodging for boarders until the coming of the railroad.

In 1902 Helen Stewart sold her property to the San Pedro, Salt Lake and Los Angeles Railroad, forerunner of the Union Pacific. The railroad had come to link the West with the East, and Las Vegas was to be a division point depot. The town was born on May 15, 1905, when the railroad auctioned off some 1,200 lots to high-bidding speculators. In two days, all the lots were sold and a

**Preceding pages:** Las Vegas, the desert oasis. **Left** and **right,** landmarks of the town.

boom town of tents and shacks soon appeared on the scene.

Las Vegas stayed a railroad town, small and sleepy, until the 1930s when the Boulder (Hoover) Dam project brought in workers from all over the country. In 1931, gambling was legalized in Nevada to funnel revenue into the state. Liberal marriage and divorce laws were also enacted in 1931, and Las Vegas became a capital for six-week residents awaiting a Nevada divorce.

**A never-never land:** Las Vegas is an easy town to navigate. Most of the gambling activity is concentrated in two main areas: the famed Las Vegas Strip and the downtown area on Fremont Street. The Strip (officially known as Las Vegas Boulevard South) begins at Sahara Avenue with the Sahara Hotel and runs south as far as the airport.

The downtown area is about 3 miles (5 km) north of the Strip area. A third area is centered just off the Strip along Convention Center Drive.

**The Strip** is a special effect made reality. Where else would you find a

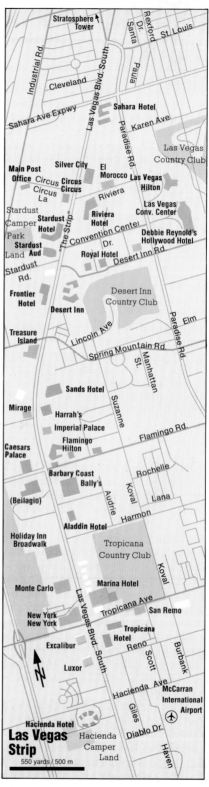

The bells toll at any hour in the Wedding Chapel, on the Strip.

colonnaded palace (Caesars Palace), a circus big top (Circus Circus), a blue pagoda (Imperial Palace) and a Mississippi River steamboat (Harrah's) sharing the same stretch of highway? Not to mention all the other hotels, motels, casinos, fountains, statues, coffee shops, gas stations, wedding chapels and shopping centers?

The hotels themselves are part of the visual excitement. They are sheathed in lights, reflective glass and marble. A recent trend is toward blindingly brilliant illuminated covered entrances called *portes cochères.*

Las Vegas properties are constantly doing face-lifting, renovating, adding on towers and making other structural changes. It is an unwritten law here that you are only as good as your latest superlative. Even McDonald's, that bastion of solid Middle America, has been swept up with Las Vegas Fever, with glittering neon tubing next to those familiar golden arches.

**Strip search:** Many of the Strip hotels are self-contained attractions. And in the last few years, there's been a determined effort to change, or at least broaden, the city's appeal. Now that gambling is legal in Atlantic City, on the Mississippi River and on certain Indian reservations, the state of Nevada has been forced to rethink its Number One attraction.

The result has been a building boom even this town of never-ending change has not witnessed before. New hotels, new casinos, new extravaganzas – most with family-style themes– have sprung up all along the Strip, with everyone from the Hard Rock Cafe to movie star Debbie Reynolds getting in on the act.

The buildings themselves are the stars of the show. At **New York, New York**, visitors can stroll in "Central Park," walk along the "Brooklyn Bridge," or ride a Coney Island-style roller coaster. The 30-story pyramid at the glass-paneled **Luxor** has an atrium big enough to hold nine Boeing 747s. At night, magnificent **Caesars Palace** is theatrically bathed in blue-green light, with an arcaded automatic "people mover" and a

Flamingo
Hilton
Casino, where
fortunes are
made and
lost.

geodesic-domed Omnimax Theater. **Treasure Island** stages a sea battle in its own lagoon. The **MGM Grand** has a casino bigger than a football field. The list – and the statistics – go on and on. The MGM stands on what is known as the Golden Corner – Las Vegas Boulevard South at Flamingo. Other Golden Corner occupants are the Flamingo Hilton and the **Barbary Coast**.

The **Flamingo Hilton's** history is decidedly more interesting than that of the more recent corporate hotels. The original Flamingo was built in 1946 by Benjamin "Bugsy" Siegel, described by newspapers of the day as "an Eastern gambler." The story is that Bugsy built the Flamingo to impress his California mistress, Virginia Hill. He spared no expense in creating a posh resort with an elegant palm-lined casino and large outdoor swimming pool.

The Flamingo's grand opening had all the trappings of a Hollywood premiere, with many of that town's celebrities in attendance. Unfortunately for Bugsy, he overlooked one small detail.

He neglected to repay a loan he had obtained from his investors, a cheery New York City gang known as Murder, Inc. Siegel was gunned down in his mistress's Beverly Hills home one year after he opened the fabulous Flamingo.

Siegel's gruesome slaying added a note of titillating notoriety to little Las Vegas. Sightseers came to town wanting to play in the casino a gangster had built. The underworld overtones became part of the Las Vegas mystique.

A construction boom of luxurious ranch-style resort hotels followed the success of the Flamingo. Las Vegas launched a national publicity blitz promoting the desert oasis as "the gambling and entertainment capital of the world." Leggy showgirls were a fixture in every publicity shot.

Other colorful early characters include the gambler known as Nick the Greek, hotelmen Del Webb, Benny Binion and Kirk Kerkorian, and of course, the reclusive Howard Hughes.

Hughes arrived in Las Vegas in 1967, taking up residence in a suite of rooms

**Hotels are luxurious and lavish.**

at the Desert Inn. By the time he left town in 1970, he had bought the Sands Desert Inn, Castaways, Silver Slipper, Frontier and Landmark hotels, along with a country club, television station, airport, ranch, mining claims and parcels of vacant land. There are those who regard the Hughes takeover of the Las Vegas casinos as a watershed in the town's history.

Early Las Vegas entrepreneurs were freewheeling types who operated their establishments with a certain carefree abandon. Howard Hughes turned over the management of his casinos to "the guys in the three-piece suits from back East." In Las Vegas, "the good old days" refers to the period preceding inflation and corporate ownership.

**Trial marriages:** All up and down the Strip are establishments where couples come to try a gamble of another sort – marriage. The marriage business is drawing people to Las Vegas in larger numbers each year, according to the Las Vegas News Bureau. Couples can be wed (or "hitched," as one chapel sign puts it) at any hour, providing they have a license from the Marriage Bureau.

The bureau is located downtown and is conveniently open from 8am to midnight Monday through Thursday and from 8am Friday through 12 midnight Sunday, including holidays. There's no blood test or waiting period. Las Vegas wedding chapels run the gamut from the barely picturesque to the outright garish. **The Little Church of the West** is a historic building by Las Vegas standards, dating back to 1942.

**Downtown** Las Vegas is not without its own special excitement. Unlike the Strip, which had miles of empty desert on which to build sprawling resort hotels, the downtown gambling area was always limited to just a few blocks of Fremont Street in the commercial center. A recent $47 million refurbishment as a pedestrian mall called the **Fremont Street Experience** has given the area a whole new lease on life. Just a mile nearer to the Strip, however (and where Downtown is said officially to begin), is the **Stratosphere Tower**. Soaring to

Westward Ho provides a paradise for gamblers.

1,825 feet (556 meters), it is the tallest building in the West. Elevators whisk visitors to the top in 30 seconds, where there is a revolving restaurant, observation decks and thrilling rides. Visitors with romantic inclinations and little fear of heights can get married near the top.

The oldest and newest in promotional advertising is very much in evidence on Fremont Street. Visitors stroll along a five-block, casino-lined mall, gathering in jam-packed crowds every hour to enjoy a computer-generated high tech light and sound show projected onto a screen. (It takes 45 hours to input the six-minute show into the computers.) The latticework unveils a spectacular moving picture show in which cartoon characters and animals dance to music, buffalo stampede, and jet fighters scream overhead. No fewer than two million light bulbs are used in the display.

High technology is also put to less extreme use on Fremont Street, as represented by the **Golden Nugget**'s computerized marquee, which spells out messages and flashes pictures.

Downtown is also home of the **Four Corners**, the intersection of Fremont and Casino Center Boulevard. The lights of the Golden Nugget, Four Queens and Fremont hotels combine to make this the most brilliantly illuminated intersection in the world. Nevada Power Company estimates the monthly electric bill of an average downtown hotel runs well into six figures, nearly half of which is eaten up by air-conditioning or heating, depending on the season.

Years ago, the downtown area was known to one and all as Glitter Gulch. The merchants ran a contest to find a more sophisticated name for the district and "Casino Center" was the winner. Nonetheless, the old names are still in everyday use – Downtown, Glitter Gulch or simply Fremont Street.

Downtown has changed considerably in recent years. Fremont Street, always a great place to gamble, did not have hotel accommodation until recently. Today the Golden Nugget, Four Queens and the Plaza are among the major casinos that boast hotel space and gourmet

**Fountain spray fronting Caesars Palace on the Strip.**

204

dining rooms as fine as any to be found on the Strip. The downtown area has its own mini-convention facility, the **Cashman Field Center**.

As a rule, it costs less to gamble downtown than on the Strip. Stakes are lower and it is still possible to find inexpensive craps tables. Some people think downtown dealers are friendlier and more tolerant too. Downtown casinos are said to have loose slots, machines that have been adjusted to pay out up to 90 percent of the money deposited in them. The volume of slot enthusiasts is so high that frequent payoffs are good promotions for the casino because they bring in more traffic. There is no skill involved in playing the slots, so they are often a tourist's first foray into casino gambling. The attraction of hitting a jackpot keeps casinos humming incessantly with the noise of machines in action. The newest versions are dollar carousels, which collect and pay out in dollars. They are very popular and may mean the demise of the standard casino coin machines.

This is not to say that the high rollers or big shooters do not frequent the downtown area. **Binion's Horseshoe** is a downtown property known for its players. (A player in Las Vegas parlance means someone who plays for very high stakes, as opposed to a grind, who makes only small bets.)

**Gambling or gaming?:** There is no place on earth where a little knowledge is more dangerous than in a casino. They don't call this place "Lost Wages" for nothing. It will be worth your while to study some of the books available on casino gambling and to learn gaming etiquette and strategies.

Several casinos offer seminars in blackjack (or "21"), craps and baccarat. It is a mistake to assume that you can rely on the assistance of the dealer, however. Although some dealers can be very helpful, you must remember that they are all employees of the casino and in most cases are forbidden to take interest in the activity around them.

It is generally acknowledged that baccarat, blackjack and craps offer the

lowest house odds. Because of the way most people play, however, the return to the house is 19 percent on craps and baccarat and 21 percent on blackjack. The lowest return to the house, only 7 percent, is from bingo. Roulette returns 27 percent to the house, keno 28 percent, and the "Wheel of Fortune" or "Big Six" 51 percent.

Is there a pattern here? Yes. The games in which you can exercise some control generally present you with better opportunities to win. "An intelligent craps player can do well," says a casino executive. "The problem is that so few people bother to understand the complicated betting involved in craps."

Dealers, who receive low salaries from casinos and therefore are very dependent on tips from customers, will appreciate a tip (or toke, as it is called here). The custom here is to make a bet for the dealer, usually half the size of your own. Dealers are required to tap a casino chip against the table or employ some other signal to indicate to the pit boss (or supervisor) that he is pocketing his tip.

All of the casinos serve complimentary drinks. If you are gambling and have not been served by a cocktail waitress, ask a dealer to summon one for you. You should tip her with cash or a casino chip.

The nonstop activity of Nevada casinos results in billions of dollars in gross gaming revenues for the state. The industry is carefully monitored by the Nevada Gaming Commission. (The state prefers the term "gaming" to "gambling".) The Gaming Commission is an effective policeman. The casinos have to be honest – cheating could result in the loss of a casino license worth millions of dollars.

The Strip offers a parade of entertainment nightly. There are big-name performers appearing in the major showrooms and world-famous production shows with lavish costumes and sets and enormous casts. Several casinos present shortened versions of popular Broadway musicals.

If your heart is set on seeing a particular performer, it is best to book a room

**Vegas is just as colorful by day...**

206

at the hotel where he or she is performing, since showrooms give preferential treatment to hotel guests. You should make a reservation the day of the show with the hotel guest-relations coordinator or the bellcap. Show admission is by reservation, not ticket. You will have a choice of a dinner show (with a minimum price) or a cocktail show. There is usually a two- or four-drink minimum at a cocktail show. Be forewarned that the evening could get pricey – your showroom tab will be subject to a considerable entertainment tax as well as the sales tax. The *maitre d'* who seats you will be much more considerate in selecting a table for you if you palm him a tip when you first enter the showroom.

If you do not have a reservation for a show, you will be allowed to wait in the "no reservations" line. This is akin to flying stand-by.

The bare-breasted beauties in the chorus line are no longer the wicked attractions they once were back in the early 1950s, when production shows made their debut on the Strip. Audiences are more worldly now and more demanding. These days the special effects are the stars of the show, major recording or even Hollywood stars who play to packed houses.

Las Vegas casinos have been plying customers with inexpensive, bountiful food buffets since the early 1950s. Prices keep nudging up toward reality, but food is still a bargain here. You can find steak-and-egg breakfasts and all-you-can-eat lunch and dinner buffets which may or may not include champagne. Sunday brunches at some of the hotels are events in themselves. Every hotel also has a 24-hour coffee shop, where you may have everything from the proverbial cup to a full-course dinner. If you're a keno buff, you can relax and play a game or two in hotel coffee shops while you eat. In addition, each major hotel has several restaurants, one of which is designated the gourmet room. These restaurants are carefully decorated showpieces. The meals here are generally memorable for the expense as well as the setting.

...as it is by night.

208

# ALBUQUERQUE

Albuquerque began in 1705, a cluster of mud huts near a simple mud chapel in a place where the Rio Grande makes a wide bend, leaving rich bottomlands where settlers could plant corn and orchards. For a century and a half it was a Spanish farming community on El Camino Real, the road from Santa Fe to Mexico City. When the railroad came in 1880 New Albuquerque moved 2 miles east, leaving Old Town to enjoy a long *siesta* – but without losing any of its identity at all.

Albuquerque is the largest city in the state of New Mexico, with some 450,000 people in the metropolitan area. It is the trade center of the state, headquarters for regional governmental agencies, a medical center of some renown, home of the state university and a private college and, since World War II, a center for Space Age research and development. Slightly more than a mile above sea level, it has a dry, crisp climate and a relaxed life-style.

Any visit to Albuquerque begins with **Old Town Plaza**. Galleries there and in other parts of town represent some of the most prestigious artists in the state. Jewelry, pottery, rugs and weavings are good buys of dependable quality.

Most activity in Old Town revolves around **San Felipe de Neri Church**, which hasn't missed a Sunday service in more than 275 years. In May it is the scene of The Blessing of the Animals, and in June the Old Town Fiesta. For nine days before Christmas, Las Posadas processions circle the plaza in candlelit reverence, reminding the faithful how Mary and Joseph sought shelter for the birth of baby Jesus.

On Christmas Eve the plaza glows with thousands of *luminarias,* an Old Spanish custom to light the pilgrim's way to the Christ Child. Original *luminarias* were small bonfires of crossed sticks called *farolitos,* today's version is a small brown paper bag with a votive candle inside, held steady by a fairly thick layer of sand in the bottom.

**Albuquerque Museum** in Old Town is a modernistic, solar-heated adobe building with changing exhibits in art, history and science. The major permanent exhibit covers 400 years of New Mexican history. A new museum of natural history across the street was opened in 1985, the first such museum built in this country in over 100 years. New Mexico is rich in paleontological material, and for years it has gone to museums in the East. Now it remains where it should.

The **Indian Pueblo Cultural Center**, a few blocks from Old Town, is owned by the 19 pueblos of New Mexico, each of which has an exhibit area showing its own unique arts and crafts. It is a good place, for example, to see the difference between a Zuni and an Acoma pot. One floor is devoted to the history of the Pueblo Indians, and there is a shop and small restaurant. On weekends during the summer different tribes perform dances on the patio, where photography is permitted free.

**Preceding pages**: the International Balloon Festival at Albuquerque. **Left**, Laguna Indian all dressed for a festival. **Right**, hiking some of the many trails in the Sandia Mountains, east of Albuquerque.

**The Rio Grande Zoological Park**, to the south of Old Town, rates among the best in the country. A rain forest, reptile house and great ape house are many people's favorites.

**Downtown** Albuquerque has made a successful comeback in recent years after almost succumbing to that common illness, *suburbia exodium*. The new civic plaza sparkles with flowers and a fountain, serving the same purpose as the plaza in any Spanish town, that of a communal gathering spot. The old buildings on Central Avenue are becoming a center for art galleries and studios, and the **Kimo Theater**, a marvel of ornate Indian-style art of the 1930s, was restored to its former glory by the city.

The architecture at the **University of New Mexico** farther east along Central Avenue shows how adaptable the basic Pueblo style is. Traditional buttressed walls with protruding *vigas* (rafters) sit happily beside modern angular lines with lots of glass. In the center of the campus are the seven-story library and the president's home, both outstanding examples of Pueblo architecture. Also on campus are the **Maxwell Museum of Anthropology**, the **Fine Arts Museum** and **Popejoy Hall**, which has a full schedule of symphony, light opera, Broadway shows and many other forms of live entertainment.

The **Sandia Mountains**, hard against the east side of Albuquerque, dominate aesthetically, recreationally and climatically. The mountainsides facing the city are rugged and steep; the other side is gentler, with forested slopes. Both sides offer miles of hiking trails. **Sandia Peak Aerial Tram**, the longest in North America, goes up the west (city) side in about 15 minutes. The tram ride is a must. By day you can see mountain ranges a hundred miles to the north, west and south. At night you can eat at a restaurant at the top while the lights of Albuquerque, Santa Fe and Los Alamos twinkle like stars below you. In winter, skiers take the tram to the top of Sandia Peak Ski Area or drive up the other side.

**Mountains and monuments:** Of special interest geologically and historically is

*Luminarias on Christmas Eve at Old Town, Albuquerque.*

a drive through the **Jemez Mountains** northwest of Albuquerque. The sights on this tour range from red and saffron cliffs to mountain streams, from forested slopes and alpine meadows to Indian pueblos. It covers 200 miles (320 km) and can be done in a day, but two would be better.

The first stop is **Coronado State Monument**, 20 miles (32 km) north of town where you leave Interstate 25 and turn northwest on State Highway 44. These are the ruins of a large prehistoric Indian pueblo, thought to be the spot where Coronado's expedition headquartered during the winter of 1540–41. The Indians never reoccupied it. Of special interest is a kiva (underground ceremonial chamber) with rare restored murals. This is probably the only chance you will ever have to enter a kiva.

Just beyond the village of **Jemez Springs** are the ruins of a Spanish mission built around 1617, preserved as **Jemez State Monument**, with a visitors center and walking trails. The highway follows the Jemez River past the camping and picnic sites and the hiking trails of the Santa Fe National Forest.

Where the road turns east you'll see **Valle Grande**, a lush, grassy valley 12 miles (19 km) across, cupped in high mountains. A few million years ago this was the seething innards of a volcano which, layer by layer, gradually built up the entire 50-mile-long (80-km) mountain range. Finally the volcano collapsed, creating Valle Grande. The volcanic ash and dust from this cataclysmic event added another 1,500 ft (450 meters) to the basalt plateau. Erosion cut the plateau into deep canyons, and where layers of volcanic ash were exposed, natural caves were hollowed out by the wind. Eons later Indians used the caves for homes. **Bandelier National Monument** preserves these cliff dwellings and a large circular pueblo on the floor of the canyon, probably occupied by the Pueblo Indians before they moved into the Rio Grande Valley.

Not far from Bandelier is **Los Alamos**, a city built in secrecy during World War II for scientists developing the atomic

**Bandelier National Monument, New Mexico.**

bomb. It is now an open city with attractive residential and business areas, in addition to the research laboratories.

Head east from Albuquerque on Interstate 40 and turn south on State 14, which follows the east side of the **Manzano Mountains**. In the early 1600s the Spanish built the missions to serve the Pueblo Indians on the eastern face of the mountains, but within 50 years raids from the fierce Plains Indians became unbearable and the peaceful Pueblo abandoned their mountain homes for the Rio Grande Valley. Together the three missions make up **Salinas Pueblo Missions National Monument**, headquartered at Mountainair on US 60.

At **Quarai** and **Abó** stand high walls of red sandstone, like primitive cathedrals open to the sky. Farther south along State 14, **Gran Quivira**, built of gray limestone, stands lonely on a high, windswept hill. Most of the pueblo has been excavated, as have the ruins of two large mission churches, one of which was abandoned before it was finished. There is a visitors center with picnic sites at Gran Quivira and Quarai. You can turn to Albuquerque by going west on US 60 and then north on Interstate 25, about 200 miles (320 km) total.

The scenic road from Albuquerque to Santa Fe goes around the back (the east side) of the Sandia Mountains, through ghost towns and Hispanic villages. The **Turquoise Trail**, otherwise known as State 14, begins at the Tijeras-Cedar Crest exit from Interstate 40, east of Albuquerque.

At the village of San Antonio, State 44 bears left to **Sandia Peak Ski Area** and on to **Sandia Crest**, which at 10,447 ft (3,166 meters) is the highest part of these mountains. Many picnic areas and hiking trails are marked as the highway gradually climbs through **Cibola National Forest**. In fall, aspen glades turn golden, and scrub oak lights red flares on the mountainsides. In winter, cross-country skiers seek out these trails.

To continue on the Turquoise Trail, return to State 14 at San Antonio and turn north again to **Golden**, an inhabited "ghost town." But it's a ghost of what it

**Caretaker at Salinas National Monument, New Mexico.**

used to be. Nearby, the first gold strike west of the Mississippi was made in 1826. Look sharply and you will see the ruins of foundations in the narrow canyon. At the north end of Golden, on a hill beside the road, stands **St Francis**, a mission church built in the 1830s and restored in 1958. The church and cemetery still serve the parish. The gate is usually locked, but you can drive up to the gate to photograph it . This is one of the most photographed mission churches in New Mexico, and if you are there on a day of brilliant cobalt skies and whipped-cream clouds you will understand why.

Eleven miles (18 km) beyond Golden is **Madrid**, once a coal mining town of thousands. It died in 1952 when diesel fuel replaced coal on the Santa Fe Railroad. Many of the cottages have been restored, but on entering the town you look down a desolate street of abandoned houses in all stages of decay.

Lively ghosts inhabit Madrid now, and they operate the **Mine Shaft Tavern**, a melodrama theater, art galleries and several stores. Bluegrass, jazz or country-and-western bands belt out thigh-slapping, foot-stomping music on weekend evenings at the Tavern, and, during the summer on Sunday afternoons, at the baseball diamond of the abandoned school. In winter things slow down at Madrid, but the Tavern always has a welcoming fire stoked in the stove and a spot of grog at the bar.

The turquoise mines of **Cerrillos**, the last town on the Turquoise Trail, gave the name to this back road to Santa Fe. In the early 1600s, the Spaniards found Indians already working turquoise mines here, but when the veins played out, the Indians left.

Cerrillos turquoise is a rare and expensive collectors' item today. Hobbyminers still find enough lead, gold, zinc or silver in the dry hills and arroyos near here to keep them in chewing tobacco. Several small, interesting shops are clustered around the plaza, and quite a few movies and TV series have been filmed in this colorful little village at the end of the Turquoise Trail.

**Around the old wood stove, San Jose.**

# SANTA FE

*Santa Fe* is "in" now, but fads come and go, and when the faddists tire of it and leave, *voila!* There's old Santa Fe, timeless and mellow, calmly waiting.

Santa Fe was founded in 1610 as the capital of the Spanish province of New Mexico. The governor's residence and official buildings were on the north side of the Plaza. Today they are the heart of the state's museum system. In the early days there was much internal bickering between secular and civic officials, with the Indians caught in the middle.

In 1680, the Indians rebelled against heavy-handed missionaries and taxes, gleefully burned all records, books and churches, smashed bells and religious accoutrements, and tortured and killed every Spaniard who didn't get away. Governor Diego de Vargas reconquered the province in 1692 without firing a shot, but the Spaniards had learned an important lesson. They no longer forbade the Indians' ancient ceremonies, so long as they went to Mass first.

Santa Fe remained the capital during the Mexican period (1821–46) and when the Americans took over. It has seen many races, creeds and politics, and will see more. Today Santa Fe has a population of about 62,000. In the winter it swells with skiers; in the summer with vacationers. Narrow and crooked old *burro* trails have become paved streets and have a rough time handling traffic, so you're better off walking the downtown areas. In any case, you'll get the feel of Santa Fe better on foot.

The city sits at 7,000 ft (2,100 meters) at the base of the **Sangre de Cristo Mountains**, the southernmost part of the Rockies. The sun is bright and warm, the air cool. Blankets feel good at night, and light wraps are needed after dark, even in summer.

The **Palace of the Governors** runs the length of the north side of the Plaza. Indians spread their jewelry and pottery on blankets along the *portal* much as they have for centuries. Exhibits in the museum relate to the history of New Mexico's Indian, Spanish, Mexican and Territorial periods. In one area the original walls are exposed under glass, showing adobe almost 400 years old.

**Museums:** Across the street to the west is the **Museum of Fine Arts**. Built in 1917, this branch of the state museum is a classic example of Pueblo Revival architecture. The permanent collection features painters whose art has been synonymous with New Mexico for 60 years, including Georgia O'Keeffe and Ernest Blumenschein. Other exhibits are changed frequently as a showcase for outstanding New Mexican artists.

On pinõn-dotted Museum Hill at the southeast edge of town (too far to walk) is a complex of three eminent museums. The **Museum of International Folk Art**, a state museum, exhibits religious and other folk art, highlighted by the **Girard Exhibit**, a collection of 120,000 pieces of folk art from around the world. Of the many museums in New Mexico, this is perhaps the most distinctive and, if possible, it should not be missed.

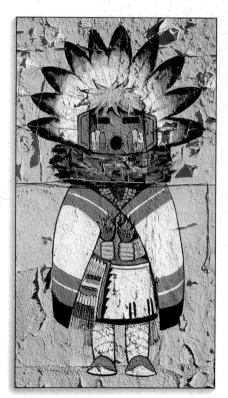

**Preceding pages:** cow skulls form a graphic image. **Left,** a San Juan dancer in New Mexico. **Right,** colorful local artwork.

Also on Museum Hill is the **Wheelwright Museum of the American Indian**, a privately endowed museum once devoted exclusively to Navajo ceremonial art but now including culture and art from other tribes. Nearby, the **Museum of Indian Art and Culture** has excellent displays of pottery, kachinas and other Native-American artifacts.

Back downtown, the **Cathedral of St Francis**, a block east of the Plaza, stands in Romanesque grandeur a monument to Jean Baptiste Lamy, Archbishop of Santa Fe. Willa Cather's novel, *Death Comes for the Archbishop,* immortalizes Lamy's work in the Southwest. Five minutes north on Bishop Lodge Road is the **Bishop's Lodge**, one of Santa Fe's most luxurious resorts. Here Bishop Lamy's private chapel is open to the public. The lodge is closed in winter.

To the south of the Plaza is **Loretto Chapel**, also known as Our Lady of Light, housing the **Famous Staircase**, built without nails or visible support. Legend says an itinerant carpenter appeared at the convent of the Sisters of Loretto in 1878 in answer to a novena and built the circular, freestanding stairway. The carpenter disappeared, but the sisters believed he was St Joseph.

**San Miguel Mission**, on the Old Santa Fe Trail two blocks east of the plaza, is sometimes called "the oldest church in America." It isn't, but it stands over the foundations of a church built around 1636 and burned during the Pueblo Revolt of 1680. It has been rebuilt and remodeled five times since then. Across the street is **The Oldest House in America**, housing a gift and souvenir shop. There are many adobe houses that are older, but it nevertheless serves as a good example of ancient construction.

**Cristo Rey Church**, at the east end of Canyon Road, holds the most remarkable piece of Spanish colonial art in the US: a huge stone altar screen – *reredos* – carved with saints and intricate designs. Measuring 40 feet wide, 18 feet high (12 by 5 meters) and weighing many tons, it was made in 1760 for an older church on the Plaza and kept in storage for over 200 years before a church big enough to hold it was built.

**Southwestern art:** The best people-watching spot in town is **La Fonda Hotel** on the plaza. Sit in the lobby and you'll see movie stars, politicians, Native Americans, artists, poets and maybe your next-door neighbor. There has always been a hostelry here at the end of the Santa Fe Trail.

The present establishment dates well before World War II and is built like a multistoried Indian pueblo with protruding *vigas*, smooth, flowing lines, flagstone floors, interior patios, colored glass, carved corbels, and furniture. The lounge is a place to sit in comfortable dimness, listen to classical guitar, sip margaritas and crunch nachos. When the guy nearby finishes his drink, he sets his glass on the bar like any good New Mexican cowboy.

For shops and galleries two general areas are outstanding: the **Plaza** and **Canyon Road**. East of the Plaza, **Sena** and **Prince** plazas off Palace Avenue have some of the most interesting shops in Santa Fe. Collectors of Indian or Spanish Colonial art will be especially

**A Santa Fe doorway.**

rewarded, as will anyone interested in contemporary Southwestern art. Several of Santa Fe's best art galleries are on Washington and San Francisco streets within one block of the Plaza.

**Canyon Road**, once a crooked trail used for hauling wood where artists could rent adobe houses for $10 a month, is now Santa Fe's other great shopping area. The cheap huts are now pricey condominiums and the finest shops, galleries and restaurants in Santa Fe.

**Ski country:** Outdoor recreation is important in Santa Fe. The season at **Santa Fe Ski Area** is one of the best in the state. Only 16 miles (26 km) from downtown, it gets 160 inches (406 cm) of powder snow a year, and the runs are mostly expert to intermediate. A day lodge and cafeteria are located at the base, but overnight lodging is not available. The road to the ski basin, State Highway 475, passes through **Hyde Memorial State Park** in **Santa Fe National Forest**, a favorite place for hiking and walking in the summer in order to admire the brilliant colors.

Over 25 years, the **Santa Fe Opera** has built a world-wide reputation for excellence. The season is July to August, and performances are usually sold out. Those without reservations can try at the gate for standing room. The Opera House is in the hills north of town, and with the sides and part of the roof open to the stars, the setting becomes part of the performances.

**El Rancho de las Golondrinas** (Ranch of the Swallows), 10 miles (16 km) south of town, is a reconstructed Spanish colonial village, once a stopping place on El Camino Real. Open June–September, there is a moderate admission fee. Fiestas are held on the first weekends in May and October, with colonial folk-art demonstrations and activities. The village of **La Cienega** grew up around the hacienda.

The **High Road to Taos**, State 76, winds through colonial New Mexico and mountain villages like Chimayo, Truchas, Las Trampas, Peñasco. During the 1700s a blanket of isolation covered New Mexico. Gone were the

**Santa Fe, 1880s.**

swashbuckling days of the conquistadors. Small villages away from the capital were isolated, and customs became so ingrained that they linger today, a relic of New Mexico 300 years ago.

From Santa Fe go north on US 84/285 to **Santa Cruz** and then onto State 76. **Holy Cross Church** in Santa Cruz was built in the 1740s and is one of the largest of the old mission churches. Its buttressed walls are 3-ft (1-meter) thick and sheltered the villagers when Plains Indians came through the mountains to steal crops, women and children.

**El Santuario** in **Chimayo** is called the Lourdes of America. During Holy Week (the week before Easter), pilgrims from miles around drive, walk and even crawl toward it. The altar, screen and Stations of the Cross are fine examples of religious folk art. To the left of the altar a room is hung with crutches, braces, photographs, poems, letters and other offerings from the devout. In a small adjoining room is a hole in the dirt floor where pilgrims get a pinch of the holy earth of Chimayo.

Several families of Chimayo weavers have achieved national fame for their tightly woven, brightly colored blankets. The **Chimayo Weavers Showroom** is open to the public.

**Village with a view:** The village of **Truchas** sits high on a timbered plateau beneath the snow-covered Truchas Peaks. On the main street are a *morada*, a church of the Penitente sect, and a plastic-roofed Pentecostal church. Truchas is not known for its hospitality, but the setting is superb.

A few miles on is **Las Trampas**, best known for its church, said to be the best example of Pueblo architecture in the state. The village was founded in 1760 as a buffer for Santa Cruz and Santa Fe against marauding Comanches. The church, **San Jose de Gracia**, is on the State and National Historic registers. Find the kindly neighbor who keeps the key, and he will let you inside.

At **Peñasco**, the next village, the route divides. Jogging right 6 miles (10 km) to State 3, travelers drive through the mountains into Taos. Or turning left

**The Harvest Procession at Las Golondrinas heralds a gathering of Hispanics.**

onto State 75, they reach the intersection with State 68, the main road to Taos. If you choose the second route, stop at Picurís pueblo for a visit.

**Pecos National Historical Park:** Earliest Spanish records mention a large Indian pueblo in the mountains east of present-day Santa Fe. Lying in a high green valley watered by the Pecos River, the pueblo had communal dwellings 4–5 stories high with over 700 rooms. There were five separate plazas and 23 *kivas*, attesting to the size and importance of the pueblo. Around 1620, the Spaniards built a large mission church there with thick adobe walls, mortared and solidly buttressed, with fine carved corbels.

The Pecos Indians joined the revolt of 1680 and burned the church. Pecos was resettled after the reconquest, and a smaller adobe church was built inside the burnt foundations. But Pecos was dying, and in 1838 the last two dozen people went west to live with the Jemez Indians, the only other tribe that spoke their language. The ruins of both the churches and the pueblo are preserved at the **Pecos National Historical Park**.

The drive to Pecos from Santa Fe on Interstate 25 follows the old Santa Fe Trail. State 63 goes north from the monument for 20 miles (32 km) where it dead-ends at Cowles, a summer home area and trail-head for horse and back-packing trips into Santa Fe National Forest and Pecos Wilderness.

You can continue east on I-25 past the Pecos turn-off for another 15 miles (24 km) to State 3, which goes to several villages as pastoral and quiet as they were a hundred years ago. At **San Miguel**, 3 miles (5 km) south of I-25, you can still see where the Santa Fe Trail forded the Pecos River. In the Mexican Period, 1821–46, San Miguel was the portal to New Mexico, where wagon trains had to stop and pay duty.

**Villanueva State Park**, 9 miles (14 km) south of San Miguel, has picnic and camping facilities on the Pecos River. The drive down this narrow valley where the stream is bordered with small fields and villages is the heart of rural Hispanic New Mexico.

**Below**, El Santuario in Chimayo, New Mexico. **Right**, the altar inside San Jose de Gracia.

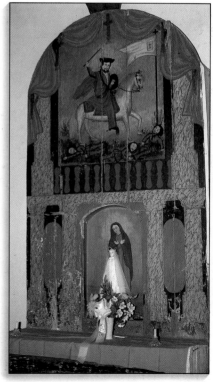

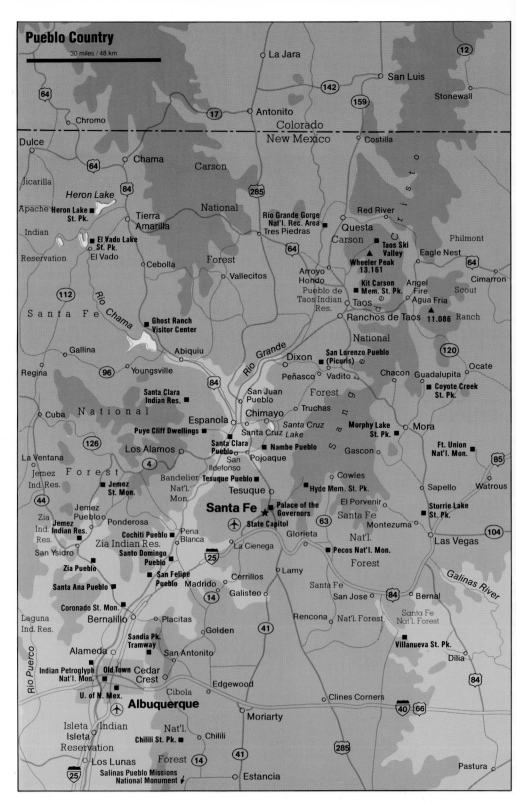

**Pueblo Country**

30 miles / 48 km

La Jara

12

San Luis

142

Stonewall

64

159

17

Antonito

Chromo

**Colorado**

Dulce

**New Mexico**

Costilla

Chama

Carson

64

Jicarilla

84

285

Heron Lake

National

Red River

Apache

Heron Lake
St. Pk.

Rio Grande Gorge
Nat'l. Rec. Area
Tres Piedras

Questa

Philmont

Indian

El Vado Lake
St. Pk.

Carson

Taos Ski
Valley

Eagle Nest

64

Reservation

El Vado

Cebolla

Forest

Wheeler Peak
13,161

112

Rio Chama

Vallecitos

Arroyo
Hondo

Kit Carson
Mem. St. Pk.

Angel
Fire

Cimarron

Agua Fria

Scout

Santa Fe

Pueblo de
Taos Indian
Res.

Taos

11,086

Ranch

Ghost Ranch
Visitor Center

Abiquiu

Ranchos de Taos

National

120

Gallina

Rio Grande

Dixon

San Lorenzo Pueblo
(Picuris)

Ocate

Regina

96

Youngsville

Peñasco

Vadito

Chacon

Guadalupita

Coyote Creek
St. Pk.

Santa Clara
Indian Res.

84

San Juan
Pueblo

Forest

Truchas

Cuba

**National**

Chimayo

Santa Cruz

Morphy Lake
St. Pk.

Mora

Puye Cliff Dwellings

Espanola

Santa Cruz
Lake

Gascon

Ft. Union
Nat'l. Mon.

126

Los Alamos

Santa Clara
Pueblo

Nambe Pueblo

85

La Ventana

4

San
Ildefonso

Pojoaque

Jemez Forest

Bandelier

Tesuque Pueblo

Cowles

Ind. Res.

Jemez
St. Mon.

Nat'l.
Mon.

Tesuque

Hyde Mem. St. Pk.

Sapello

Watrous

44

Jemez
Pueblo

Ponderosa

El Porvenir

Storrie Lake
St. Pk.

Zia
Ind.
Res.

Jemez
Indian Res.

Pena
Blanca

**Santa Fe**

Palace of the
Governors

Santa Fe

Montezuma

104

Cochiti Pueblo

State Capitol

Nat'l.

Las Vegas

San Ysidro

Zia Indian Res.

Santo Domingo
Pueblo

Glorieta

Pecos Nat'l. Mon.

Zia Pueblo

San Felipe
Pueblo

Madrido

25

La Cienega

Lamy

Forest

Galinas River

Santa Ana Pueblo

Cerrillos

Santa Fe

San Jose

84

Bernal

Coronado St. Mon.

14

Galisteo

Rencona

Nat'l. Forest

Santa Fe
Nat'l. Forest

Laguna
Ind. Res.

Bernalillo

Placitas

Villanueva St. Pk.

Rio Puerco

Sandia Pk.
Tramway

Golden

41

Dilia

Alameda

San Antonito

84

Indian Petroglyph
Nat'l. Mon.

Old Town

Cedar
Crest

Edgewood

U. of N. Mex.

Cibola

Clines Corners

40

66

**Albuquerque**

Moriarty

Isleta Indian

Nat'l.

Chilili

Isleta

Chilili St. Pk.

Reservation

285

25

Los Lunas

Forest

14

41

Estancia

Pastura

Salinas Pueblo Missions
National Monument

# PUEBLO COUNTRY

Thousands of years ago the odyssey of prehistoric humans took them through the misty migrations of the Ice Age to the peak of their Stone Age civilization at around AD 1100 in the Four Corners states: New Mexico, Arizona, Colorado and Utah. By the time the Spaniards came north from Mexico in 1540 the descendants of the Anasazi, the Ancient Ones, were well settled in their communal villages along the Rio Grande and its tributaries, from Isleta in the south to Taos in the north. A few tribes had moved west, and the Spaniards called them Pueblo Indians because they lived in villages, unlike the nomadic, warlike tribes such as the Navajo, Apache and Ute of the northern plains.

Today more than 80,000 Indians live in the 19 pueblos of New Mexico. For the most part, they live where they were living when the Spaniards came. Each pueblo has its own governor and council and is subject to federal and most state laws but remains autonomous in many ways. Elaborate ceremonial dances are performed as they have been for thousands of years. They may appear to be social events (they are), but they are also prayer meetings for rain, good harvests, fertility, peace and a thanksgiving for all the good things of life. Outsiders are permitted to attend dances at Indian pueblos, but they should never forget that they are guests.

Never take photographs or make audio recordings or drawings unless you have obtained permission at the tribal office and have paid the fee, if there is one. Some pueblos do not permit photography at all; others allow it some of the time at certain events. In all pueblos there are some ceremonies to which outsiders will not be admitted, but in those cases there will be a sign or a guard at the entrance of the village. The best time to visit is on a feast day. All the pueblos mentioned here except Zuni are within driving distance of Albuquerque, Santa Fe or Taos.

**Ancient architecture:** Often called Sky City, **Acoma** is 65 miles (105 km) west of Albuquerque off Interstate 40 in New Mexico. Perched on a 400-foot (125-meter) high rock mesa, the old pueblo had a strong defensive position. Most Acomans live in two newer villages below, raise cattle and sheep, operate highway businesses or work in nearby towns. Some are chosen each year to live on top of the rock and keep the old village and church in good repair. Most of the tribe returns to the hilltop for special feast days.

An overwhelming sense of history pervades the church, **San Esteban del Rey**, built in 1629 of flagstone and adobe mud. Every timber had to be carried from the distant mountains, and water and mud for the adobe were carried up the steep trail to the mesa top. The high ceiling, hand-hewn beams, thick walls, square towers and adjoining priests' quarters are a masterpiece in primitive architecture.

A visitors center is located near the base of the mesa, where tourists must

*Preceding pages: even New Mexico gets its share of snowy winters. Below, Acoma Church Tower.*

board a bus to the village. An Acoma guide conducts them through the pueblo. Photography is permitted for a fee.

Acoma pottery is thin, well-fired and watertight. It is usually white and painted with black geometric designs; a newer style is all white with fingernail marks pressed into the wet clay.

**Cochiti** is 36 miles (58 km) south-west of Santa Fe or 45 miles (22 km) north of Albuquerque. Cochiti potters are famous for their earth-tone pots in the shape of or decorated with animal figures and painted with black designs. The most sought after designs are of storytellers, pueblo mothers or some-times fathers, with anything from one to 30 children crawling all over them.

Cochiti people farm and work in town. The resort community of **Cochiti Lake**, a few miles north, is on reservation land. The Indians sit on decision-making boards, and many of them work at the lake, where water sports are available. They also operate a campground there. The annual feast day is July 14 when there is a corn dance.

**Isleta**, only 13 miles (21 km) south of Albuquerque, manages to retain a strong identity nevertheless. Its people farm the good bottomlands along the river and hold jobs in Albuquerque. Most of the Isletans remained friendly with the Spaniards during the revolt of 1680 and fled south with them, returning with de Vargas in 1692–94. Their magnificent mission church, built around 1615, was gutted during the rebellion and restored on their return. It is still in use, one of the most venerable in New Mexico. San Agustín, the patron saint, is honored on September 4 but they perform many other dances during the fall and summer.

**Cliff dwelling craftsmen: Jemez**, 48 miles (77 km) northwest of Albuquer-que, is set among the red and ocher cliffs of the Jemez Mountains. It was one of the last tribes to submit to Spanish rule after the reconquest, and many of its people went west to live with the Na-vajo. Even today, at any feast day in Jemez, a surprising number of Navajo will be there. A craft cooperative on the highway sells Jemez pottery, usually

**Acoma Indian pueblo, one of the oldest continuously inhabited villages in North America.**

reddish-brown and tan, painted black.

About 12 miles (19 km) up the canyon, just beyond the resort village of Jemez Springs, **Jemez State Monument** preserves the ruins of a mission church built by and for the Jemez people around 1617. It too was gutted in the rebellion, and never rebuilt. Jemez celebrates its patron San Diego on November 12, and in August they perform the Pecos Bull Dance to honor the Pecos people who moved in with them in 1838.

**Laguna** is along Interstate 40 about 45 miles (75 km) west of Albuquerque. A turnout gives travelers a good view of the pueblo – a church and squat, square adobe homes on a low hill a few hundred yards away. For a better view, drive into the pueblo. This is one of the largest pueblo groups, with almost 5,000 members living in seven villages on the reservation. Uranium mines there provided much employment until recently. Once again, cattle ranching and other jobs in Albuquerque provide a livelihood for most families.

**Nambe**, 21 miles (34 km) north of Santa Fe, has been largely Hispanicized, but its impressive mission church is well-maintained and dominates the area. San Francisco is celebrated on October 4, and on July 4 there is a popular festival at the foot of Nambe Falls, where many dances are performed and photography is permitted. A campground has recently been built near the falls.

**Picurís**, 20 miles (32 km) southwest of Taos, was once much larger than it is today. Being on the eastern edge of the pueblo world, it was subject to attack by Plains Indians more than any other pueblo. This pueblo is believed to have been founded around 1250 AD by a group of Taos Indians, and the two tribes speak the same language. (The 19 pueblos speak six distinct languages.) Their annual feast day and corn dance is August 10 in honor of San Lorenzo. Women potters produce utilitarian cooking pottery. It is reddish brown with highlights of mica and not decorated, but it is serviceable.

**Pojoaque**, 16 miles (26 km) north of Santa Fe, shrank almost to extinction. It

A place of worship for Indians in Cochiti, New Mexico.

was reorganized and now has a tribal structure. On December 12 of each year there is a tribute to Our Lady of Guadalupe, patron saint of New Mexico and Mexico.

**Sandia**, 14 miles (22 km) north of Albuquerque, has fertile river bottomland for farming and has capitalized on its nearness to Albuquerque by encouraging tourist-related industries. The reservation extends to the top of the Sandia Mountains. On the road to the Sandia Peak Tram, is a large arts and crafts center selling the work of many tribes. On June 13 San Antonio is honored with a corn dance.

**San Felipe**, 28 miles (45 km) north of Albuquerque, is one of the most conservative pueblos, never permitting photography under any circumstances. The lovely 18th-century mission church is open only during religious services. On Christmas Eve, the spirits of the animal kingdom pay homage to the Christ Child as dancers representing deer or buffalo. Elaborately dressed women dancers enter the church after Midnight Mass. In hushed closeness, onlookers await the arrival of the procession. No one is supposed to be around to see the dancers come from their kiva. Buffalo dancers wear the dark fur and horned headdress of the buffalo, with their exposed skin darkened, and stomp on the floor. Deer dancers, their headdresses bedecked with antlers, move more lightly. One by one, the dancers move to the altar to greet the figure of the holy infant.

**San Ildefonso**, 20 miles (32 km) northwest of Santa Fe, is best known as the home of the famous potter, Maria Martinez. Inspired by ancient Anasazi pottery, she and her husband, Julian, developed San Ildefonso's trademark black-on-black ware and sparked a new interest in Pueblo pottery of every style. Julian died in 1943 and Maria's son Popovi Da, took up the painting chores. His son Tony Da, also an artist, became well-known for integrating turquoise, incising techniques and unconventional shapes into his pottery designs.

San Ildefonso has a large, clean plaza for the performance of an exciting dance

**Making mud bricks for the construction of adobes.**

# THE ART OF ADOBE

Adobe has long been the traditional building material of the Southwest. Structures made from it are undulating and sculptural in nature, yet their mass gives them a sense of permanence and timelessness. The word *adobe* comes from Arabic and was brought to the US by Spanish colonists at the end of the 15th century. It refers to the structures, the unbaked clay bricks made from earth, and the earth used to make the bricks.

In New Mexico, archaeologists have discovered remnants of adobe walls built by the Pueblo Indians that date back to 1200, 400 years before the Spanish arrived. There is evidence of two types of earthen walls built from the 13th to the 15th centuries. One was coursed adobe, using a stiff mixture of mud blended with anything from stones to pot shards. The mud was applied by the handful, course on top of course, until the desired height was reached. A more sophisticated method made use of hand-formed, unbaked clay bricks. Mud mortar cemented the bricks in place.

The Spanish colonists brought with the word *adobe* a new method of making the bricks. Wooden bottomless moulds were made with a handle on each end. They could generally hold from one to eight bricks. The moulds were set on the ground and filled with a mixture of mud and straw. The straw helped dry the bricks by conducting moisture from the center of the adobe and kept the bricks from cracking as they dried. The excess mud was scraped off the top. When the bricks were dry enough not to sag, the forms were lifted, moved to a new spot and filled again to repeat the process.

These were the two primary methods of building with adobe until the coming of the railroad in the 1880s, which almost eliminated the use of adobe for several decades. American settlers brought new technology as well as prejudice against the long-established culture of the native populations. Red-fired brick, board and batten, concrete block and frame-stucco are just a few of the construction materials and methods that dominated the Southwest landscape. The coming of the railroad also had tremendous impact on the already existing architecture. Elaborate ornamentation and new rooflines gave the simple, flat-roofed buildings a radical face lift.

Not until after World War I was there any significant reemergence of adobe architecture. An awareness of decreasing natural resources turned builders' and architects' eyes toward a building material of infinite supply, which also had excellent passive solar properties. Adobe has the ability, when properly oriented to the sun, to retain its temperature for long periods of time. In this energy-conscious age of high utility bills and interest in conservation, this becomes an attractive feature.

With the reemergence of adobe came commercial adobe yards, which are now producing a stabilized adobe block. As the word implies, a stabilizer is an additive, such as an asphalt emulsion, that when mixed with mud produces an unbaked clay brick that resists moisture penetration, adobe's worst enemy.

Building adobe structures with brick is only one method of construction. *Pise' de terre*, better known as rammed earth, was developed in France in the 16th century. Wooden forms are placed on the wall and filled with a blend of moist soils. The soil is compressed with a hand or pneumatic tamper. The forms are moved to another section of wall and filled again.

Unfortunately the amount of labor required in adobe construction often makes it too expensive for the average home-buyer, though its use by owner-builders is steadily increasing. Solutions are slowly being found. Recently architects and builders have been looking for more innovative methods that will increase productivity and decrease the dollar margin between adobe and conventional building materials. ∎

**Mellow adobe walls at Taos Indian Pueblo**

on January 23. It is an animal or hunting dance and it begins at daylight and continues throughout the day.

**San Juan**, 29 miles (47 km) north of Santa Fe, is across the river from the place chosen by Juan de Oñate as the first capital of New Mexico in 1598. Only a cross on the mound of an unexcavated pueblo marks the spot today, but the modern pueblo is large and active. Their feast day is celebrated on June 24, and on Christmas Day they perform the Matachines Dance, an adaptation of a Spanish morality play.

**Santa Ana**, 30 miles (48 km) northwest of Albuquerque, keeps the entrance to the pueblo chained except on special feast days, when visitors are permitted to come in. Most of the people live in three smaller villages down by the river near Bernalillo and return to the old pueblo only on feast days. Photography is not permitted. Traditional polychrome pottery almost became a lost art until Endora Montoya undertook teaching the younger women. This has revived the art. **Coronado State Monument**, near Bernalillo, preserves the ruins of a pueblo said by the Santa Ana Indians to be their ancestral home.

**Santa Clara**, 30 miles (48 km) northwest of Santa Fe, has several outstanding potters. Among the best known are Lonewolf and Medicine Flower, members of the Naranjo family. It is red or black ware, polished and incised with intricately carved designs.

In Santa Clara Canyon each July, the Puye Cliff Ceremonial, a thrilling weekend event, takes place high atop the mesa. A modest craft show accompanies traditional dances performed against a backdrop of stone and adobe ruins. Puye, which is part of the Pajarito Plateau, is a majestic place to see a pair of Eagle dancers, wearing white feathered headdresses, with feather wings strapped to their arms, swooping and gliding in solemn mimicry of the eagles whose aeries are on the clifftops.

**Santo Domingo**, 31 miles (50 km) southwest of Santa Fe and 39 miles (63 km) north of Albuquerque, is best known for its jewelry, particularly *heishi*, small

**Race Day at San Juan Pueblo Church.**

shells polished to a silky smoothness. These Indians are born traders and most of the artisans you see selling on the portals of public buildings in Santa Fe and Albuquerque are from Santo Domingo. Theirs is a large pueblo, and the people are active in Indian affairs and conservative about pueblo life, strictly forbidding photography.

Santo Domingo holds its Corn Dance on August 4, the feast of Saint Dominic, in an open-air extravaganza involving 500 dancers from age two to 80. Each barefoot woman dancer has a blue stepped *tablita* painted to symbolize a mountain with an indication of rain. She wears a one-shouldered *manta* – a woven sash – the best family jewelry, and holds a pine bough in each hand. The men wear short white embroidered kilts with long bold sashes, armbands and moccasins, and they too carry pine boughs. The entry of two long files of dancers into the plaza is pageantry at its finest, but the purpose is sacred – to raise the spirits of rain and fertility, to stamp the earth, beat the drum and chant

and raise the vibrations of the earth to ensure a fine harvest in the fall. On Christmas and Easter they have dances which last several days.

**Taos Pueblo**, 2 miles (3 km) north of the city of Taos, is the most photographed and familiar of all Indian pueblos, with its large, multistoried pueblos facing each other across the plaza. Taos marked the northern frontier of the Spanish province, and it was here that the Comanche and other Plains Indians came to trade with the Spaniards and Pueblo Indians. All year long they might raid and plunder, but during the trade fair a truce prevailed. Even today, Taos Indians show traits of their Plains brothers: long braids, beaded moccasins, aquiline noses, high cheekbones. The Plains war dances sometimes performed at Taos are unlike the traditionally quieter dances of the pueblos. Taos potters produce a good red-brown micaceous pottery, like that at Picurís, not ornamental but useful. On September 29 and 30 they pay homage to San Geronimo with dances.

At dawn, male members of North

**The Santa Clara Dance is a well-attended annual event.**

House race against those of South House; at the end of the race the teams are showered with Crackerjacks and oranges by *Taoseños* from the stepped roofs of North House. The Chifonetti are male clowns painted with black and white stripes and adorned with cornhusks in their hair, who cavort through the on-lookers, cart off children and tease the crowd. (In other pueblos similar figures are known as Koshares.) Their joking has a moral purpose – chastising mis-creants and warning others.

Immediately after the races, an inter-tribal trade fair begins. Selected artisans show their wares in booths set up on the wide dirt plaza between North House and the stream that divides the pueblo. Except for a few special feast days, photography is permitted in Taos. A visitor center is at the entrance to the plaza to collect fees and issue permits.

**Tesuque**, 10 miles (16 km) north of Santa Fe, is a small pueblo, but it has some excellent potters, usually working with earth-colored clay in animal fig-ures. Its patron saint day, November 12,

celebrates San Diego. They perform animal dances in the winter.

**Zia**, 36 miles (58 km) northwest of Albuquerque, sits on a volcanic mesa, its mud-plastered houses blending so well with the landscape that they are easily missed. Zia pottery, usually earth tones painted with stylized figures of birds and flowers, and well-fired, is sought by collectors; especially prized are the pots made by Candelaria Gauch-pin. Zia is a small pueblo and conserva-tive, never allowing photography. Zia watercolor paintings are also prized. The Zia ancient sun symbol appears on New Mexico's state flag as a symbol of "perfect friendship." The feast day is August 15, with a corn dance.

**Zuni**, in the far western part of New Mexico, 40 miles (64 km) south of Gallup, was the first New Mexican pueblo seen by Spaniards. In 1539 sol-diers and priests leading an advance party for Coronado's expedition saw the cluster of flat-roofed adobe build-ings, the straw in the mud glinting in the afternoon sun, and immediately went back to report that they had seen the "Seven Cities of Gold." Zunis are su-perb jewelry and pottery craftsmen. The silver inlay jewelry is usually made with small pieces of turquoise, jet, coral, mother-of-pearl and tortoise shell set in intricate patterns. Their crafts are avail-able at a cooperative store and several trading posts just outside the old village. The most famous Indian dance in the Southwest is the Shalako Dance at Zuni, held in late November or early Decem-ber. Beginning at sundown, towering, grotesque figures come into the village to dance and sing all night at certain designated homes.

The extremely costly costumes are draped over a wooden framework with pulleys to move parts like a puppeteer. The covering is of feathers, paint, ani-mal skins and other materials. The head is bird-like, the body is conical. To be chosen as a Shalako is an honor, and the role demands training, both physical and spiritual. Zuni is at an elevation of over 7,000 ft (2,100 meters) and the night of the Shalako is almost always bitterly cold and snowy.

**Left**, San Felipe de Neri Church in Old Town Albuquerque; the city was founded in 1706. **Right**, concha belts and bracelets are common ornaments among Indians.

# TAOS

Taos glows with a physical radiance, white sunlight and lavender shadows, blue distance and golden earth. In 1912 this light drew eight young artists from the East who formed the Taos Society of Artists, the start of a legacy. Whether the spell lies in the physical beauty, the legends or the history, few people visit Taos without feeling its magic.

Taos was settled by the Spaniards in the early 1600s, close to the Taos Indian Pueblo. Taos plaza has seen a lot of history go by – Indians, Spanish conquistadors, mountain men and merchants. The American flag flies 24 hours a day in the plaza, a special honor commemorating the bravery of Kit Carson and other frontiersmen during the Civil War. When Confederate sympathizers tried to replace the American flag with the Confederate flag, Carson and friends nailed the stars and stripes to the tallest pine tree they could find, and stood armed guard until the Confederates had been driven back to Texas.

Taos has more than 80 art galleries, its major industry, and you will be missing the meaning of Taos if you don't explore them. Walk up **Ledoux Street**, a couple of blocks west of the plaza. Mellow adobe walls crowd the winding street, and turquoise-colored gates stand ajar, inviting you in.

**Murdered governor:** The first American governor of New Mexico was murdered in 1847, a few months after the American occupation. The **Governor Bent House Museum and Gallery** preserves this historic site. Kit Carson, famous scout and soldier, lived in Taos with his Mexican wife during his later years, and their house is now the **Kit Carson Home and Museum**. The cemetery where he and other Taos personalities are buried is part of **Kit Carson Memorial State Park** off the main street of Taos.

During the 1920s, the flamboyant Mabel Dodge Luhan brought many artists, including D.H. Lawrence, to Taos. She married a Taos Indian and built a rambling adobe home (now a bed-and-breakfast inn) on the edge of the reservation where she entertained talented and famous people in great style. She gave the Lawrences a ranch in the Sangre de Cristo Mountains about 15 miles (24 km) north of town.

After his death in Europe, Lawrence's wife brought his ashes back and built a shrine for him on the ranch, which she willed to the University of New Mexico. Visit the **D.H. Lawrence Ranch and Memorial** and admire the view which influenced him so much.

The **Church at Ranchos de Taos** (1722) on the south edge of town, though not one of the oldest in New Mexico, is probably the best-known and most-photographed because of its classic pueblo-style architecture. Georgia O'Keeffe and other artists have captured the flowing lines that seem to be part of the earth.

The Rio Grande river runs a few miles west of Taos through a deep gorge. Its first 50 miles (80 km) south of the Colorado border make up the nation's

**Preceding pages:** painting the Sangre de Cristos. **Left,** Park Service staff member as mountain man, Bent's Fort. **Right,** interior of St James Hotel, Cimarron.

first officially designated Wilderness River Area. The **Rio Grande Gorge** is accessible by hiking down from the rim of the steep volcanic mesas which confine it. In May and June white-water rafters find this part of the Rio Grande a real challenge with some rapids classed Grade VI, the most dangerous kind of white water. Nine miles (14 km) west of Taos on US Highway 64, a dramatic bridge spans the green and white ribbon flowing between black basalt walls 650 ft (200 meters) below. South of town at **Pilar**, a road leads down to the river to **Rio Grande Gorge State Park**, a favorite spot for trout fishermen.

**Taos Ski Valley**, 20 miles (32 km) northeast of town, is the best known of New Mexico's 12 ski areas. The runs are on the slopes of Wheeler Peak, over 13,000 ft (4,000 meters) high, and the ski area has dozens of powder bowls, glades and chutes. The season usually lasts from at least early November into April. Ernie Blake, a Swiss transplant known as The Godfather of the Slopes, developed Taos Ski Valley over many

years, earning a reputation for high standards. Miles of hiking trails lead from the ski valley into the forests and wilderness areas fringing Taos.

**Sipapu Ski Area** is 25 miles (40 km) southeast of Taos, and its gentle slopes are popular with young families and beginners. Twenty-six miles (42 km) east of Taos, on the other side of the mountains is **Angel Fire**, a new year-round resort. The ski runs are long and challenging, and facilities include condos, lodges, restaurants and a private airport. The drive from Taos over **Palo Flechado Pass** on US 64 is a beauty, especially in the fall.

**Trips out of Taos:** Just 34 miles (55 km) north of Taos, the town of **Red River** has two developed ski areas. One has expert and intermediate runs, the other mostly beginner and intermediate runs. Other winter sports, including snowmobiling and cross-country skiing, are popular, and all equipment can be rented. Summer guests can fish, hike, camp and visit ghost towns. Reservations are almost always necessary for

**The west end of the church at Ranchos de Taos (Saint Francis Assisi Mission).**

240

lodging. The Taos Valley Resort Association acts as a central reservations system and can provide information about shuttle buses from Albuquerque.

**Chama** is the New Mexico terminal for the **Cumbres and Toltec Scenic Railroad** which runs to Antonito, Colorado, and is about 60 miles (95 km) west of Taos on US 64. The sturdy little train has authentically restored cars that chugged over this route carrying ore and timber a hundred years ago. The ride takes you through alpine meadows, over passes and deep gorges, and across sagebrush flats. The route zigzags across the state line and is owned and operated by both states. Reservations can be made at either terminal. It is a long day's trip, with visitors returning by bus to their point of departure. Or a half trip may be taken from either terminal, returning by train. In winter Cumbres Pass is buried under many feet of snow, so the train runs only from mid-June to October. The New Mexico portion is very scenic.

Chama lies in the Sangre de Cristo Mountains at an elevation of around 7,680 ft (2,340 meters). Fishing is good in the Chama River, as it is at two lakes south of town, El Vado and Heron lakes. Elk and deer hunting parties are headquartered here, and snowmobiling is popular in winter.

**Alamosa** is in the San Luis Valley of Colorado, a productive farmland 50 miles (80 km) wide between the San Juan Mountains to the west and the Sangre de Cristos to the east. **Great Sand Dunes National Monument** lies 35 miles (56 km) northeast of Alamosa against the base of the Sangre de Cristos like piles of soft brown velvet. Prevailing winds blow across the valley from the west, picking up particles of sand and dust and dropping them when they reach the solid barrier of the mountains. The dunes are over 700 ft (215 meters) high and 10 miles (16 km) long. A visitor center has exhibits describing the history, plants and animals of the area. There are no trails on the dunes, so you walk where you please. When storms sweep in from the northeast, the winds reverse the pattern of the ridges.

**Cross-country skiers try their hand at telemarking on a New Mexico peak.**

**Santa Fe Trail country:** Starting in 1821 the Santa Fe Trail was the channel of commerce and communication between the Spanish Rio Grande and the United States. Because of the social and business relationships already established, commerce made victory easy when the United States took the Southwest in the Mexican War (1846–48). Forts protected settlers, pioneers and miners as they fulfilled the nation's "manifest destiny."

The main branch of the trail came across southeast Colorado into New Mexico, over Raton Pass, through Cimarron, Las Vegas, and all around the southern end of the Rocky Mountains to Santa Fe.

Strangers sometimes doubt it, but you can still see parts of the Santa Fe Trail in northeastern New Mexico. Wherever the ground has not been plowed, as in the areas north of Las Vegas and Fort Union, the grass-grown ruts are plainly visible from the train or from Interstate 25 in Apache Canyon.

**Bent's Fort**, 8 miles (13 km) east of La Junta in Colorado on US 350, was built by the Bent brothers in 1833 and became one of the most famous forts and trading posts in the West, doing brisk business with both pioneers and Indians. It has been authentically reconstructed and is a national historic landmark, open year-round except for Christmas and Thanksgiving.

Bent's Fort was the meeting place for fur trappers from all over the Rockies, the most famous of whom was scout Kit Carson. Military and government surveying parties, wagon freighters and stagecoaches stopped for supplies, food and rest. Indians came to trade buffalo hides and furs for food and tobacco. Charles Bent became the first American governor of New Mexico Territory, which at that time included southern Colorado. He was murdered in 1847.

Another stopping place on the Santa Fe Trail was on *El Rio de las Animas Perdidas en Purgatorio* (River of Lost Souls in Purgatory) – generally shortened to Purgatory or Purgatoire – just before it crossed over the mountains into New Mexico. Today the town of **Early-morning breakfast on a cattle drive.**

Trinidad is on that spot, a coal mining and trade center with many brick buildings dating back to the last century. The **Baca House**, built of adobe in 1869, was the home of a prominent rancher and merchant of Spanish ancestry. **Bloom Mansion** was built in 1882 by a pioneer merchant, cattleman and banker. The **Pioneer Museum** is in a 12-room adobe building behind the Baca House.

**A town by the spring:** Across the mountains from Trinidad, a good spring provided another stopping place on the trail, and here the town of **Raton** grew. A historic district on First Street preserves several old buildings which now house specialty shops, a theater museum and the **Palace Hotel**, which does not rent rooms but has a fine restaurant.

**Raton Ski Basin** is really in Colorado, but the only way to get to it is through Raton. It is a small, family-oriented ski area.

One of the colorful men in Raton's past, Uncle Dick Wootton, trapped beavers, hunted and scouted for the Fremont Expedition with his close friend Kit Carson. He is best remembered for his toll road over Raton Pass. He moved boulders and trees from 27 miles (43 km) of extremely rough terrain to make what was, for the time, a fair wagon road. He built a home and way station at the summit, and not many people argued with this 6-ft 6-inch (198 cm) tall frontiersman, rifle in hand, when he stood at his toll gate and asked $1.50 a wagon, or a nickel or dime a head for livestock. Anyone who chose not to pay could go around the mountains, a detour of over a hundred miles (160 kms). He never charged Indians. He sold his road to the railroad, and the site is marked today. The Santa Fe Railroad still follows the same route, and Interstate 25 is on the hillside just above it.

**Capulin Mountain National Monument**, 34 miles (55 km) east of Raton on US 64/87, is a perfectly shaped volcanic cone that served as a landmark on one of the branches of the Santa Fe Trail. At the base there is a visitors center with picnic area, and a road circles the cone to the top where the view reaches into

**Bison roam the meadows of New Mexico.**

Colorado, Oklahoma, Texas and Kansas. Trails lead into the crater.

**Cimarron**, 35 miles (56 km) southwest of Raton, was another stop on the Santa Fe Trail. Cimarron was started by Lucien Maxwell, another trapper-trader-scout-freighter friend of Kit Carson. Through inheritance and purchase he became sole owner of the 1.7 million-acre (694,480-hectare) Maxwell Land Grant which covered most of northeastern New Mexico and some of southern Colorado. Maxwell became a legend of the Santa Fe Trail, entertaining lavishly in his baronial adobe mansion in Cimarron. Weary stagecoach travelers were drawn into gambling at cards or on horse racing when they stopped at Cimarron. Maxwell paid his rare losses from a chest of gold coins. He sold the grant in 1870 and it was subsequently broken up into ranches and townsites.

The **Old Aztec Mill Museum** is the four-story gristmill Maxwell built in Cimarron in 1865. The **St James Hotel** (sometimes called the Don Diego) was built around 1872 by a French chef from Lincoln's White House and has been restored as a museum. The tin ceiling of the original bar, now a gift shop, is pierced by 30 bullet holes, reminders of Cimarron's wild past.

Four miles (6 km) south of Cimarron on State Highway 21 is **Philmont Scout Ranch**, where as many as 17,000 Boy Scouts and their leaders come every summer. The 127,000-acre (51,000-hectare) ranch was given to the Scouts by the wealthy oil baron Waite Phillips. It contains grassy valleys, timbered mountains, streams and a mansion with a 14-room guest house.

Visitors are welcome at Philmont, especially to visit its two museums. One is the **Kit Carson Museum**, a home he rebuilt and enlarged, where he lived briefly in the 1850s. The other houses a library and art collection which contains much of the work of the famous naturalist, Ernest Thompson Seton, one of the founders of scouting. The museums are open to the public daily in the summer at no charge.

**Fort Union**, 9 miles (14 km) off Interstate 25 and 19 miles (30 km) north of Las Vegas, used to be one of the largest and most important forts in the West. Built in 1851 (two replacements were built during the next 30 years), it was a supply depot for other forts throughout the Southwest. Almost at the end of the Santa Fe Trail, many a Conestoga wagon thundered through its protecting walls barely ahead of the Comanche. Fort Union was closed in 1891 and is a national monument today.

**Las Vegas** (not to be confused with the Nevada gambling center) was the capital of New Mexico for two months during the Civil War when the Confederates held Santa Fe, and it is still a major trade center for the big cattle and sheep ranches in the area. Most of the older part of town around the plaza has been designated a historic district. Las Vegas began as a land-grant village during the Mexican period and was an important stop on the Santa Fe Trail, as well as a division point on the railroad. When the railroad bypassed the old plaza by 2 miles (3 km), a new Las Vegas quickly grew up there.

Interior design, Southwestern style.

244

# GEORGIA O'KEEFFE

**F**ew artists are as closely identified with the Southwest as Georgia O'Keeffe. Although born in Wisconsin and trained primarily in Chicago and New York, much of her most distinctive work was produced in northern New Mexico. Her sensuous depictions of the sun-washed hills and mesas near her Abiquiu home and of the bleached bones, vivid blossoms and Spanish churches she encountered on long rambles have come to represent the spirit of the Southwestern landscape.

O'Keeffe first came to public attention in 1916 when Alfred Stieglitz, an influential photographer and art collector, exhibited her drawings at his New York gallery. "The purest, finest, sincerest things to have entered [the gallery] in a long while," he said of the work. The two artists had an immediate rapport and moved in together shortly after. They were married in 1924.

It was an often stormy relationship, although O'Keeffe, some 24 years her husband's junior, later characterized the union as "really very good." An independent woman, she kept her name long before it was fashionable. "I've had a hard time hanging on to my name, but I hang on to it with my teeth. I like getting what I've got on my own," she explained. She often craved solitude while Stieglitz preferred to surround himself with family and fellow artists.

At times, she felt frustrated by the unwillingness of the male-dominated art world to take her seriously. "All the male artists I knew... made it very plain that as a woman I couldn't make it – I might as well stop painting," she said to a friend. Stieglitz strongly refuted this: "Women can only create babies, say the scientists, but I say they can produce art – and Georgia O'Keeffe is the proof of it."

Nor was she comfortable with the elaborate interpretations critics made of her work. She once scolded a writer who asked about the meaning of a painting: "The meaning is there on the canvas. If you don't get it, that's too bad. I have nothing more to say than what I painted."

Despite her frustrations, her years in New York and at the Stieglitz house at Lake George were extremely productive and resulted in dozens of important works, including the first of her giant close-ups of flowers, a subject she revisited many times over the years.

O'Keeffe first stayed in New Mexico in 1929 and realized immediately she had found a new home. "Sometimes I think I'm half mad with love for this place. I've climbed and poked into every hill and mountain in sight." She spent her first summer in Taos as a guest of Mabel Dodge

Luhan, a patron of the arts and "collector of people" whose acquaintances included D.H. Lawrence and Ansel Adams. She later moved to the Ghost Ranch southwest of Taos and, in 1945, bought an adobe home in the tiny village of Abiquiu. She settled there in 1949, three years after Stieglitz's death.

The landscape continued to inspire O'Keeffe. She wandered on foot or horseback or in her beloved Model A Ford. It's a "perfectly mad looking country – hills and cliffs and washes too crazy to imagine all thrown up into the air by God and let tumble where they would." She was particularly intrigued by the sun-bleached bones she found in the desert – a recurring motif in subsequent work. "The bones seem to cut sharply to the center of something that is keenly alive on the desert even tho' it is vast and empty and untouchable – and knows no kindness with all its beauty." She was also drawn to works of man like San Francisco de Asis church in Rancho de Taos, various crosses and her own home.

O'Keeffe died in Santa Fe in 1986 aged 92, one of the best-known American artists of the 20th century and a painter of singular vision. "I have never cared about what others were doing in art, or what they thought of my own paintings," she once said with typical straightforwardness. "Why should I care? I found my inspirations and painted them." ∎

**Georgia O'Keeffe in Taos, 1929.**

245

# SOUTHEASTERN NEW MEXICO

Southeastern New Mexico and the part of Texas that runs south of it hold surprises and contrasts, from snowcapped peaks to desert, from historic towns to the Space Age, from irrigated fields to the empty distance of the *Llano Estacado* (Staked Plains).

The subterranean passages of **Carlsbad Caverns National Park** underlie part of a reef laid down by an ancient sea. The Guadalupe Mountains are part of that same reef, which was pushed up to give Texas its four highest peaks. In the central portion is the green, mountainous homeland of the Mescalero Apache. Far to the south are Las Cruces and El Paso. This is big country, capable of absorbing as much time as you want to give it.

Carlsbad Caverns is not just another cave. To enter the caverns is to leave behind a familiar environment of sunlight and wind, of night and day, of temperatures changing with the clouds, rain, snow and sun. As you descend into a strange underground universe, you cease to hear the sounds of men, animals and machines. Your eyes adjust to the dimness, your ears to the silence. You begin to feel the awesome beauty of the limestone fantasyland, to see curtains spun of translucent stone, pillars so mighty they seem to hold up the earth. Time is eternal. You are in an alien but benign world.

A complete 3-mile (5-km) walking tour begins at the natural entrance near the visitors center, where a series of switchbacks quickly descends 200 ft (60 meters) below the surface. As natural light gradually disappears, subtle electric lighting takes over, focusing on ethereal rock formations. The trail then descends gradually but steadily to the lowest point, 830 ft (250 meters) below the surface, then rises a little bit more to accommodate the **Big Room**, which is the size of 14 football fields (1¼ miles)

**Limestone shapes, Carlsbad Caverns.**

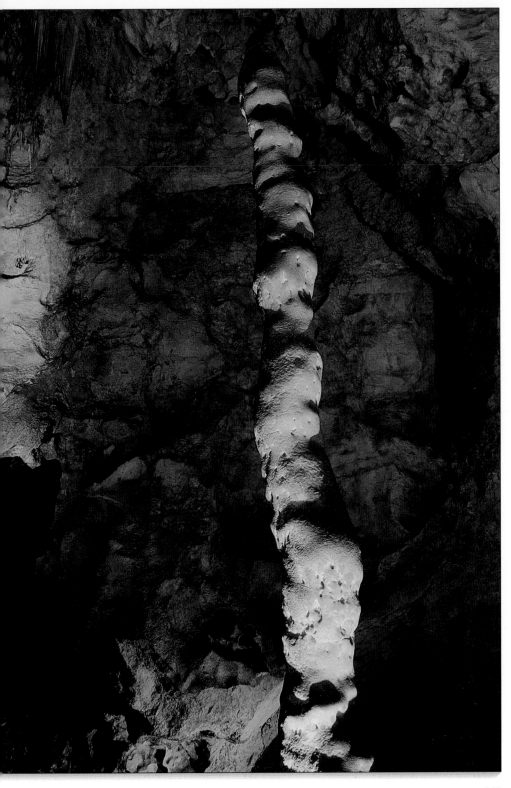

and as high as a 22-story building. You can take an elevator back up to the surface once you've descended to see it.

Depending on how much time you have, you can also view several other nearby sites. The **Kings Palace**, the **Queens Chamber** and the **Papoose Room** all require a guided tour (check at the information desk for times), where the action of acidic rainwater percolating through the Permian Reef Formation has hollowed out great chambers in the pale rock.

The process that made Carlsbad Caverns began 3 million years ago during the Permian Period. A limestone reef formed around the edge of a shallow sea. When the sea dried up, the reef was covered with sediment, but groundwater seeped through, dissolving the limestone and creating the caverns.

Millions of years later the earth's crust buckled, causing one side of the reef to be pushed up. This elevated limestone became the Guadalupe Mountains, and the caverns were exposed. Water still dripped into the caverns,

depositing minute limestone crystals to create the formations seen there today.

For an experience in real spelunking, sign up for the hike into **New Cave**, 23 miles (37 km) south of the visitors center. Only 25 people at a time may take the trip, which starts with a hike up a rocky hill and goes 1½ miles inside the cavern. This cave is not lighted, and the trail is sometimes wet, slick and steep. Everyone carries a flashlight, but in the immense blackness each one is only a pinprick of feeble light. At one point during the trip, the ranger asks everyone to remain quiet, sit down and turn off their flashlights. For many people, this is the first time in their lives that they experience total blackness and almost complete silence.

**Neighboring national parks:** The highway to the caverns (US Highway 62/180) continues on to the **Guadalupe Mountains National Park** in Texas. The two national parks are in the same range of mountains, divided only by the state line. In contrast to the Caverns on the New Mexico side, the Texas side is

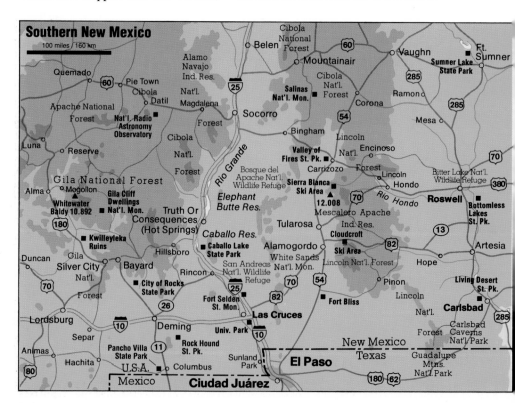

famous for the spectacular rock formations of the **Permian Reef**.

There, a big wedge of the reef was pushed up to form limestone crags and deep canyons. Guadalupe Mountains National Park is not as developed as the Carlsbad Caverns, but it does have one campground, a visitors center and miles of trails going up to the peaks and into the canyons, where the geology of the mountains is best exposed. In the fall, the canyons that have springs become unexpected oases of color.

The Guadalupes were the last stronghold of the Mescalero Apache before they settled on their reservation 100 miles (160 km) to the north. The first transcontinental mail route, known as the Butterfield Trail, touched the southern tip of the Guadalupes for a brief period, and cattle and sheep ranches skirt the foothills.

Northwest of Carlsbad, the **Mescalero Apache Reservation** occupies almost a half-million acres (200,000 hectares) in the Sacramento Mountains. Though composed of limestone like the Guadalupes, the Sacramentos have a far different character. Higher, cooler, wetter, they are covered with big stands of timber and meadows.

Cattle ranching, lumber and tourism are the main occupations of the Mescalero. The tribal celebrations on July 3 and 4 feature powwow dancing and a rodeo at the fairgrounds in the town of Mescalero. At the northern end of the reservation, and 3 miles (5 km) south of the city of Ruidoso, is the Mescalero's **Inn of the Mountain Gods**, a complete luxury resort. The grounds are situated at the base of Sierra Blanca, the tribe's sacred mountain.

Immediately north of the reservation boundary is **Ruidoso**, a year-round vacation town. With races every weekend from May through Labor Day, **Ruidoso Downs** is one of the most popular racetracks in the Southwest. The world's best quarterhorses are bought, sold and raced here. The season ends with two of the richest horse races in America.

The finale, the **All-American Futurity**, has a purse of over $2 million.

**Branding cattle.**

Concerts, art shows, fishing and hiking in the mountains fill the summer recreation bill. In winter, nearby **Ski Apache Resort** in Lincoln National Forest, also owned by the Mescalero Apache, draws skiers from Texas and the Midwest.

**Where Billy the Kid found favor:** Over the mountains north of Ruidoso is **Old Lincoln Town**. A hundred years ago this was the scene of the Lincoln County War, a brief but bloody battle involving ranchers, merchants, cowboys and politicians. Billy the Kid happened to be on the side of the good guys this time, and the courthouse where he was jailed is a state museum.

Several other buildings along the main street are owned by the state and comprise a historic district. The **Wortley Hotel**, across from the courthouse, is a bed-and-breakfast inn. During the first weekend in August the citizens of Lincoln stage an outdoor drama about Billy the Kid and the Lincoln County War. There is an authentic Pony Express race that runs from the ghost town of White Oaks to Lincoln. The riders carry mail that has been especially cancelled to mark the event for stamp collectors.

**White Sands National Monument** lies along US 7082 between two mountain ranges west of Alamogordo. The white "sand" is a 50-mile (80-km) expanse of fine gypsum eroded from the Sacramento Mountains. Dunes up to 200 ft (68 meters) high look like the waves of a giant sea, domed by an incredibly blue sky.

White Sands is a place to be young, to run and fall and roll down the dunes. The visitors center at the entrance has geological exhibits, and an 8-mile (13-km) drive goes to the heart of the dunes, where there are picnic facilities. The monument is open all year, and the entrance is off US 70. Surrounding White Sands are two giant military installations, Holloman Air Force Base and White Sands Missile Range.

A 20-mile (32-km) drive east of Alamogordo on US 82 leads to the mountain resort village of **Cloudcroft**. The road climbs abruptly from 4,350 ft (1,325 meters) at Alamogordo to almost 9,000

**Yucca plant growth at White Sands National Park, near Alamogordo.**

ft (2,700 meters) at Cloudcroft. Several parts along the way give grand panoramic views of the White Sands below.

Cloudcroft has a family-oriented ski area, and old logging roads make good cross-country ski trails. Summer visitors seek the relief of cool days and chilly nights. Soaring in at around 9,000 ft (2,700 meters), the golf course at Cloudcroft Lodge is the highest one in the country.

**Land of black and white dunes:** Nowhere are the contrasts of this region more noticeable than between the dunes of White Sands and the **Valley of Fires Recreation Area** directly north. The Valley of Fires was formed when lava flowed from a small peak near the northern end of the *malpais* (badlands) 44 miles (70 km) down the valley, solidifying for eternity into a black, tormented mass. Trails lead from the campground and picnic area.

**Las Cruces** took its name from a forlorn cluster of crosses that marked the place where Franciscan missionaries were killed by Apache in the early 1800s. The town was not established until after the area became a US territory, but early Spanish trails passed through here. With a population of more than 45,000, it is one of New Mexico's largest towns. The Mesilla Valley to the north and south is a rich agricultural area, though desert claims the hills above the Rio Grande.

Two miles (3 km) south of Las Cruces is **Mesilla**. Although about the same age as Las Cruces, Mesilla has remained a sleepy village while Las Cruces has developed into a modern city. In Mesilla the Gadsden Purchase was signed in 1853, fixing the boundary of the United States and Mexico.

Twelve miles (19 km) north of Las Cruces lie the ruins of **Fort Selden**, built in 1865 and now preserved as a state monument. The fort played an important role in protecting the pioneers and miners who traveled along the overland trail to California.

**Sunland Park Racetrack**, 35 miles (56 km) south of Las Cruces and only five minutes from El Paso, was built

**Church at Laguna Indian Pueblo, New Mexico.**

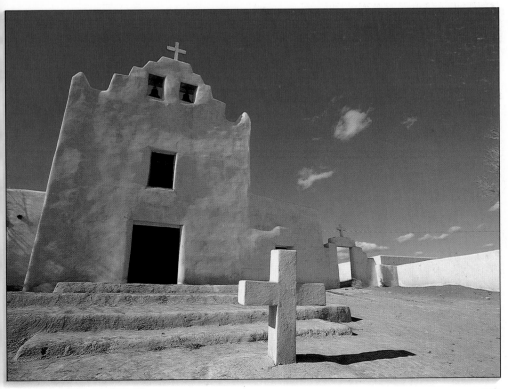

close to the Texas border to suit racing fans. Winter season lasts from early October to early May.

**El Paso**, Texas, was originally a place where Spanish trails crossed the Rio Grande. Travelers called it *El Paso del Norte*, the Pass of the North. In 1659, a small colony was established on the south side of the river, and, in 1827, another began on the north side.

After the war with Mexico when the US border was set, the two colonial villages became El Paso, on the north side of the river, and **Ciudad Juárez, Mexico**, on the south. The two comprise an international city of well over a million people.

**Cowboys and Indians:** El Paso used to be a tough, gunslinging border town, and a bit of that flavor persists in the number of cowboy boots and Stetson hats you see on the streets. Five major boot factories are located in El Paso. The annual **Sun Carnival**, which is held between Christmas and the New Year, culminates in one of the oldest college football bowl games.

Traces of three Indian villages lie within 10 miles (16 km) down the Rio Grande. During the Pueblo Revolt of 1680 in New Mexico, refugee Spaniards and nonhostile Indians fled to El Paso, where they established new villages. After the reconquest 12 years later, many chose to stay, and these villages – Ysleta del Sur, Socorro and San Elizario – are the vestiges of those settlements.

At least three bridges cross over to Juarez, but the Juarez exit from Interstate 10 is the best. It sweeps grandly down Avenida de las Americas about a mile to the **Pronaf Center**.

Daytime driving to the Pronaf Center is easy for visitors, but if you go for a night out at one of the fabulous supper clubs, you would be best advised to put your life in the hands of one of the Mexican cab drivers, who wait in droves at the border for just this occasion. If you like to haggle over prices – which isn't done in the better shops – ask directions to the **Public Market**, a cacophony of smells, sights and sounds.

**Trading posts like this one can still be found in the Southwest.**

# BILLY THE KID

**W**hatever he was like as a real kid in the Irish slums of New York City is lost to history, but his bloody exploits as a teenager in New Mexico are unlikely to be forgotten any time in the near future.

The origins of sad-eyed, buck-toothed Billy the Kid, legendary man-killer, have long been disputed, but it is now generally agreed that he was born Patrick Henry McCarty on September 17, 1859, at 210 Green Street, in lower Manhattan. His parents were Patrick McCarty and the former Catherine Devine; he had an older sister named Bridget (her very existence has been questioned) and a younger brother named Joseph. From almost the beginning, he was called by his middle name, Henry. By 1864, Catherine McCarty was a widow. She apparently left New York City with her children that year but doesn't surface again in the historical record until 1870 in Wichita, Kansas.

Also in Wichita was one William Henry Harrison Antrim, who became "Uncle Bill." Despite financial success, the McCartys and Antrim left Kansas in 1871, probably in search of a healthier climate, as Catherine had been diagnosed as having tuberculosis. On March 1, 1873, 13-year-old Henry McCarty watched as his mother and "Uncle Bill" married in Santa Fe in New Mexico Territory.

The family moved down to Silver City, where the Kid's mother died of tuberculosis on September 16, 1874. A year later, Henry Antrim – as he now called himself – was arrested for the first time. The charge: stealing clothes from a Chinese laundry. He promptly escaped by climbing up a chimney and high-tailing it over to Arizona. His family ties were severed, and the Kid was now on the run, even if there was nobody actually chasing him.

In Arizona, the Kid stole livestock and killed his first man, Francis P. "Windy" Cahill, on September 16, 1877, during a saloon fight at Camp Grant. The Kid then fled back to New Mexico, where he joined up with Jesse Evans's gang of thieves near Silver City and took on the moniker William Bonney.

That association didn't last long. Soon he had a new set of friends and was living in the vast and volatile Lincoln County, where he would earn his notoriety. The killing of rancher John Tunstall on February 18, 1878, touched off the Lincoln County War, a violent clash of commercial and political interests. Tunstall had hired William Bonney the previous December, and Billy sought vengeance for his boss's death. The Kid succeeded, taking part in the slaying of William "Buck" Morton, Frank Baker, William McCloskey, Sheriff William Brady and Manuel Segovia. The Lincoln County War ended in July with the death of lawyer Alexander McSween, the not-too-competent leader of the late Tunstall's supporters, the Regulators.

In the aftermath of the fighting, newly elected territorial governor Lew Wallace refused to pardon Billy, and the Kid turned his hand to rustling in the Fort Sumner area. The new Lincoln County sheriff, Pat Garrett, captured the Kid at Stinking Springs on December 21, 1880. The following March in Mesilla, Billy was convicted of murdering Sheriff Brady and sentenced to be hanged in the town of Lincoln on May 13, 1881. On April 28, when Sheriff Garrett was out of town collecting taxes, Billy shot down two deputies and escaped from the Lincoln courthouse.

The Kid elected to remain among friends in New Mexico instead of fleeing the territory. He had both Anglo and Hispanic to call upon, as he was often a likable chap.

After following up on numerous "Billy sightings," Garrett caught up with the 21-year-old outlaw on the night of July 14, 1881, at Pete Maxwell's place in Fort Sumner. In a darkened bedroom early on the morning of the 15th, Billy saw the shadow of a man and asked, "*Quien es?*" ("Who is it?") Garrett answered by firing a bullet into Billy's chest. ∎

**Shop in Lincoln, New Mexico.**

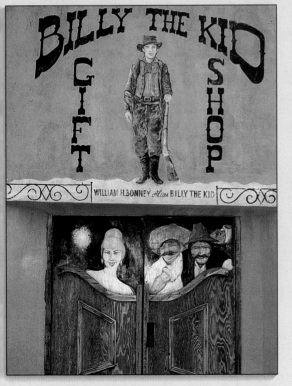

# SOUTHWESTERN NEW MEXICO

The unifying theme in southwestern New Mexico is vastness. Most of it is made up of mountains and wilderness areas, but where the Rio Grande flows there are old Spanish settlements and small farms. Points of interest here range from ghost towns to astronomical observatories and modern art.

As early as 1598 the Spaniards noted how helpful the Indians were at a certain place on the Rio Grande, and when a town grew there it was named **Socorro** (succor, or help, in Spanish). The first church was built in 1628, but the village was abandoned during the Pueblo Revolt of 1680 and was not resettled until 1815. Socorro is in the middle of a rich mining district and was a boom town during the last two decades of the 19th century. When the railroad came in 1880, it became a ranching headquarters town. The original plaza is a block off the main street, and several buildings around it are designated historic landmarks. The **New Mexico Institute of Mining and Technology** is a few blocks west of the plaza, and the **Rock and Mineral Museum** there is worth seeing.

**Birds of a different feather:** Twenty miles (32 km) south of Socorro, on old US Highway 85 (which parallels Interstate 25), is the **Bosque del Apache National Wildlife Refuge** where, from November through February, thousands of waterfowl make a winter home. Most beautiful are the snow geese with their white bodies and black-tipped wings. Sandhill cranes, a soft gray color, with a wingspan bigger than a man's height, graze the stubble fields. The most exotic bird at Bosque del Apache is the whooping crane, the object of an experimental effort to save it from extinction. Whoopers are pure white and almost a foot taller than the sandhill cranes, so they are easy enough to spot, even though there are only a few of them in comparison to their more numerous cousins.

When you go to Bosque del Apache National Wildlife Refuge, allow time to drive around the ponds and fields and to hike trails through the cottonwood groves. Almost 300 kinds of birds live here as well as foxes, bobcats, raccoons, eagles, coyotes, deer and many other kinds of wildlife. To see the waterfowl, go to the north end of the refuge to the lookout tower by 4.30. Far in the distance a dark wavy line will appear on the horizon, and soon the plaintive purr of the cranes and the continuous honk of the geese will be heard. The sky turns from blue to rose, saffron and orange as the birds settle on their icy beds. It is cold this time of year; make sure you dress warmly and carry a thermos of something to warm you up.

West of Socorro is **Magdalena**, railhead for the Magdalena Livestock Driveway. Cattle were driven here from Arizona and western New Mexico to be shipped to market. Even as late as the 1950s the trail was used occasionally. A few remnants of wooden windmills mark the famous cattle driveway.

US 60 continues west across the **Plains of San Agustin**, the setting of

**Preceding pages:** rodeo round-up. **Left,** antennae at the National Radio Astronomy Observatory's Very Large Array. **Right,** open-pit copper mine.

Conrad Richter's novel, *Sea of Grass*. In the middle of this ancient sea-floor valley, completely encircled by mountains, is the **National Radio Astronomy Observatory's Very Large Array**. Twenty-seven huge antennae mounted on a Y-shaped railroad track probe the skies. A visitors center is at the entrance just off the highway.

The Rio Grande is dammed at **Truth or Consequences** (known as T or C), 75 miles (120 km) south of Socorro, to form **Elephant Butte Reservoir**. Boating, fishing and other water sports are good here. This small town on the central highlands has its share of interesting history, but earned itself a place on the quizzical map when it changed its name from Hot Springs to T or C in 1948 in response to an offer from broadcaster Ralph Edwards, who originated a popular radio show of the same name.

**Towns that silver built:** A few miles south of T or C, State Highway 90 turns west toward the Black Range, part of **Gila National Forest** which makes up most of the southwestern part of the state. This is a scenic but slow route to Silver City, going through two old mining towns. **Hillsboro**, 17 miles (27 km) west of T or C, was the scene of a rich silver strike in the 1880s. Ruins of the courthouse and jail remain, but most of the people who live there today are artists or retirees. A museum has relics of the colorful days of Black Range mining, Apache attacks and ranching.

If you are a rockhound, take a detour south on US 180 to **Rockhound State Park**, 14 miles (22 km) southeast of **Deming**. This may be the only park in the country where you can take part of it home with you – up to 15 lbs (7 kilos) of quartz, jasper, agate, amethyst and other specimens. Trails fan out from the campground and visitors center.

The border of Mexico is 35 miles (56 km) south of Deming, with **Columbus** on the American side and **Las Palomas** on the Mexican side. Both are small and don't offer much in the way of shopping or amusement, but each has an interesting history. **Pancho Villa State Park** at Columbus commemorates much more

**Mule deer downed by a hunter.**

than the revolutionary figure for whom it is named. In 1916 Pancho Villa led a band of rebels across the border in an attack that killed eight civilians and soldiers at Columbus and nearby Camp Furlong. This was the only time since the War of 1812 that the continental United States had been invaded by foreign troops. It is also the first time in American history that air power was used in war. General John J. "Black Jack" Pershing led a pursuit party into Mexico after Pancho Villa. They were given air cover by eight little single-engine planes from Fort Sam Houston in Texas. Also in the park at Camp Furlong are ruins of truck ramps which are reminders that here in this forgotten border outpost mechanized warfare was born before World War I. Only a few adobe ruins remain of the camp. The campground and park are a cactus-land-scaped winter hideaway.

Twenty-eight miles (45 km) north of Deming is **City of Rocks State Park** and campground. Like a Stonehenge on the desert, boulders rise 50 to 60 ft (15 to 18 meters) high. Some look like sky-scrapers, others tilt at crazy angles. In a state where prehistoric ruins are so common, you might suppose these to be ruins, but they are the products of erosion on ancient rhyolite outcroppings. This was a favorite lookout place for Apache waiting to ambush stagecoaches on the Butterfield Trail. Camp and picnic areas are among the rocks and sheltered by gnarled alligator juniper trees.

**A different kind of ghost:** Two miles south of **Lordsburg** in the far southwestern corner of New Mexico is the classic ghost town of **Shakespeare**, now privately owned. The town boomed and died through successive silver strikes and a great diamond hoax, and saw its share of hangings and brothels. It was once on the Butterfield Trail. Some of the mining promoters had read English literature and they named it for their favorite poet.

**Silver City** was born of a silver boom in 1870, but, unlike most mining boom towns, it never died. It is the gateway to the **Gila National Forest** and the **Gila**

*Citellus teveticaudus, a ground squirrel; mule deer.*

**Wilderness Area** and is the largest town in this part of the state. **The Inner Loop**, a paved, 100-mile (160-km) scenic drive (States 15, 35 and 90), goes from the edge of the Wilderness Area to Gila Cliff Dwellings National Monument. The loop returns to Silver City past lakes and farms. Several guest ranches and outfitters along here take pack and hunting trips into the wilderness.

Six miles (10 km) out of Silver City is **Pinos Altos**, the oldest mining town in the district. The first school you see has been converted to a small museum, and across the street are the Buckhorn Restaurant and Saloon and the Opera House. In the Buckhorn, whitewashed adobe walls, heavy-beamed ceilings, carved furniture and velvet draperies add a touch of Spanish elegance. Though not the original building, the Opera House has excellent exhibits of historic photographs and Mimbres pottery, and in the summer it often provides entertainment like melodrama or old movies.

The road continues through the mountains to **Gila Cliff Dwellings National Monument**, in a secluded canyon where prehistoric Mogollon Indians lived for a thousand years. They have been gone for seven centuries. A mile-long trail leads up the canyon and into the dwellings, built 180 ft (55 meters) above the canyon floor. To learn more about the Mogollon, pay a visit to the **Fleming Hall Museum** on the campus of **Western New Mexico University** in Silver City, where you'll find a large exhibit of Mimbres pottery produced by the Mogollon from 900 to 1100 AD. Other trails lead from the visitor center into the Gila Wilderness Area. A permit from the forest ranger is necessary if you wish to make a wilderness trip.

The Gila Wilderness was established in 1924, a half-million acres (200,000 hectares) of rugged mountains through which no roads or wheeled vehicles of any kind may travel, not even firefighting equipment. A few years ago that point was made clear when some men drove into a remote canyon in a Jeep, became hopelessly stuck, and were not only fined heavily, but also had to dismantle

**New Mexico characters.**

the Jeep and pack out every part, down to the last bolt, on foot or horseback.

**Catwalking along a canyon:** Sixty miles (97 km) north of Silver City on US 180 is the village of **Glenwood**, another headquarters for pack trips into the wilderness. There are a couple of small motels, restaurants and a district ranger station here. Near Glenwood is the **Catwalk of Whitewater Canyon**, remnants of a pipeline built to bring water down the canyon to a silver mill. The canyon was so narrow the pipe had to be fastened to the sheer walls, and the men who worked on it had to have the agility of cats. Today a metal mesh fence encloses the catwalk, making it safe for anyone. In some places, splashing waterfalls and quiet pools are 30 ft (9 meters) below the walk and the canyon is so narrow the sun reaches the bottom only at midday.

Three miles (5 km) north of Glenwood a road turns toward **Mogollon Ghost Town** (1878–1930s), 9 miles (14 km) up in the mountains. This was the heart of a rich gold and silver district that produced millions of dollars of ore from 1875 until World War II. Relics of mines, tailings dumps and many foundations on the hills show the prominence the mining district once had.

About 20 people live in Mogollon now, mostly along Main Street, which follows Silver Creek. The buildings are weathered gray, the metal rusted red. Some of them were built years ago for a Henry Fonda movie, but they were built so well that most people can't tell the ghosts from the new buildings.

Catron County in west central New Mexico is the least populated part of the state – about 3 sq. miles (8 sq. km) for every person. The county seat and largest town is **Reserve**, population 400. The second largest town is **Quemado**, population 200. About 30 miles (50 km) north of Quemado is the **Lightning Field**, a work of art of unbelievable magnitude. In 1970 Walter de la Maria won a commission from the Dia Art Foundation in New York City to create a work of land art that would be the essence of isolation. The land was to be

**Mogollon Ghost Town.**

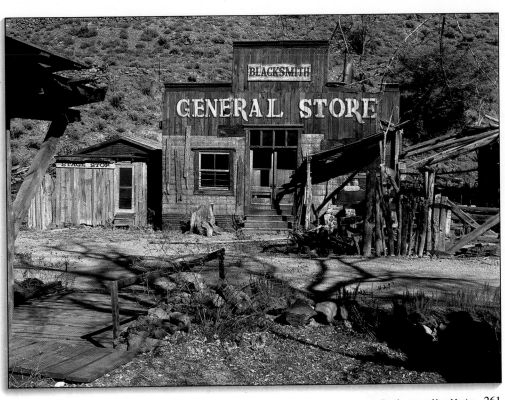

not only the setting but also a part of the work itself. For five years de la Maria roamed the West before finding this lonely high plateau surrounded by jagged mountains on all sides.

**Dazzling Lightning Field:** The Lightning Field took several years to construct. It is made of 400 thin, pointed stainless-steel poles, arranged in a mile long grid, 16 rows by 25. In the flat light of midday the poles almost disappear, but in late afternoon, early morning and even by full moonlight, light catches on the poles like spots of gold or silver shining in perfect symmetry to a diminishing point that seems to go to eternity. The poles are so precisely set that if a giant sheet of glass were laid on top, every pole would touch it.

Visitors are meant to experience the Lightning Field, not just look at it. Only six guests may go at a time and only from May to October. You meet at the foundation's office in Quemado, 175 miles (280 km) from Albuquerque, leave your car and camera there, and go by pickup to the field. An old homesteader's cabin, rustic but comfortably modernized, is your home for the next 24 hours. No one is allowed to go to Lightning Field for less than 24 hours. Food for three meals is in the refrigerator, records are there for the stereo. The manager lives over the hill, out of sight, and after dropping off guests he disappears until the next day after lunch.

State 117 goes north from Quemado about 75 miles (120 km) to Interstate 40 near **Grants**. There are no towns and few houses on this road, but it's a beautiful drive and two natural phenomena are noteworthy. About 30 miles (48 km) of the highway runs alongside a black and angry river of lava. Called **El Malpais National Monument**, it is composed of five distinct lava flows originating around 3,000 years ago, with the last one as recent as about 500 years ago. Indian legends tell of rivers of fire in the region. A few early Indian and Spanish trails went across the southern end where the lava flow spreads out, but generally travelers avoided it. The best place to see and appreciate the form and

El Morro Rock, a landmark on early trails, is now El Morro National Monument.

magnitude of the lava flow is at the north end, 10 miles (16 km) south of Interstate 40 at a designated viewing point and picnic area. As you drive along State 117, there are places to explore along the edges, but it is dangerous to walk very far on the lava. It quickly shreds shoe leather.

The other point of geological interest is **La Ventana**, New Mexico's second largest natural arch, located in the bluffs that run along the east side of the lava flow. The arch is a mile or two south of the turnoff to the lava vista point.

**Essence of New Mexico:** At the west edge of Grants, State 53 turns south down the west side of the Malpais. More timber and grass grow on this side, and one or two dirt roads go to the edge of the flow. Signs point to the **Bandera Crater and Ice Caves**, privately owned but an integral part of the Malpais. Bandera, a perfect cinder cone, was one of the sources of the lava flow. Trails go to the top of Bandera, and steps lead down into the ice caves, frozen green sheets that have been there longer than

anyone remembers. Buy authentic Indian jewelry, pottery and kachina dolls at the trading post here.

State 53 continues to **El Morro National Monument**, 50 miles (80 km) southwest of Grants. The sandstone mesa juts up from the plateau like the prow of a ship. This was a landmark on early trails, especially since there is a pool of never-failing spring water there under an overhang. Beginning with Indian petroglyphs, hundreds of inscriptions have been carved around the base, including one by Don Juan Oñate who passed through the region in 1605. On top of the mesa are ruins of a prehistoric pueblo, believed to be the ancestral home of the Zuni, whose present pueblo is 30 miles (48 km) to the west. A visitors center, camp and picnic grounds, firelight programs and the well-maintained trails over and around the mesa and bluff make this lesser-known national monument a special place to visit. This is the essence of New Mexico: space, sparkling air, mountains and the ever-present signs of older civilizations.

**Gila Cliff Dwellings National Monument, on the edge of the Gila Wilderness.**

# INSIGHT GUIDES
# Travel Tips

Boxell

# FOR THOSE
# WITH MORE THAN
# A PASSING INTEREST
# IN TIME...

Before you put your name down for a Patek Philippe watch *fig. 1*, there are a few basic things you might like to know, without knowing exactly whom to ask. In addressing such issues as accuracy, reliability and value for money, we would like to demonstrate why the watch we will make for you will be quite unlike any other watch currently produced.

**"Punctuality", Louis XVIII was fond of saying, "is the politeness of kings."**

We believe that in the matter of punctuality, we can rise to the occasion by making you a mechanical timepiece that will keep its rendezvous with the Gregorian calendar at the end of every century, omitting the leap-years in 2100, 2200 and 2300 and recording them in 2000 and 2400 *fig. 2*. Nevertheless, such a watch does need the occasional adjustment. Every 3333 years and 122 days you should remember to set it forward one day to the true time of the celestial clock. We suspect, however, that you are simply content to observe the politeness of kings. Be assured, therefore, that when you order your watch, we will be exploring for you the physical—if not the metaphysical— limits of precision.

**Does everything have to depend on how much?**

Consider, if you will, the motives of collectors who set record prices at auction to acquire a Patek Philippe. They may be paying for rarity, for looks or for micromechanical ingenuity. But we believe that behind each $500,000-plus

bid is the conviction that a Patek Philippe, even if 50 years old or older, can be expected to work perfectly for future generations.

In case your ambitions to own a Patek Philippe are somewhat discouraged by the scale of the sacrifice involved, may we hasten to point out that the watch we will make for you today will certainly be a technical improvement on the Pateks bought at auction? In keeping with our tradition of inventing new mechanical solutions for greater reliability and better time-keeping, we will bring to your watch innovations *fig. 3* inconceivable to our watchmakers who created the supreme wristwatches of 50 years ago *fig. 4*. At the same time, we will of course do our utmost to avoid placing undue strain on your financial resources.

**Can it really be mine?**

May we turn your thoughts to the day you take delivery of your watch? Sealed within its case is your watchmaker's tribute to the mysterious process of time. He has decorated each wheel with a chamfer carved into its hub and polished into a shining circle. Delicate ribbing flows over the plates and bridges of gold and rare alloys. Millimetric surfaces are bevelled and burnished to exactitudes measured in microns. Rubies are transformed into jewels that triumph over friction. And after many months—or even years—of work, your watchmaker stamps a small badge into the mainbridge of your watch. The Geneva Seal—the highest possible attestation of fine watchmaking *fig. 5*.

**Looks that speak of inner grace** *fig. 6.*

When you order your watch, you will no doubt like its outward appearance to reflect the harmony and elegance of the movement within. You may therefore find it helpful to know that we are uniquely able to cater for any special decorative needs you might like to express. For example, our engravers will delight in conjuring a subtle play of light and shadow on the gold case-back of one of our rare pocket-watches *fig. 7*. If you bring us your favourite picture, our enamellers will reproduce it in a brilliant miniature of hair-breadth detail *fig. 8*. The perfect execution of a double hobnail pattern on the bezel of a wristwatch is the pride of our casemakers and the satisfaction of our designers, while our chainsmiths will weave for you a rich brocade in gold *figs. 9 & 10*. May we also recommend the artistry of our goldsmiths and the experience of our lapidaries in the selection and setting of the finest gemstones? *figs. 11 & 12.*

**How to enjoy your watch before you own it.**

As you will appreciate, the very nature of our watches imposes a limit on the number we can make available. (The four Calibre 89 time-pieces we are now making will take up to nine years to complete). We cannot therefore promise instant gratification, but while you look forward to the day on which you take delivery of your Patek Philippe *fig. 13*, you will have the pleasure of reflecting that time is a universal and everlasting commodity, freely available to be enjoyed by all.

*Should you require information on any particular Patek Philippe watch, or even on watchmaking in general, we would be delighted to reply to your letter of enquiry. And if you send us*

fig. 1: The classic face of Patek Philippe.

fig. 4: Complicated wristwatches circa 1930 (left) and 1990. The golden age of watchmaking will always be with us.

fig. 5: The Geneva Seal is awarded only to watches which achieve the standards of horological purity laid down in the laws of Geneva. These rules define the supreme quality of watchmaking.

fig. 9: Harmony of design is executed in a work of simplicity and perfection in a lady's Calatrava wristwatch.

fig. 10: The chainsmith's hands impart strength and delicacy to a tracery of gold.

fig. 2: One of the 33 complications of the Calibre 89 astronomical clock-watch is a satellite wheel that completes one revolution every 400 years.

fig. 6: Your pleasure in owning a Patek Philippe is the purpose of those who made it for you.

fig. 7: Arabesques come to life on a gold case-back.

fig. 11: Circles in gold: symbols of perfection in the making.

fig. 8: An artist working six hours a day takes about four months to complete a miniature in enamel on the case of a pocket-watch.

fig. 12: The test of a master lapidary is his ability to express the splendour of precious gemstones.

fig. 3: Recognized as the most advanced mechanical regulating device to date, Patek Philippe's Gyromax balance wheel demonstrates the equivalence of simplicity and precision.

# PATEK PHILIPPE
## GENEVE
fig. 13: The discreet sign of those who value their time.

your card marked "book catalogue" we shall post you a catalogue of our publications. Patek Philippe, 41 rue du Rhône, 1204 Geneva, Switzerland, Tel. +41 22/310 03 66.

# Wherever you're going we'll be there.

**F**rom Alice Springs to Zimbabwe, you can be sure Hertz will be at your service.

**W**ith over 500,000 cars in more than 150 countries, and 5,000 rental locations with 2,000 at airports, you can always rely on Hertz to offer the car you want, when you want it, and at the right price.

**A**nd wherever you go you'll always find the same friendly quality service that is second to none.

**I**t's not surprising then that our combination of unbelievable prices and unbeatable service has made us the world's #1 car rental company.

**S**imply call your local travel agent, or Hertz direct for further information.

Highest Quality. Low, Low Prices.

**Hertz**

Hertz rents and leases Fords and other fine cars.

# Getting Acquainted

## The Place

### Time Zones

All the Southwest runs on Mountain Standard Time except for Nevada, which uses Pacific Standard Time (one hour earlier than Mountain Time). In spring, Colorado, Utah, Texas and New Mexico move the clock ahead one hour for Daylight Savings Time. In fall, the clock is moved back.

Arizona does not observe Daylight Savings Time, but the Navajo Nation does. Thus, during spring and summer, Arizona is one hour behind the Navajo Nation. Mexico does not observe Daylight Savings Time.

### Climate

The Southwest spans half a dozen climate and life zones, but by and large you will find sunny skies, low humidity and limited precipitation.

Climate varies widely with elevation. Climbing 1,000 ft (300 meters) is equivalent to traveling 300 miles (500 km) north. In temperature, traveling from the lowest to the highest points of Arizona is like traveling from Mexico to the north of Hudson Bay in Canada.

### ARIZONA

Arizona gets 80 percent of available sunshine annually. Annual rainfall averages 12.55 inches (30 cm). Wind velocity for most cities is under 8 mph (13 kph). Northern regions average around 73 percent sunshine; southern areas average around 90 percent. Average temperatures in Phoenix reach 100°F (38°C) in summer and fall to 30°F (–1°C) in winter. Phoenix gets about 7 inches (18 cm) of rain per year. In Flagstaff, 145 miles (230 km) to the north, temperatures range from 75–80°F (24–27°C) in summer and fall to around 15°F (–10°C) in winter. Annual rainfall in Flagstaff averages 84 inches (210 cm), most of it falling in July, August and December.

### GRAND CANYON

At its hottest, the south rim of the Grand Canyon reaches 90°F (32°C) rising to 100°F (38°C) at the bottom of the gorge. Flash thunderstorms are common. Generally, the weather is more comfortable in the spring and fall. Always bring sweaters when visiting the Canyon.

### LAS VEGAS

June through September, daytime temperatures rarely register below 100°F (38°C). Spring and fall seasons are short, with temperatures around 75°F (24°C). Daytime winter temperatures are generally 50–70°F (10–20°C) with January and February nights near freezing point.

### NEW MEXICO

Every part of the state gets at least 70 percent sunshine year-round, with July and August thunderstorms providing most of the precipitation. From December to March, snowfalls vary from 2 inches (5 cm) in the lower Rio Grande Valley to 300 inches (750 cm) or more in the north-central mountains. Albuquerque registers highs just over 90°F (32°C) in summer; winter lows are below 30°F (–1°C) in January. Only 59 miles (95 km) to the north, but at a higher elevation, Santa Fe reports July highs above 90°F (32°C) and January lows below 20°F (–7°C).

### UTAH

Southern Utah has sunny days, cool nights and little precipitation. Occasional summer days warm up past 100°F (38°C), which makes hiking inadvisable during the day. Arches National Park is the warmest spot in Utah, with consistent summer temperatures of 110–115°F (43–46°C). Bryce Canyon is much higher and so much cooler, with July and August temperatures of 70–90°F (21–32°C) falling to around a brisk 45°F (7°C) overnight. Thunderstorms, usually brief, occur in all the parks. Visitors can count on warm to hot days and should prepare for nights requiring heavier clothing.

# Planning the Trip

## What To Bring

### Clothing

Weather can be unpredictable in any season, so be prepared for just about anything. Dress in layers that can be peeled off or put on as conditions dictate. Rain gear is always a good idea. A high-factor sunblock, wide-brimmed hat and sunglasses are advisable too, even if the day starts out cloudy. The sun can be merciless, especially in deserts or prairies where there is little shade.

If you plan on doing a lot of walking or hiking, it's worth investing in a sturdy pair of hiking shoes or boots. Consider buying them a half or full size larger than usual and be sure to break them in properly before arriving. A thin, inner polypropylene sock and a thick, outer sock will help keep your feet dry and comfortable. If blisters or sore spots develop, quickly cover them with moleskin, available at just about any pharmacy or camping supply store.

With few exceptions, western dress is informal. A pair of jeans or slacks, a polo or button-down shirt, and boots or shoes are appropriate at all but the fanciest places and events.

### Electrical Adapters

Standard American electricity is at 110 volts. An adapter is necessary for UK appliances, which run on 240 volts.

### Film

A variety of 35-mm, 110 and cartridge films are available in most grocery stores, pharmacies and convenience stores. If you need professional-quality photographic equipment or film, consult the local telephone directory for the nearest camera shop. If you don't have a camera, consider the relatively inexpensive disposable cameras available at many supermarkets, pharmacies and convenience stores.

CAMEL
BAGS

YOUR TRAVEL PARTNER

# You close your laptop and adjust your footrest. A taste of Brie. A sip of Bordeaux. You lean back and hope you won't be arriving too soon.

## That depends on how far you're going.

The fact that Lufthansa flies to 220 global destinations comes as a surprise to some. Perhaps we've been too busy with our award-winning service to tell everybody that we are one of the world's largest airline networks. A network that can offer you fast and convenient connections to anywhere. A network that offers rewards with Miles and More, one of the world's leading frequent flyer programmes. And above all, a network that makes you feel at home, however far you're going. So call Lufthansa on 0345 252 252 and we'll tell you the full story.

 **Lufthansa**

## Maps

Accurate maps are indispensable in the Southwest. You can usually find a good selection at bookstores, convenience stores and gas stations.

Free maps may be available by mail from state or regional tourism bureaus (see below). Free city, state and regional maps as well as up-to-date road conditions and other valuable services are also available to members of the Automobile Association of America. If you are driving any distance, the service is well worth the membership fee.

Maps of national parks, forests and other natural areas are usually offered by the managing agency (see below). Good topographical maps are available from Trails Illustrated, PO Box 3610, Evergreen, CO 80439, tel: (303) 670-3457 or toll-free 800-962-1643. Topographical maps are also available from the **US Geological Survey**, PO Box 25286, Denver Federal Center, Denver, CO 80225, tel: (303) 236-7477.

## Entry Regulations

### Passports & Visas

A passport, visitor's visa and evidence of intent to leave the US after your visit are required for entry into the US by most foreign nationals. Visitors from the United Kingdom and several other countries staying less than 90 days may not need a visa if they meet certain requirements. All other nationals must obtain a visa from the US consulate or embassy in their country. An international vaccination certificate may be required depending on your country of origin.

Canadians entering from the Western Hemisphere, Mexicans with border passes and British residents of Bermuda and Canada do not normally need a visa or passport, but it's best to confirm visa requirements before leaving home.

Once in the US, you may visit Canada or Mexico for up to 30 days and re-enter the US without a new visa. If you lose your visa or passport, arrange to get a new one at your country's nearest consulate or embassy. For additional information, contact the US consulate or embassy in your country or the US State Department, tel: (202) 663-1225.

## Customs

All people entering the country must go through US Customs, a time-consuming process. To speed things up, be prepared to open your luggage for inspection and keep the following restrictions in mind.

• If you are bringing in more than $10,000 you must fill out a report.
• Anything for personal use may be brought in duty- and tax-free.
• Adults are allowed to bring in one liter (1.06 quarts) of alcohol for personal use.
• You can bring in gifts worth less than $400 duty- and tax-free. Anything over the $400 limit is subject to duty charges and taxes.
• Agricultural products, meat and animals are subject to complex restrictions. Leave these items at home if at all possible.

For more details contact a US consulate or write the Department of Agriculture, or US Customs, 1301 Constitution Avenue NW, Washington, DC 20520, tel: (202) 514-4330.

## Health

### Precautions

**Insurance**: It's vital to have insurance when traveling. Unless you go to a free clinic, you may have to prove you can pay for your treatment. Know what your policy covers and have proof of the policy with you at all times. Check with your travel agent.

**Sunburn:** A beautiful day of rafting can result in sunburn, so protect yourself with a sunscreen and sunglasses. The elderly and ill, small children and people with fair skin should be especially careful. Excessive pain or redness and blistering or numb skin mean you need professional medical attention. Minor sunburn can be soothed by taking a cold bath.

**Dehydration**: Drink plenty of water in the American Southwest and, if outdoors, try to carry liter bottles of water and something to eat. Don't wait to get thirsty – start drinking extra liquids as soon as you get up. Also avoid the sun at its hottest: 2–4pm.

**Cacti**: To avoid being stuck, stay on the trail and wear long pants and sturdy boots. Some people may have allergies to the prickly varieties of these beautiful desert plants.

**Hypothermia** occurs when the core body temperature falls below 95°F (35°C). At altitude, combinations of alcohol, cold, and thin air can produce hypothermia. Watch for drowsiness, disorientation and sometimes increased urination. If possible get to a hospital, otherwise blankets and extra clothing should be piled on for warmth. Don't use hot water or electric heaters and don't rub the skin. The elderly should be especially careful in extremely cold weather.

**Drinking water:** All water from natural sources must be purified before drinking. *Giardia* is found throughout the West, even in crystal-clear water, and it can cause severe cramps and diarrhea. The most popular purification methods are tablets or filters (both from camping supply stores) or by boiling for at least 15 minutes. Drink only bottled water (including ice cubes) in Mexico.

**Frostbite** occurs when living tissue freezes. Symptoms include numbness, pain, blistering and whitening of the skin. The most immediate remedy is to put frostbitten skin against warm skin. Simply holding your hands for several minutes over another person's frostbitten cheeks or nose, for example, may suffice. Otherwise, immerse frostbitten skin in warm (not hot!) water. Refreezing will cause even more damage, so get the victim into a warm environment as quickly as possible. If one person is frostbitten, others may be too. Check all members of your party for frostbite.

**Altitude sickness**: The air thins as you go higher. Unless properly acclimatized, you may feel uncharacteristically winded. If you experience nausea, headache, vomiting, extreme fatigue, light-headedness or shortness of breath, you may be suffering from altitude sickness. Although the symptoms may be mild at first, they can develop into a serious illness. Head lower down and try to acclimatize gradually.

**Swimming**: Strong currents and cold water can drown even experienced swimmers. Wear a life vest when boating, and avoid hypothermia by staying out of cold water.

**Ghost Towns**: Exercise caution around old buildings and abandoned mines. Structures may be unstable and the ground may be littered with broken glass, nails and other debris. Mine shafts are particularly dangerous. Never enter a mine shaft or cave unless accompanied by a park ranger or other professional.

### INSECTS & PESTS

**Snakes:** There are rattlesnakes and coral snakes in the Southwest, but not in great numbers.

According to the late writer Ed Abbey, only 3 percent of people bitten by a rattlesnake die, and these are mainly small children. Walk in the open; proceed with caution in rocks; make noise in grass; do not step close to dark places or dense, overgrown areas where snakes might lurk; shake out bedding or clothing that has been lying on the ground; and wear sturdy hiking boots. Snakes lie on the pavement at night because of the heat, so use a flashlight if you are walking on a desert highway after dark. Don't poke under rocks or let your children pick things up in the desert.

Snakebite kits are good psychological protection, but there is controversy over how effective they really are. If bitten, apply a tourniquet lightly above the bite toward the heart. Try to identify the species, and then go immediately to a doctor. If that's not possible, try and keep the bitten person quiet and get a doctor.

**Gila monsters** are the only poisonous Southwestern lizards on record. They are big and menacing but easily recognized and rarely encountered.

**Insects**: Bees are abundant, which should concern only those allergic to the sting. The kissing bug is an unusual looking black bug with an unpleasant bite. There are stinging fire ants and some varieties of wasp. These bugs are neither friendly nor normally dangerous.

Black widow spiders and scorpions can be a problem if encountered. Scorpions are nocturnal, so use flashlights if you walk barefoot in the desert at night. They crawl into things, so shake out clothes and bedding and check stores in the morning.

## Money Matters

### Credit Cards & Automatic Teller Machines

Major credit cards are widely accepted at shops, restaurants, hotels and gas stations, although not all cards are accepted by every vendor. Try to carry at least two card types. Some credit cards allow withdrawals of cash from the automatic teller machines (ATM) in larger towns and cities. Out-of-town ATM cards may also work. Check with your bank or credit-card company for the systems your card will operate.

Money may be sent or received by wire at any Western Union office, toll-free tel: 800-325-6000, or American Express Money Gram office, toll-free tel: 800-926 9400 or 1-800 MONEY-GRAM.

### American Currency & Exchange

American money runs on a decimal system. A dollar ($1) is 100 cents 100¢). There are four coins, each worth less than a dollar. A penny (1¢); a nickel (5¢); a dime (10¢); and a quarter (25¢).

There are seven notes: $1, $5, $10, $20, $50, $100 and, rarely, $2. Each bill is the same color, size and shape, so check the dollar amount on the face of the bill.

Arrive with at least $100 in small bills to pay for taxis and other incidentals. Instead of cash, it's a good idea to carry traveler's checks – they are accepted by most retailers and can be exchanged for cash at banks if presented with your passport. Major credit cards will be generally useful and essential to rent a car.

Foreign currency is rarely accepted in the US. You can exchange currency at major big-city banks, hotels, international airports and currency-exchange offices.

## Holidays

On holidays, post offices, banks, most government offices and quiet a few shops and restaurants are closed. Public transport usually runs less frequently.

**New Year's Day:** January 1
**Martin Luther King, Jr.'s Birthday:** January 15
**Presidents Day:** The third Monday in February

**Texas Independence Day:** March 2 (Texas)
**Good Friday**: March/April – date varies
**Easter Sunday**: March/April – date varies
**San Jacinto Day:** April 21 (Texas)
**El Cinco de Mayo:** May 5
**Memorial Day:** Last Monday in May
**Emancipation Day:** June 19 (Texas)
**Independence Day:** July 4
**Pioneer Day:** July 24 (Utah)
**Lyndon B. Johnson's Birthday:** August 27 (Texas)
**Labor Day:** First Monday in September
**Columbus Day:** Second Monday in October
**Veterans Day:** November 11
**Thanksgiving Day:** Fourth Thursday in November
**Christmas Day:** December 25

## Getting There

### By Air

If driving to the Southwest is impractical because of distance, the next best way to get there is to fly to a nearby city and rent a car. The major hubs in the Southwest are:
**Arizona**: Phoenix Sky Harbor International, Tucson International.
**Colorado**: Denver International, Colorado Springs Airport.
**Nevada**: McCarran International (Las Vegas).
**New Mexico**: Albuquerque International.
**Texas**: El Paso International.
**Utah**: Salt Lake City International.

### NATIONAL AIRLINES

| | |
|---|---|
| American Airlines | 800-433-7300 |
| Continental Airlines | 800-525-0280 |
| TWA | 800-221-2000 |
| United Airlines | 800-241-6522 |
| US Air | 800-428-4322 |

### REGIONAL AIRLINES

| | |
|---|---|
| Air Nevada Airlines | 800-634-6377 |
| Havasu Airlines | 800-764-2487 |
| Las Vegas Airlines | 800-634-6851 |
| Scenic Airlines | 800-634-6801 |
| Sky West Airlines | 800-453-9417 |
| Southwest Airlines | 800-273-1221 |

# HOLIDAY MAKER

**18 CAPSULES**

FAST AND EFFECTIVE

## ARRET™

### THERE'S NO QUICKER WAY TO STOP DIARRHOEA

If diarrhoea disrupts your holiday, remember Arret can relieve the symptoms within one hour.

So you lose as little holiday time as possible.

To make the most of your holiday, make sure you pack Arret.

### ARRET. HOLIDAY INSURANCE FROM YOUR PHARMACIST.

Always read the label. Contains loperamide.

PRIMA SUPER 135 38-135 MM

PRIMA SUPER 115 38-115 MM

# YOUR TRAVEL COMPANION FOR THOSE PRICELESS MOMENTS

PRIMA SUPER 28V 28-70 MM

PRIMA ZOOM 70F 35-70 MM

There's no better way to capture life's most cherished moments than with a Canon Prima Zoom camera. All Prima Zoom cameras are durable and light and come with easy-to-use features like an intelligent Automatic Focusing system, and a special feature that reduces the undesirable "red-eye" effect. Buying a Canon Prima Zoom also means you're getting Canon's reputation for optical excellence. It's your guarantee for breathtaking pictures, every time.

**Canon**
**PRIMA ZOOM**

Canon Europa N.V., P.O. Box 2262, 1180 EG Amstelveen, the Netherlands

PRIMA ZOOM SHOT 38-60 MM

## By Train

Amtrak offers more than 500 destinations across the US. Generally speaking, the trains are comfortable and reliable, with lounges, restaurants, snack bars and, in some cases, movies and live entertainment.

Amtrak's **Southwest Chief** runs from Chicago to Los Angeles. Stops include Dodge City, Kansas; La Junta, Colorado; Albuquerque and Gallup, New Mexico; Winslow, Flagstaff (Amtrak Thruway bus service to Grand Canyon) and Kingman, Arizona; and Barstow, California.

The **Sunset Limited** runs from Miami to Los Angeles. Stops on this route include Alpine and El Paso, Texas; Deming, New Mexico; and Tucson and Phoenix, Arizona.

The **Desert Wind** runs from Chicago to Los Angeles. Stops on this route include Denver and Grand Junction, Colorado; Thompson and Salt Lake City, Utah; Las Vegas, Nevada; and Barstow, California.

Be sure to ask about two- or three-stopover discounts, senior citizens and children's discounts, and Amtrak's package tours. Tel: 800-USA-RAIL for detailed scheduling.

## By Bus

One of the least expensive ways to travel in America is by bus. The biggest national bus company is Greyhound, tel: 800-231-2222. The company routinely offers discounts such as a $99 go-anywhere fare and a $1 ticket for moms on Mother's Day. Call the Greyhound office nearest you for information on special rates and package tours. However, Greyhound generally does not service remote areas. A rental car or other transport will be necessary from the major hubs.

## Hitchhiking

Hitchhiking is illegal in many places and ill-advised everywhere. It's an inefficient and dangerous method of travel. Don't do it!

## By Car

Driving is by far the most flexible and convenient way to travel in the Southwest. Major roads are well-maintained, although back-country roads may be unpaved. If you plan on driving into remote areas or in heavy snow, mud or severe weather, it's a good idea to use a four-wheel-drive vehicle with high chassis clearance.

Your greatest asset as a driver is a good road map. They can be obtained from state tourism offices, filling stations, supermarkets and convenience stores. Although roads are maintained even in remote areas, it is advisable to listen to local radio stations and to check with highway officials or police officers for the latest information on weather and road conditions, especially if you plan on leaving paved roads. Driving conditions vary dramatically depending on elevation. During fall, winter and early spring, your car should be equipped with snow tires or chains, a small collapsible shovel, and an ice scraper. Also, be prepared for the extra time required to drive along winding, narrow mountain roads.

If you plan to drive in desert areas, carry extra water – at least 1 gallon (4 litres) per person per day. It' is advisable to take along some food, too. Flash floods may occur during the rainy season, from early summer to fall. Stay out of arroyos, washes and drainage areas.

Service stations can be few and far between in remote areas. Not every town will have one, and many close early. Check your gas gauge often. It's always better to have more fuel than you think you will need.

A word of caution: If your car breaks down on a back road, do not attempt to strike out on foot, even with water. A car is easier to spot than a person and gives shelter from the elements. Sit tight and wait to be found.

Finally, if you intend to do a lot of driving, it's a good idea to join the **American Automobile Association**. The AAA offers emergency road service, maps, insurance, bail bond protection and other services. AAA, 1000 AAA Drive, Heathrow, FL 32746, tel: (407) 444-4300.

## Car Rentals

National car rental agencies are located at all airports, cities and large towns. In most places, you must be at least 21 years old (25 at some locations) to rent a car, and you must have a valid driver's license and at least one major credit card. Foreign drivers must have an international driver's license. Be sure that you are properly insured for both collision and personal liability. Insurance may not be included in the base rental fee. Additional cost varies depending on the car and the type of coverage, but it is usually $10–20 per day. You may already be covered by your own auto insurance or credit-card company, so be sure to check with them first.

Be sure to inquire about an unlimited mileage package. If not, you may be charged an extra 10–25¢ or more per mile over a given mileage. Rental fees vary depending on time of year, location, how far in advance you book your rental, and if you travel on weekdays or weekends. Inquire about discounts or benefits for which you may be eligible, including corporate, credit-card or frequent-flyer programs.

| | |
|---|---|
| Alamo | 800-327-9633 |
| American Int. | 800-669-7312 |
| Avis | 800-331-1212 |
| Budget | 800-527-0700 |
| Dollar | 800-800-4000 |
| Enterprise | 800-325-8007 |
| Hertz | 800-654-3131 |
| National | 800-227-7368 |
| Thrifty | 800-331-4200 |

### RV RENTALS

No special license is necessary to operate a motor home (or recreational vehicle – RV for short), but they aren't cheap. When you add up the cost of rental fees, insurance, gas and campsites, you may find that renting a car and staying in motels or camping is less expensive.

Keep in mind, too, that RVs are large and slow and may be difficult to handle on narrow mountain roads. If parking space is tight, driving an RV may be extremely inconvenient. Access to some roads may be limited. For additional information about RV rentals, call the **Recreational Vehicle Rental Association**, tel: 800-336-0355.

# Practical Tips

## Business Hours

Standard business hours are Monday–Friday 9am–5pm. Many banks open a little earlier, usually 8.30am, and nearly all close by 3pm. A few open on Saturday morning. Post offices tend to be open Monday–Friday 8am–5pm and Saturday 8am–noon. Most stores keep weekend hours and may stay open late one or more nights a week.

## Tipping

Service personnel depend on tips for a large part of their income. With few exceptions, tipping is left to your discretion; gratuities are not automatically added to the bill. In most cases, 15–20 percent is the going rate for tipping waiters, taxi drivers, bartenders, barbers and hairdressers. Porters and bellmen usually get about 75¢–$1 per bag, but never less than $1 total.

## Media

### Newspapers

*Albuquerque Journal*, 7777 Jefferson NE, Albuquerque, NM 87109, tel: (505) 823-4400.
*Albuquerque Tribune*, 7777 Jefferson NE, Albuquerque, NM 87109, tel: (505) 823-4400.
*Arizona Republic*, 120 E. Van Buren, Phoenix, AZ, tel: (602) 257-8300.
*Las Vegas Sun*, 800 S. Valley View, Las Vegas, NV 89107, tel: (702) 385-3111.
*Las Vegas Review-Journal*, 1111 W. Bonanza Road, Las Vegas, NV 89107, tel: (702) 383-0211.
*New Mexican*, 202 E. Marcy, Santa Fe, NM 87501, tel: (505) 983-3303.
*Phoenix Gazette*, 120 E. Van Buren, Phoenix, AZ, tel: (602) 257-8300.
*Salt Lake Tribune*, 143 S. Main Street, Salt Lake City, UT 84111, tel: (801) 237-2045.
*Tucson Citizen*, 4850 S. Park Avenue, Tucson, AZ 85714, tel: (520) 573-4400.

## Magazines

The magazines below often feature articles about the Southwest.
*Arizona Highways*, 2039 W. Lewis Street, Phoenix, AZ 85009, tel: (602) 258-6641.
*Nevada Magazine*, Capitol Complex, Carson City, NV 89710, tel: (702) 687-5416.
*New Mexico Magazine*, 1100 Saint Francis Drive, Joseph Montoya Building, Santa Fe, NM 87503, tel: (505) 827-0220.
*Phoenix Magazine*, 5555 N. Seventh Avenue, Phoenix, AZ 85013, tel: (602) 207-3750.

## Postal Services

Even the most remote towns are served by the US Postal Service. Smaller post offices tend to be limited to business hours (Monday–Friday 9am–5pm), although central, big-city branches may have extended weekday and weekend hours.

Stamps are sold at all post offices. They are also sold at some convenience stores, filling stations, hotels and transportation terminals, usually in vending machines.

For reasonably quick delivery at a modest price, ask for first-class or priority mail. Second- and third-class mail is cheaper and slower.

For expedited deliveries, often overnight, try US **Express Mail** or one of several international courier services: **Fedex**, tel: 800-238-5355; **DHL**, tel: 800-345-2727; **United Parcel Service**, tel: 800-272-4877. There may be other local services listed in the telephone directory.

## Telephones

Public telephones are located at many highway rest areas, service stations, convenience stores, bars, motels and restaurants. The quickest way to get assistance is to dial 0 for the operator; or if you need to find a number, call information on 555-1212. Local calls cost 25¢ and can be dialed directly. Rates vary for long-distance calls, but they can also be dialed directly with the proper area and country code. If you don't know the codes, call information or dial 0 and ask for the international operator.

Make use of toll-free numbers whenever possible. For information on toll-free numbers, dial 800-555-1212. For personal calls, take advantage of lower long-distance rates on weekends and after 5pm on weekdays.

To telephone beyond the US and Canada (which follows the US system), first dial the international access code 011, then the country code. If using a US phone credit card, dial the company's access number below, then 01, then the country code. **Sprint**, tel: 10333; **AT&T**, tel: 10288.

### COUNTRY CODES

| | |
|---|---|
| Australia | 61 |
| New Zealand | 64 |
| United Kingdom | 44 |

**Western Union**, tel: 800-325-6000, can arrange telegrams and mailgrams. Check the local phone directory or call information for local offices. There are fax machines at most hotels and some motels. Printers, copy shops, office-supply shops and some convenience stores may also have them.

## Useful Addresses

### State Tourism Offices

#### ARIZONA

**Arizona Office of Tourism**, 1100 W. Washington Street, Phoenix, AZ 85007, tel: (602) 542-8687 or toll free 800-842-8257.
**Flagstaff Convention and Visitors Bureau**, 211 W. Aspen Avenue, Flagstaff, AZ 86001, tel: (520) 779-7611.
**Grand Canyon Chamber of Commerce**, PO Box 3007, Grand Canyon, AZ 86023, tel: (520) 638-2901.
**Navajo Nation Tourism Office**, PO Box 663, Window Rock, AZ 86515, tel: (520) 871-6436.
**Phoenix & Valley of the Sun Convention and Visitor Bureau**, 400 E. Van Buren #600, Phoenix, AZ 85004, tel: (602) 254-6500.
**Prescott Chamber of Commerce**, 117 W. Goodwin Street, Prescott, AZ 86302, tel: (520) 445-2000.
**Tombstone Office of Tourism**, PO Box 917, Tombstone, AZ 85638, tel: (520) 457-3929 or toll free 800-457-3423.
**Tucson Convention & Visitors Bureau**, 130 S. Scott Avenue, Tucson, AZ 85701, tel: (520) 624-1817 or toll free 800-638-8350.

## COLORADO

**Colorado Tourism Authority**, 1625 Broadway, Suite 1700, Denver, CO 80202, tel: toll-free 800-265-6723.

**Cortez Chamber of Commerce**, PO Box 968, Cortez, CO 81321, tel: (970) 565-3414 or toll free 800-346-6528.

**Durango Chamber Resort Association**, 111 S. Camino del Rio, Durango, CO 81301, tel: (970) 247-0312.

**Pueblo Chamber of Commerce**, 210 N. Santa Fe Drive, Pueblo, CO 81002, tel: (719) 542-1704 or toll free 800-233-3446.

**Silverton Chamber of Commerce**, PO Box 565, Silverton, CO 81433, tel: (970) 387-5654 or toll free 800-752-4494.

**Telluride Chamber Resort Assocation**, 666 W. Colorado Avenue, Telluride, CO 81435, tel: (970) 728-3041.

## NEVADA

**Nevada Tourism**, Capital Complex, Carson City, NV 89710, tel: (702) 687-4322 or toll free 800-237-0774.

**Las Vegas Chamber of Commerce**, 711 E. Desert Inn Road, Las Vegas, NV 89104, tel: (702) 735-1616.

**Las Vegas Convention and Visitors Authority**, Convention Center, 3150 Paradise Road, Las Vegas, NV 89109, tel: (702) 892-0711 or toll free 800-332-5333.

**Greater Reno Chamber of Commerce**, 405 Marsh Avenue, Reno, NV 89505, tel: (702) 686-3030.

**Reno-Sparks Convention and Visitors Authority**, 4590 S. Virginia Street, Reno, NV 89504, tel: (702) 827-7667 or toll free 800-367-7366.

## NEW MEXICO

**New Mexico Tourism**, Lamy Building, 491 Old Santa Fe Trail, Santa Fe, NM 87503, tel: (505) 827-7400 or toll 800-545-2040.

**Alamogordo Chamber of Commerce**, PO Box 518, Alamogordo, NM 88311, tel: (505) 437-6120.

**Albuquerque Convention and Visitors Bureau**, PO Box 26866, Albuquerque, NM 87125, tel: (505) 243-3696 or toll free 800-284-2282.

**Fort Sumner Chamber of Commerce**, PO Box 28, Fort Sumner, NM 88119, tel: (505) 355-7705.

**Gallup Convention and Visitors Bureau**, PO Drawer Q, Gallup, NM 87305, tel: (505) 863-3841.

**New Mexico North**, PO Box 547, Angel Fire, NM 87710, tel: 505-377-6353.

**Old West Country**, 1103 N. Hudson, Silver City, NM 88061, tel: (505) 538-0061 or toll free 800-548-9378.

**Santa Fe Convention & Visitors Bureau**, PO Box 909, Santa Fe, NM 87501, tel: (505) 984-6760.

**Taos County Chamber of Commerce**, PO Drawer I, Taos, NM 87571, tel: (505) 758-3873 or toll free 800-732-8267.

## TEXAS

**Texas Tourism**, PO Box 12728, Austin, TX 78711, tel: (512) 478-0098 or toll free 800-888-8839.

**El Paso Convention and Visitors Bureau**, 1 Civic Center Plaza, El Paso, TX 79940, tel: (915) 534-0658.

## UTAH

**Utah Travel Council**, Council Hall, Capitol Hill, Salt Lake City, UT 84114, tel: (801) 538-1030 or toll free 800-200-1160.

**Canyonlands**, 117 S. Main, Monticello, UT 84535, tel: (801) 587-3235.

**Color Country**, 906 N. 1400 West, St George, UT 84771, tel: (801) 628-4171 or toll free 800-233-8824.

## National Parks & Wilderness Areas

**National Park Service**, Southwest Region, PO Box 728, Santa Fe, NM 87504-0728, tel: (505) 988-6016.

**Bureau of Land Management**, US Department of the Interior, 1849 C Street NW, Washington, DC 20240, tel: (202) 208-5717.

**Fish and Wildlife Service**, US Department of the Interior, 1849 C Street NW, Washington, DC 20240, tel: (202) 208-5634.

**Forest Service**, US Department of Agriculture, 14th and Independence Avenue SW, S. Agriculture Building, Washington, DC 20250, tel: (202) 205-8333.

## State Parks

**Arizona State Parks**, 800 W. Washington, Phoenix, AZ 85007, tel: (602) 542-4174.

**Colorado State Parks**, 1313 Sherman Street #618, Denver, CO 80203, tel: (303) 866-3437.

**Nevada State Parks and Recreation**, 123 W. Nye Lane, Carson City, NV 89702, tel: (702) 687-4384.

**New Mexico State Parks**, 408 Galisteo, Santa Fe, NM 87501, tel: (505) 827-7465.

**Utah Division of Parks and Recreation**, 1636 W. North Temple, Suite 116, Salt Lake City, UT 84116, tel: (801) 538-7221.

## Embassies

**Australia**: 1601 Massachusetts Avenue NW, Washington, DC 20036, tel: (202) 797-3000.

**Canada**: 501 Pennsylvania Avenue NW, Washington, DC 20001, tel: (202) 682-1740.

**Great Britain**: 3100 Massachusetts Avenue NW, Washington, DC 20008, tel: (202) 462-1340.

**Mexico**: 1911 Pennsylvania Avenue NW, Washington, DC 20006, tel: (202) 728-1600.

**New Zealand**: 37 Observatory Circle NW, Washington, DC 20008, tel: (202) 328-4800.

## Security & Crime

A few common-sense precautions will help keep you safe while traveling in the Southwest. For starters, know where you are and where you're going. Whether traveling on foot or by car, bring a map and plan your route in advance. If you get lost, ask a passerby, shopkeeper or police officer for directions. Most people are happy to help.

Don't carry large sums of cash or wear flashy or expensive jewelry. Keep them locked in your trunk or in a hotel safe. Lock unattended cars and keep your belongings in the trunk. If possible, travel with a companion, especially after dark.

If you are a witness to or victim of a crime, or need to report an emergency situation of any kind, immediately contact the police (dial 911 or 0 for an operator). If you are involved in a traffic accident, remain at or very near the site. It is illegal to leave the scene of an accident. Find a nearby telephone or ask a passing motorist to call the police, and then wait for emergency vehicles to arrive.

If you plan on drinking, ask a companion to be a "designated driver," a person who forgoes alcohol and drives the others home. Otherwise, use public transport or a taxi. Driving under the influence of alcohol carries stiff penalties, including fines, jail, community service and suspension of your license. As the slogan goes, impairment begins with the first drink.

Buckle up! Wearing seatbelts is required in most states. Children under four must be in a child's seat or (depending on age and size) in a seatbelt.

## Weights & Measures

The US still uses the Imperial System of weights and measures.

| | |
|---|---|
| 1 inch | 2.54 centimeters |
| 1 foot | 30.48 centimeters |
| 1 yard | 0.9144 meter |
| 1 mile | 1.609 kilometers |
| 1 pint | 0.473 liter |
| 1 quart | 0.946 liter |
| 1 ounce | 28.4 grams |
| 1 pound | 0.453 kilogram |
| 1 acre | 0.405 hectare |
| 1 sq. mile | 259 hectares |
| 1 centimeter | 0.394 inch |
| 1 meter | 39.37 inches |
| 1 kilometer | 0.621 mile |
| 1 liter | 1.057 quarts |
| 1 gram | 0.035 ounce |
| 1 kilogram | 2.205 pounds |
| 1 hectare | 2.471 acres |
| 1 sq. kilometer | 0.386 sq. mile |

# Where to Stay

## Hotels

| | |
|---|---|
| Budget | $50 or less |
| Moderate | $50–100 |
| Expensive | $100–150 |
| Very expensive | $150+ |

### Arizona

**Arizona Biltmore**, 24th Street and Missouri Avenue, Phoenix, AZ 85016, tel: (602) 955-6600 or toll free 800-950-0086. An elegant grand hotel designed by Frank Lloyd Wright and in landscaped grounds. Amenities: air conditioning, television, pools, fitness room, golf courses, biking, restaurants, bars, shops, parking. Credit cards: all major. Very expensive.

**Best Western Grand Canyon Squire Inn**, Highway 64, Grand Canyon, AZ 86023, tel: (520) 638-2681. Comfortable, modern hotel located just outside of Grand Canyon National Park. Amenities: air conditioning, television, pool, tennis, restaurant, bar, parking. Credit cards: all major. Moderate to expensive.

**Bisbee Grand Hotel**, 61 Main Street, Bisbee, AZ 85603, tel: (520) 432-5900. An elegantly restored Victorian building with period decor in a historic southern Arizona mining town. Amenities: parking, saloon, billiard room, free breakfast; no in-room telephones or televisions. Credit cards: American Express, Discover, MasterCard, Visa. Moderate.

**Bright Angel Lodge**, W. Rim Drive, Grand Canyon, AZ 86023, tel: (520) 638-2631. An old rustic lodge and bungalows with simple accommodation set in Grand Canyon National Park. Amenities: television, restaurant, parking, bar. Credit cards: all major. Moderate.

**Copper Queen Hotel**, 11 Howell Avenue, Bisbee, AZ 85603, tel: (520) 432-2216. A turn-of-the century Victorian landmark built during the heyday of the Copper Queen Mine; guests have included John Wayne and Teddy Roosevelt. Amenities: parking, television, restaurant, saloon, pool. Credit cards: all major. Moderate.

**Desert Rose**, 3424 E. Van Buren Street, Phoenix, AZ 85008, tel: (602) 275-4421. A modest but comfortable small hotel a short drive from downtown. Amenities: air conditioning, television, pool, restaurant, parking. Credit cards: all major. Budget.

**El Tovar Hotel**, Grand Canyon National Park Lodges, PO Box 699, Grand Canyon, AZ 86023, tel: (520) 638-2401. A rustic lodge built in 1905 on the edge of the South Rim. Amenities: air conditioning, television, parking, restaurant, bar, gift shop, some rooms with balcony. Credit cards: all major. Very expensive.

**Grand Canyon Lodge**, Bright Angel Point, AZ 86052, tel: (520) 638-2611. Basic motel accommodations and cabins on the North Rim of the Grand Canyon; open seasonally. Amenities: air conditioning, restaurant, bar, parking. Credit cards: all major. Moderate.

**Innsuites Hotel, Tucson Randolph Park**, 102 N. Alvernon Way, Tucson, AZ 85711, tel: (520) 795-0330. Spanish-style hotel with comfortable rooms and attractive setting. Amenities: air conditioning, television, pool, in-room refrigerator and microwave, some rooms with kitchenette. Credit cards: all major. Moderate.

**Loews Ventana Canyon Resort**, 7000 N. Resort Drive, Tucson, AZ 85750, tel: (520) 299-2020. Luxurious hotel in the desert outside the city. Amenities: air conditioning, television, pools, tennis, golf courses, fitness room, restaurants, bar, shops, parking. Credit cards: all major. Very Expensive.

**Navajo Nation Inn**, Highway 264, Window Rock, AZ 86515, tel: (520) 871-4108. Simple, comfortable motel located in the capital of the Navajo Nation. Amenities: air conditioning, television, restaurant, parking. Credit cards: American Express, Diners Club, MasterCard, Visa. Moderate.

**Ritz Carlton Phoenix**, 2401 E. Camelback Road, Phoenix, AZ 85016, tel: (602) 468-0700 or toll free 800-241-3333. Luxurious grand hotel with plush furnishings. Amenities: air conditioning, television, pool, fitness room, tennis, restaurants, bar, parking. Credit cards: all major. Expensive to very expensive.

**Thunderbird Lodge**, PO Box 548, Chinle, AZ 86503, tel: (520) 674-5841. Simple but comfortable accommodations at Canyon de Chelly National Monument in the Navajo Nation. Amenities: air conditioning, television, cafeteria, Jeep tours, parking. Credit cards: All major. Moderate.

**Wahweap Lodge and Marina**, 100 Lakeshore Drive, Page, AZ 86040, tel: (520) 645-2433. Modern, comfortable hotel on Lake Powell. Amenities: air conditioning, television, pools, boating, restaurants, bar, fitness room, parking. Credit cards: all major. Moderate to expensive.

### Colorado

**Far View Lodge**, PO Box 277, Mancos, CO 81328, tel: (970) 529-4421. A motel located within Mesa Verde National Park; open seasonally. Amenities: private balconies, restaurant, interpretive presentations, parking, no in-room telephone or television. Credit cards: all major. Moderate.

**General Palmer Hotel**, 567 Main Avenue, Durango, CO 81301, tel: (970) 247-4747 or toll free 800-523-3358. A gracious, midsized Victorian house fully restored with period furnishings. Amenities: air conditioning, television, parking, library, restaurant, bar, one room with Jacuzzi. Credit cards: all major. Moderate to expensive.

**Strater Hotel**, 699 Main Avenue, Durango, CO 81301, tel: (970) 247-4431 or toll free 800-247-4431. A fine Victorian mansion built in 1887 with authentic period furnishings and an Old West saloon. Amenities: air conditioning, television, parking, restaurant, saloon. Credit cards: all major. Moderate to expensive.

**Tamarron Resort**, 40292 Highway 550 North, Durango, CO 81301, tel: (970) 259-2000 or toll free 800-678-1000. A plush full-service resort in San Juan National Forest. Amenities: air conditioning, television, pool, fitness room, tennis, golf, horseback riding, restaurants, bars. Credit cards: all major. Expensive to very expensive.

**Tomboy Inn**, 619 W. Columbia Street, Telluride, CO 81435, tel: (970) 728-6621 or toll free 800-446-3192. Small, comfortable hotel in a popular ski resort. Amenities: television, some rooms with refrigerator, fireplace, kitchenette and/or balcony, parking. Credit cards: American Express, Discover, MasterCard, Visa. Expensive.

## Nevada

**Caesars Palace**, 3570 Las Vegas Blvd South, Las Vegas, NV 89109, tel: (702) 731-7110 or toll free 800-634-6001. A glitzy pleasure palace in Roman theme; a monument to Vegas style. Amenities: air conditioning, television, pools, tennis, fitness club, restaurants, bars, nightclub, Omnimax theater, casino, entertainment, shops, parking. Credit cards: all major. Moderate to very expensive.

**Center Strip Inn**, 3688 Las Vegas Blvd South, Las Vegas, NV 89109, tel: (702) 739-6066 or telephone toll free 800-777-7737. Comfortable motel on the Strip. Amenities: air conditioning, television, pool, free breakfast, parking. Credit cards: American Express, Discover, MasterCard, Visa. Moderate to expensive.

**Circus Circus**, 2880 Las Vegas Blvd South, Las Vegas, NV 89109, tel: (702) 734-0410 or toll free 800-634-3450. This comfortable hotel takes the circus theme to extremes; high-wire artists perform above the casino floor. Amenities: air conditioning, television, pools, restaurants, bars, casino, shops, parking. Credit cards: all major. Budget to moderate.

**MGM Grand Hotel**, 3799 Las Vegas Blvd South, Las Vegas, NV 89109, tel: (702) 891-1111 or toll free 800-929-1111. The world's largest hotel is Las Vegas at its most extravagant; worth visiting for the spectacle alone. Amenities: air conditioning, television, pool, tennis, fitness club, restaurants, bars, casino, entertainment, sports arena, 33-acre theme park, shopping mall, parking. Credit cards: all major. Moderate to very expensive.

## New Mexico

**Albuquerque Hilton**, 1901 University Blvd NE, Albuquerque, NM 87102, tel: (505) 884-2500. Big, spacious hotel with many amenities and downtown location. Amenities: air conditioning, television, pools, tennis courts, restaurants, bar, fitness room, tennis courts, parking. Credit cards: all major. Expensive to very expensive.

**Doubletree**, 201 Marquette Avenue NW, Albuquerque, NM 87102, tel: (505) 247-3344. Comfortable, contemporary downtown hotel popular with business people. Amenities: air conditioning, television, restaurant, bar, workout room, pool, parking. Credit cards: all major. Expensive to very expensive.

**Eldorado Hotel**, 309 W. San Francisco Street, Santa Fe, NM 87501, tel: (505) 988-4455 or toll free 800-955-4455. Luxurious contemporary hotel with lovely Southwestern design. Amenities: air conditioning, television, pool, workout room, restaurants, bars, shops, parking. Credit cards: all major. Expensive to very expensive.

**Hyatt Regency**, 330 Tijeras SW, Albuquerque, NM 87102, tel: (505) 842-1234. Elegant and contemporary downtown hotel. Amenities: air conditioning, television, pool, fitness room, restaurant, bar, gift shop, parking. Credit cards: all major. Moderate to expensive.

**Inn of the Anasazi**, 113 Washington Avenue, Santa Fe, NM 87501, tel: (505) 988-3030 or toll free 800-688-8100. New, luxurious hotel near the Plaza with Pueblo-style decor. Amenities: air conditioning, television, restaurant, fireplaces, parking. Credit cards: all major. Very expensive.

**Inn of the Mountain Gods**, PO Box 269 Mescalero, NM 88340, tel: (505) 257-5141 or toll free 800-545-9011. Owned by the Mescalero Apache tribe, this resort hotel is located on a lake in the Sacramento Mountains and offers a variety of recreational activities. Amenities: air conditioning, television, golf course, tennis courts, pool, fishing, boating. Credit cards: all major. Moderate to expensive.

**La Fonda**, 100 E. San Francisco Street, Santa Fe, NM 87501, tel: (505) 982-5511 or toll free 800-523-5002. Historic Pueblo Revival-style hotel on the Plaza rebuilt in 1919. Amenities: air conditioning, television, parking, pool, restaurant, bars, nightclub, some rooms with fireplaces, shops. Credit cards: all major. Expensive to very expensive.

**La Posada de Albuquerque**, 125 2nd Street NW, Albuquerque, NM 87102, tel: (505) 242-9090 or toll free 800-621-7231. Comfortable old hotel with nice architectural touches from the 1930s. Amenities: air conditioning, television, restaurant, bar, parking. Credit cards: all major. Moderate.

**La Posada de Santa Fe**, 330 E. Palace Avenue, Santa Fe, NM 87501, tel: (505) 986-0000 or telephone toll free 800-727-5276. Comfortable older hotel in a lovely Spanish colonial design. Near the Plaza. Amenities: air conditioning, television, pool, restaurant, bar, some rooms with fireplace, parking. Credit cards: all major. Moderate to very expensive.

**St Francis**, 210 Don Gaspar Avenue, Santa Fe, NM 87501, tel: (505) 983-5700 or toll free 800-666-5700. Charming older hotel built in the 1920s and now fully restored with period decor. Amenities: air conditioning, television, restaurant, bar, parking. Credit cards: All major. Moderate to expensive.

## Utah

**Apache Motel**, 166 S. 4th Street, Moab, UT 84532, tel: (801) 259-5727. Basic motel accommodation. Amenities: air conditioning, television, pool, parking. Credit cards: all major. Budget to moderate.

**Bryce Canyon Lodge**, TW Recreational Services, PO Box 400, Cedar City, UT 84720, tel: (801) 586-7686. Built in 1923 by the Utah Pacific Railroad and on the Register of Historic Places. Set in the heart of Bryce Canyon National Park. Amenities: some rooms with air conditioning, television, parking, pool, horseback riding, restaurant. Credit cards: all major. Expensive.

**Capitol Reef Inn**, 360 W. Main Street, Torrey, UT 84775, tel: (801) 425-3271. Small seasonal hotel with simple accommodation. Amenities: air conditioning, television, parking, restaurant. Credit cards: Discover, MasterCard, Visa. Budget.

**Goulding's Monument Valley Lodge**, PO Box 1, Monument Valley, UT 84536, tel: (801) 727-3231. Simple accommodation in Monument Valley. Amenities: air conditioning, television, restaurant, pool, Indian shop, parking. Credit cards: All major. Moderate to expensive.

**The Lodge at Brianhead**, 314 Hunter Ridge Drive, Brianhead, UT 84719, tel: (801) 677-3222. Comfy hotel in Dixie National Forest near Cedar Breaks National Monument. Amenities: air conditioning, television, parking, pool, fitness room, restaurant. Credit cards: American Express, MasterCard, Visa. Budget to moderate.

**Recapture Lodge**, Highway 191, Bluff, UT 84512, tel: (801) 672-2281. Rustic accommodations about 45 minutes from Monument Valley. Amenities: television, air conditioning, slide shows and interpretive talks, tours of Monument Valley by reservation, some rooms with kitchenettes, pool, playground, parking. Credit cards: American Express, Discover, MasterCard, Visa. Budget to moderate.

**Zion Lodge**, TW Recreational Services, Cedar City, UT 84720, tel: (801) 586-7686 or 801-772-3213. Rustic but comfortable amenities in the glorious scenery of Zion National Park. Amenities: air conditioning, parking, restaurant, horseback riding, bus tours. Credit cards: all major. Moderate.

Chain hotels and motels are reliable and convenient but tend to lack character. You can usually depend on a clean, comfortable room for a reasonable cost. In general, prices range from $25–75 depending on location and additional amenities such as a pool, lobby or restaurant.

### Moderate

| | |
|---|---|
| Best Western | 800-528-1234 |
| Hilton | 800-HILTONS |
| Holiday Inn | 800-HOLIDAY |
| Hyatt | 800-228-9000 |
| ITT Sheraton | 800-325-3535 |
| La Quinta | 800-531-5900 |
| Marriott | 800-228-9290 |
| Radisson | 800-333-3333 |
| Ramada | 800-2-RAMADA |
| Westin | 800-228-3000 |

### Budget

| | |
|---|---|
| Comfort Inn | 800-228-5150 |
| Days Inn | 800-325-2525 |
| Econo Lodge | 800-553-2666 |
| Howard Johnsons | 800-654-2000 |
| Motel 6 | 800-466-8356 |
| Quality Inn | 800-228-5151 |
| Red Lion Inn | 800-733-5466 |
| Super 8 | 800-800-8000 |
| Travelodge | 800-578-7878 |

Bed-and-breakfasts tend to be more homey and personal than hotels. In many cases, you're a guest at the innkeeper's home. Some are historic homes or inns decorated with antiques, quilts, art and other period furnishings; others offer simple but comfortable accommodations.

Before booking, ask whether rooms have telephones or televisions and whether bathrooms are private. Ask about breakfast, too. The meal is included in the price but may be anything from a few muffins to a multicourse feast. You may be served at a common table, a private table or in their rooms.

For more information contact:

**Arizona Association of Bed & Breakfast Inns**, 3101 N. Central #560, Phoenix, AZ 85012, tel: (602) 277-0775.

**Bed and Breakfast Innkeepers of Colorado Association**, 1102 W. Pikes Peak Avenue, Dept. T, Colorado Springs, CO 80904, tel: 800-756-2242.

**Bed and Breakfast of New Mexico**, PO Box 2805, Santa Fe, NM 87504, tel: (505) 982-3332.

**Bed and Breakfast Inns of Utah**, PO Box 3066, Park City, UT, tel: (801) 645-8068.

| | |
|---|---|
| Budget | $50 or less |
| Moderate | $50 - $100 |
| Expensive | $100 - $150 |
| Very expensive | $150+ |

## Arizona

**Betsy's Bed and Breakfast**, 1919 Rock Castle Drive, Prescott, AZ 86301, tel: (520) 445-0123. Modern redwood house set on a hillside above Prescott. Amenities: private baths, breakfast, parking. Credit cards: Visa, MasterCard. Budget to moderate.

**Cathedral Rock Lodge**, 61 Los Amigos Lane, Sedona, AZ 86336, tel: (520) 282-7608. Large country home near mountains. Amenities: private baths, some rooms with television, breakfast, parking. Credit cards: MasterCard, Visa. Moderate to expensive.

**Dierker House**, 423 W. Cherry, Flagstaff, AZ 86001, tel: (520) 774-3249. Well-appointed old home in historic district. Amenities: private and shared baths, parking, breakfast. Credit cards: MasterCard, Visa. Budget.

**Kennedy House**, 2075 Upper Red Rock Loop Road, Sedona, AZ 86336, tel: (520) 282-1624. A comfortable, contemporary home near Sedona's Red Rock Crossing. Amenities: private baths, breakfast, parking, guided nature hikes. Credit cards: MasterCard, Visa. Moderate.

**Maricopa Manor**, 15 W. Pasadena Avenue, Phoenix, AZ 85013, tel: (602) 274-6302. Spanish-style home built in the 1920s and furnished with antiques and art. Amenities: all rooms are suites with air conditioning, television and private bath; breakfast, pool, spa, gardens, parking. Credit cards: American Express, Discover, MasterCard, Visa. Moderate to expensive.

## Colorado

**Country Sunshine Bed and Breakfast**, 35130 Highway 550 North, Durango, CO 81301, tel: (970) 247-2853 or toll free 800-383-2853. Comfortable ranch home on the Animas River 12 miles north of Durango. Amenities: private baths, hot tub, breakfast, parking. Credit cards: all major. Moderate.

**Logwood Bed and Breakfast**, 35060 Highway 550, Durango, CO 81301, tel: (970) 259-4396. A comfortable, western-style log home set on 15 acres on the Animas River. Amenities: suite with fireplace and television, breakfast and deserts, fishing, hiking, parking. Credit cards: MasterCard, Visa. Moderate.

**Main Street Bed and Breakfast**, 322 Main Street, Ouray, CO 81427, tel: (970) 325-4871. Two historic homes in town with views of the San Juan Mountains; seasonal. Amenities: television, private baths, private decks, breakfast, parking, one house with kitchenettes. Credit cards: American Express, MasterCard, Visa. Moderate.

---

## New Mexico

**Adobe Abode**, 202 Chapelle, Santa Fe, NM 87501, tel: (505) 983-3133. Historic adobe home with eclectic decor three blocks from the Plaza. Amenities: television, private bath, some rooms with fires and private patios, breakfast, parking. Credit cards: Discover, MasterCard, Visa. Expensive.

**La Posada de Chimayo**, PO Box 463, Chimayo, NM 87522, tel: (505) 351-4605. A traditional adobe with brick floors and viga ceilings near a charming Hispanic village. Amenities: private baths, breakfast, fireplaces, parking. Credit cards: MasterCard, Visa (for deposit only). Moderate.

**Mabel Dodge Luhan House**, PO Box 3400, Taos, NM 87571, tel: (505) 758-9456. This lovely bed and breakfast inn is the former home of Mabel Dodge Luhan, socialite and patron of the arts whose guests included D.H. Lawrence and Georgia O'Keeffe. Amenities: parking, breakfast, hot tub, fireplaces; no in-room televisions or telephones. Credit cards: MasterCard, Visa. Moderate to very expensive.

**Water Street Inn**, 427 W. Water Street, Santa Fe, NM 87501, tel: (505) 984-1193. A comfortable, Southwestern-style inn within walking distance of the Plaza. Amenities: air conditioning, television, private baths, breakfast, fireplaces. Credit cards: American Express, MasterCard, Visa. Moderate to very expensive.

## Utah

**Bluff Bed and Breakfast**, PO Box 158, Bluff, UT 84512, tel: (801) 672-2220. Contemporary home set on 17 acres near the San Juan River in southern Utah's red-rock country. Amenities: private baths, breakfast, parking. No credit cards. Moderate.

**Seven Wives Inn**, 217 N. 100 West, St George, UT 84770, tel: (801) 628-3737. A comfortable inn located in town near the Brigham Young house and within driving distance of Zion and Bryce Canyon national parks. Amenities: air conditioning, television, private bath, breakfast, pool, parking. Credit cards: all major. Moderate to expensive.

**O'Toole's Under the Eaves Guest House**, 980 Zion Park Blvd, Springdale, UT 84767, tel: (801) 772-3457. Historic stone cottage near the entrance to Zion National Park. Amenities: air conditioning, private and shared baths, breakfast, parking. Credit cards: Discover, MasterCard, Visa. Moderate to expensive.

---

## Dude Ranches

Dude ranches range from working cattle operations with basic accommodation to rustic resorts with swimming pools, tennis courts and other amenities. Most ranches offer horseback riding and lessons, guided pack trips, entertainment like rodeos, square dances and storytellers and plenty of hearty food.

For additional information and an extensive list of dude ranches contact: **Dude Ranchers Association**, PO Box 471, LaPorte, CO 80535, tel: (303) 223-8440.

The price guide indicates weekly rates per person including lodging, meals and activities. Rates may vary depending on season and size of party. Some ranches offer daily rates and family or children's rates.

| | |
|---|---|
| $ | $500–1,000 |
| $$ | $1,000–1,500 |
| $$$ | $1,500–2,000 |
| $$$$ | $2,000–2,500 |
| $$$$$ | $2,500+ |

## Arizona

**Circle Z Ranch**, PO Box 194, Patagonia, AZ 85624, tel: (520) 287-2091. Adobe cottages 60 miles south of Tucson at the foot of the Patagonia and Santa Rita mountains. Amenities: horseback riding and instruction, pool, tennis courts, cookouts, pack trips. No credit cards. $

**Grapevine Canyon Ranch**, PO Box 302, Pearce, AZ 85625, tel: (520) 826-3185 or toll free 800-245-9202. In southern Arizona's Dragoon Mountains, this is a working cattle ranch with guest cabins and *casitas*. Amenities: horseback riding and instruction, pool, hot tub, cookouts, fishing, entertainment. Credit cards: American Express, MasterCard, Visa. $–$$

**Lazy K Bar Guest Ranch**, 8401 N. Scenic Drive, Tucson, AZ 85743, tel: (520) 744-3050 or toll free 800-321-7018. Guests stay in cabins in the Tucson Mountains overlooking the Santa Cruz Valley. Amenities: horseback riding and instruction, pool, spa, tennis courts, volleyball, basketball and other activities, ranch store, entertainment. Credit cards: MasterCard, Visa. $

**Tanque Verde Guest Ranch**, 14301 E. Speedway Blvd, Tucson, AZ 85748, tel: (520) 296-6275 or 800-234-3833. Guests are housed in *casitas* at this former stagecoach station situated at the base of the Rincon Mountains. Amenities: horseback riding and instruction, pools, tennis, cookouts, outdoor sports, entertainment. Credit cards: American Express, MasterCard, Visa. $$$–$$$$$

**White Stallion Ranch**, 9251 W. Twin Peaks Road, Tucson, AZ 85743, tel: (520) 297-0252 or toll free 800-782-5546. A 3,000-acre cattle ranch bordering Saguaro National Park in southern Arizona. Amenities: horseback riding, pool, tennis, hot tub, petting zoo, hayrides, cookouts. No credit cards. $$–$$$$

---

## Colorado

**Colorado Trails Ranch**, 12161 County Road 240, Durango, CO 81301, tel: (970) 247-5055 or toll free 800-323-3833. Cabins in the San Juan Mountains, southwest Colorado. Amenities: horseback riding and instruction, tennis, pool, shooting, water skiing, river rafting, fishing, children's counselors. Credit cards: all major. $$$$–$$$$$

Lake Mancos Ranch, 42688 County Road, Mancos, CO 81328, tel: (970) 533-7900. Cabins and ranch house at the base of the La Plata Mountains near Mesa Verde National Park. Amenities: horseback riding and instruction, pool, hot tub, fishing, children's program, entertainment. Credit cards: MasterCard, Visa. $$

Powderhorn Guest Ranch, Powderhorn, CO 81243, tel: (970) 641-0220 or toll free 800-786-1220. Log cabins in the historic Powderhorn Valley near Gunnison surrounded by wilderness areas. Amenities: horseback riding and lessons, fishing, pool, spa, rafting, cookouts, entertainments. No credit cards. $

Wilderness Trails Ranch, 1776 County Road 302, Durango, CO 81301, tel: (970) 247-0722 or toll free 800-527-2624. The ranch offers authentic log cabins surrounded by wilderness area in the Pine River Valley near Lake Vallecito. Amenities: horseback riding and instruction, pack trips, pool, waterskiing, fishing, children's program, playground, recreation room, guided trip to Mesa Verde, rafting, boating, entertainment. Credit cards: Discover, MasterCard, Visa. $$

Wit's End Guest Ranch and Resort, 254 County Road 500, Bayfield, CO 81122, tel: (970) 884-4113. Located in the Vallecito Valley northeast of Durango, the ranch offers beautifully appointed log cabins and a main lodge. Amenities: horseback riding and instruction, pool, tennis, hot tubs, fishing, biking, pack trips, entertainment, guided hikes, children's program. Credit cards: American Express, Discover, MasterCard, Visa. $$$$$

## New Mexico

The Lodge at Chama, PO Box 127, Chama, NM 87520, tel: (505) 756-2133. A rustic but elegant lodge with private rooms located about 100 miles north of Santa Fe. Amenities: guided horseback riding, fishing, hunting, shooting. Credit cards: MasterCard, Visa. $$$$

Los Pinos Ranch, Route 3, Box 8, Tererro, NM 87573, tel: (505) 757-6213 or (winter) 505-757-6679. The ranch offers a rustic lodge and cabins on the Pecos River in the Sangre de Cristo Mountains. Amenities: horseback riding, fishing, hiking. No credit cards. $

## Utah

Pack Creek Ranch, PO Box 1270, Moab, UT 84532, tel: (801) 259-5505. A 300-acre ranch in the foothills of the La Sal Mountains near Arches and Canyonlands national parks. Amenities: horseback riding, pack trips, hiking, pool, fishing. Credit cards: American Express, Discover, MasterCard, Visa. $ (Riding extra.)

## Camping

Most tent and RV sites in national and state parks and in national forests are available on a first-come, first-served basis. Arrive as early as possible to reserve a campsite. Campgrounds fill early during the busy summer season (spring, fall and winter in the desert parks). A limited number of campsites in the most popular parks may be reserved in advance. Contact the parks for information on availability. Fees are usually charged for campsites. Backcountry permits may be required for wilderness hiking and camping.

There are hundreds of private campgrounds, too, some with swimming pools, RV hookups, showers and other facilities. The largest network is Kampgrounds of America (KOA), PO Box 30558, Billings, MT 59114, tel: (406) 248-7444.

# Eating Out

## What To Eat

Southwestern cuisine is as varied and interesting as the land itself. A single dish may include a savory mix of red and green chilies, yellow and blue cornmeal, a dark brown mound of beans with snowy sour cream, a pile of shredded lettuce, an improbably neon-green whip called *guacamole* with salty fried tortilla chips stuck in like banners, and a parti-colored sauce of red tomatoes, green chilies, coriander and white onions.

A couple of local customs to keep in mind: you may be asked by your waiter if you prefer red or green chilies (green tends to be a bit milder); and traditional New Mexican meals usually are served with *sopapillas*, a puffy fried dough eaten with honey.

In addition to the native dishes, large towns like Santa Fe, Albuquerque, Phoenix and Tucson offer everything from pasta parlors to sushi. Many of the most interesting restaurants have built their reputations on blending Southwestern flavors with a variety of international cuisines. Still, it's hard to go wrong with the traditional repertoire: *enchiladas, tacos, burritos, posole, guacamole* and lots of red-hot chilies.

## Where To Eat

The price guide indicates the approximate cost of dinner for two excluding beverages, tax and tip. The standard tip is 15 percent, more for exceptional service or a large party. In some cases, the gratuity may be included in the bill.

Inexpensive    less than $40
Moderate       $40–100
Expensive      $100+

## Arizona

Cafe Express, Flagstaff, AZ, tel: (520) 774-0541. Lively and popular with hip college crowd; good baked goods and vegetarian dishes. Inexpensive.

Cafe Terra Cotta, 4310 N. Campbell Avenue, Tucson, AZ, tel: (520) 577-8100. Imaginative Southwestern dishes with a nouvelle influence. Inexpensive to moderate.

Christopher's, 2398 E. Camelback Road, Phoenix, AZ, tel: (602) 957-3214. Formal, intimate, contemporary French dining. Will impress your business associates, in-laws or date; the bistro is less expensive and somewhat less formal. Moderate to expensive.

Dakota Cafe, 6541 E. Tanque Verde Road, Tucson, AZ, tel: (520) 298-7188. Popular cafe with broad menu and vegetarian dishes. Inexpensive.

Depot Cantina, 300 S. Ash Avenue, Tempe, AZ, tel: (602) 966-6677. A fun place in a renovated train station with tasty Mexican standards. Inexpensive.

Ed Debevic's Short Orders Deluxe, 2102 E. Highland, Phoenix, AZ, tel: (602) 956-2760. Old-fashioned, bustling diner with the usual, almost-like-mom's fare – burgers, fries, meatloaf, etc. Inexpensive.

**El Minuto**, 354 S. Main Avenue, Tucson, AZ, tel: (520) 882-4145. Spicy and filling Mexican food in a stripped-down *cantina* that is popular with locals. Inexpensive.

**Janos**, 150 N. Main Avenue, Tucson, AZ. 520-884-9426. Inventive French-Southwestern cuisine served in a lovely, 19th-century adobe. Moderate.

**Jean Claude's Petit Cafe**, 7340 E. Shoeman Lane, Scottsdale, AZ, tel: (602) 947-5288. Contemporary French bistro good for a romantic night out. Inexpensive to moderate.

**Rox Sand**, 2594 E. Camelback Road, Phoenix, AZ, tel: (602) 381-0444. A hip, fashionable restaurant offering imaginative combinations of international cuisines. Moderate.

**The Stockyards**, 5001 E. Washington Street, Phoenix, AZ, tel: (602) 273-7378. Steakhouse with 19th-century decor and Old West specialties like Rocky Mountain Oysters (the bits you remove to make a bull into a steer) and excellent steaks. Inexpensive to moderate.

**Shogun**, 12615 N. Tatum Blvd, Scottsdale, AZ, tel: (602) 953-3264. A fine choice for sushi, tempura and other Japanese specialties when you tire of Southwestern cooking. Inexpensive to moderate.

**Tomaso's**, 3225 E. Camelback Road, Phoenix, AZ, tel: (602) 956-0836. Fine Italian food in a friendly, comfortable setting. Inexpensive to moderate.

**Vincent on Camelback**, 3930 E. Camelback Road, Phoenix, AZ, tel: (602) 224-0225. Elegant but not stuffy, this is regarded by some as one of the finest restaurants in the Southwest, combining French and Mexican tastes. Moderate.

## Colorado

**Floradora**, 103 W. Colorado Avenue, Telluride, CO, tel: (970) 728-3888. Continental and some Southwestern dishes in a warm, Victorian-style setting. Inexpensive to moderate.

**Henry's**, Strater Hotel, 699 Main Avenue, Durango, CO 81301, tel: (970) 247-4431 or toll free 800-247-4431. Hotel restaurant featuring steak and seafood in a fine Victorian building. Inexpensive to moderate.

**Palace Grill**, 1 Depot Place, Durango, CO, tel: (970) 247-2018. Filling American dishes served in a historic Victorian building. Inexpensive to moderate.

## New Mexico

**Apple Tree**, 123 Bent Street, Taos, NM, tel: (505) 758-1900. Fine Southwestern and International cuisine in a romantic setting. Moderate.

**Assets Grill Brewing Company**, 6910 Montgomery NE, Albuquerque, NM, tel: (505) 889-6400. A mixture of ethnic cuisines with a New Mexican twist in a lively country setting; a great selection of beers, including a brew made at the restaurant. Inexpensive.

**Cafe Pasqual's**, 121 Don Gaspar Street, Santa Fe, NM, tel: (505) 983-9340. Innovative International/Southwestern cuisine very popular with both residents and tourists. Moderate.

**Conrad's**, 125 2nd Street NW, Albuquerque, NM 87102, tel: (505) 242-9090. Hotel restaurant serving imaginative Mexican fare in comfy modern atmosphere. Inexpensive.

**Coyote Cafe**, 132 W. Water Street, Santa Fe, NM, tel: (505) 983-1615. American and New Mexican fare served in an imaginatively decorated site (a former bus depot); extremely popular due in part to the owner's cookbooks. Moderate.

**La Traviata**, 95 W. Marcy Street, Santa Fe, NM, tel: (505) 984-1091. Fine Italian food in a boisterous atmosphere. Moderate.

**M & J Sanitary Tortilla Factory**, 403 2nd Street SW, Albuquerque, NM, tel: (505) 242-4890. Authentic and filling Mexican dishes in a casual diner-like setting. Inexpensive.

**Michael's Kitchen**, 305 Paseo del Pueblo Norte, Taos, NM, tel: (505) 758-4178. Warm, homey place with a tasty selection of filling American and New Mexican standards. Inexpensive.

**Monte Vista Fire Station**, 3201 Central Avenue NE, Albuquerque, NM, tel: (505) 255-2424. Carefully prepared American cuisine in a restored firehouse. Inexpensive to moderate.

**Natural Cafe**, 1494 Cerrillos Road, Santa Fe, NM, tel: (505) 983-1411. Healthy and vegetarian menu served in a cozy, arty setting. Inexpensive.

**Pink Adobe**, 406 Old Santa Fe Trail, Santa Fe, NM, tel: (505) 983-7712. A very popular restaurant in a lovely historic building featuring New Mexican and Continental dishes and a good wine list. Inexpensive to moderate.

**Rancho de Chimayo**, Chimayo, NM, tel: (505) 351-4444. An old-fashioned hacienda-style restaurant with traditional New Mexican fare. A favorite for travelers visiting the Santuario de Chimayo. Inexpensive.

**Santacafe**, 231 Washington Avenue, Santa Fe, NM, tel: (505) 984-1788. Understated elegance is the theme at this historic adobe featuring a wide-ranging menu with a New Mexican flare. Moderate.

**66 Diner**, 1405 Central Avenue NE, Albuquerque, NM, tel: (505) 247-1421. Located on old Route 66 near the University of New Mexico, this spiffy diner is a walk down memory lane. Inexpensive.

**Tomasita's**, 500 S. Guadalupe Street, Santa Fe, NM, tel: (505) 983-5721. A spicy selection of New Mexican dishes at the former Santa Fe Railroad terminal; lively and informal, popular with both locals and tourists. Inexpensive.

**Truchas Mountain Cafe**, Highway 76, Truchas, NM, tel: (505) 689-2444. Casual, family restaurant with hearty Mexican food; a great stop on the High Road to Taos. Inexpensive.

**Villa Fontana**, Highway 522, Taos, NM, tel: (505) 758-5800. Gourmet northern Italian cuisine at a lovely country restaurant. Moderate.

**Wild and Natural Cafe**, 812 Paseo del Pueblo Norte, Taos, NM, tel: (505) 751-0480. A savory selection of vegetarian dishes, with Southwestern and Asian specialties. Inexpensive.

## Utah

**Adriana's Restaurant**, S. 100 West, Cedar City, UT, tel: (801) 865-1234. Romantic old-English atmosphere with steaks, seafood and pasta. Inexpensive to moderate.

**Bit and Spur Saloon and Mexican Restaurant**, 1212 Zion Park Blvd, Springdale, UT, tel: (801) 772-3498. Fine Mexican food in a casual atmosphere near the entrance to Zion National Park. Inexpensive.

**Capitol Reef Cafe**, 360 W. Main Street, Torrey, UT, tel: (801) 425-3271. Friendly restaurant with fresh and natural foods and plenty of vegetarian dishes. Inexpensive.

**New Garden Cafe**, 138 S. Main, Hurricane, UT, tel: (801) 635-9825. An informal eatery with tasty burgers, enchiladas, pizza and a few choices for vegetarians. Inexpensive.

**Libby Lorraines**, 1035 S. Valley View Drive, St George, UT, tel: (801) 673-7190. Casual Italian. Inexpensive.

**Grand Old Ranch House**, 1266 N. Highway 191, Moab, UT, tel: (801) 259-5753. A steakhouse with some seafood and German specialties; the building is listed on the National Register of Historic Places. Inexpensive.

**Sunbonnet Cafe**, Highway 63, Bluff, UT, tel: (801) 672-2201. A small-town diner with burgers, fries and Navajo Tacos. Inexpensive.

## Drinking

Laws governing liquor sales vary from state to state. The legal drinking age in New Mexico, Utah, Colorado and Nevada is 21. The drinking age in Arizona is 19, and in Texas it's 18.

In Arizona and Las Vegas, Nevada, state laws permit sale of liquor by the bottle or glass in any licensed establishment. In New Mexico, bottled liquor is sold in drug, grocery and liquor stores and sold by the glass in bars and other licensed establishments. In Texas, liquor is sold by the bottle in packaged goods stores and by the glass in licensed establishments. In Colorado, you can find bottled liquor in liquor stores and most drug stores, which also may sell by the glass, with some restrictions.

Liquor sales in Utah are made at state licensed stores. All package stores (where liquor is not consumed on the premises) are closed on Sunday and holidays. Many restaurants and hotels are licensed to sell minibottles and "splits" of wine. This is the procedure by which you purchase liquor personally, then return to your table to order mixers or "setups." Liquor purchased at a restaurant store may not be taken away. Beer is available at most restaurants, grocery and drug stores seven days a week.

## Bars & Nightclubs

### Arizona

**All That Jazz**, 333 E. Jefferson Street, Phoenix, AZ, tel: (602) 256-1437. Upscale but casual jazz club with bar and fine dining.

**Char's Has the Blues**, 4631 N. 7th Avenue, Phoenix, AZ, tel: (602) 230-0205. Popular blues club with atmospheric setting.

**Chuckwalla's**, 2000 Westcourt Way, Tempe, AZ, tel: (602) 225-9000. Upscale club with mellow live music.

**Orbit Cafe**, Central and Camelback Road, Phoenix, AZ, tel: (602) 265-2354. Low-key restaurant; live jazz.

**Phoenix Live**, 455 N. 3rd Street, Phoenix, AZ, tel: (602) 252-2112. A large and lively singles club with lots of dancing and music.

**Rhythm Room**, 1019 E. Indian School Road, Phoenix, AZ, tel: (602) 265-4842. Rollicking blues club with fine local and touring acts.

**Rustler's Roost**, 777 S. Pointe Parkway, Phoenix, AZ, tel: (602) 431-6474. Bar and restaurant with live country music and dancing.

**Timothy's**, 6335 N. 16th Street, Phoenix, AZ, tel: (602) 277-7634. Bar and restaurant with live contemporary jazz.

**Toolie's Country**, 43rd Avenue and Thomas Road, Phoenix, AZ, tel: (602) 272-3100. Live country music and dancing at a western saloon.

---

### New Mexico

**Adobe Bar**, 125 Paseo del Pueblo Norte, Taos, NM, tel: (505) 758-2233. A convivial spot for light dining while listening to local musicians.

**Bull Ring Lounge**, 414 Old Santa Fe Trail, Santa Fe, NM, tel: (505) 983-3328. Bar and restaurant with dancing, popular with singles.

**Caravan East**, 7605 Central Avenue NE, Albuquerque, NM, tel: (505) 265-7877. Live country-and-western music in a lively honky-tonk setting.

**El Farol**, 808 Canyon Road, Santa Fe, NM, tel: (505) 983-9912. Live blues and rock bands on the fashionable Canyon Road.

**El-Rey**, 624 Central Street, Albuquerque, NM, tel: (505) 242-9300. A wide range of musical acts from country to rock play in this funky old theater.

**Kachina Cabaret**, 413 Paseo del Pueblo Norte, Taos, NM, tel: (505) 758-2275. A well-known spot for hearing local and touring country and Hispanic bands.

**Midnight Rodeo**, 4901 McCloud NE, Albuquerque, tel: (505) 888-0100. Country-and-western mecca with a huge dance floor, several bars and well-known bands.

**Sagebrush Inn**, Paseo del Pueblo Sur, Taos, NM, tel: (505) 758-2254. Rock and country acts nightly.

# Culture

## Museums

### Arizona

**The Amerind Foundation**, PO Box 400, Dragoon Road, Dragoon, AZ 85609, tel: (520) 586-3666. Daily 10am–4pm.

**Arcosanti**, HC-74, PO Box 4136, Mayer, AZ 86333, tel: (520) 632-7135. Daily 9am–5pm.

**Arizona Historical Society**, 949 E. Second Street, Tucson, AZ 85719, tel: (520) 628-5774. Monday to Saturday 10am–4pm, Sunday noon–4pm.

**Arizona Mineral Resource Museum**, 1502 W. Washington, Phoenix, AZ, tel: (602) 255-3791. Monday to Friday 9am–5pm, Saturday 1–5pm.

**Arizona Science Center**, 147 E. Adams Street, Phoenix, AZ, tel: (602) 256-9388. Monday to Saturday 9am–5pm, Sunday noon–5pm.

**Arizona Sonoran Desert Museum**, 2021 N. Kinney Road, Tucson, AZ 85743, tel: (520) 883-1380. Daily 8.30am–5pm.

**Arizona State Museum**, University of Arizona, Park Avenue at University, Tucson, AZ 85721, tel: (520) 621-6281. Monday to Saturday 10am–5pm, Sunday noon–5pm.

**Bisbee Mining and Historical Museum**, 5 Copper Queen Plaza, PO Box 14, Bisbee, AZ 85603, tel: (520) 432-7071. Daily 10am–4pm.

**Desert Caballeros Western Museum**, 21 N. Frontier Street, Wickenburg, AZ 85390, tel: (520) 684-2272. Open Monday to Saturday 10am–4pm, Sunday 1–4pm.

**Fremont House Museum**, Tucson Convention Center Complex, Tucson, AZ 85701, tel: (520) 622-0956. Wednesday to Saturday 10am–4pm.

**Heard Museum**, 22 E. Monte Vista Road, Phoenix, AZ 85004, tel: (602) 252-8848. Monday to Saturday 9.30am–5pm, until 9pm on Wednesday, Sunday noon–5pm.

**John Wesley Powell Memorial Museum**, 6 Lake Powell Blvd, Page, AZ 86040, tel: (520) 645-9496. Monday to Friday 9am–5pm.

**Kitt Peak National Observatory**, 950 N. Cherry, Tucson, AZ 85719, tel: (520) 318-8000. Daily 10am–3.30pm.

**Mesa Southwest Museum**, 53 N. MacDonald, Mesa, AZ 85201, tel: (602) 644-2230. Tuesday to Saturday 9am–6pm, Sunday noon–6pm.

**Museum of the Forest**, Gila County Historical Society, 1001 W. Main Street, Payson, AZ 85541, tel: (520) 474-3483. Wednesday to Sunday noon–4pm.

**Museum of Northern Arizona**, Fort Valley Road, Route 4, Box 720, Flagstaff, AZ 86001, tel: (520) 774-5211. Daily 9am–5pm.

**Museum of the Southwest**, 1500 N. Circle I Road, Willcox, AZ 85643, tel: (520) 384-2272. Monday to Saturday 9am–5pm, Sunday 1–5pm.

**Museum of the West**, 109 S. Third Street, Tombstone, AZ 85638, tel: (520) 457-9219. Daily 9.30am–5pm.

**Phippen Museum of Western Art**, 4701 Highway 89, Prescott, AZ 86301, tel: (520) 778-1385. Monday 10am–4pm, closed Tuesday, Wednesday to Saturday 10am–4pm, Sunday 1–4pm.

**Phoenix Art Museum**, 1625 N. Central Avenue, Phoenix, AZ, tel: (602) 257-1222. Tuesday to Saturday 10am–5pm, Sunday noon–5pm.

**Sharlot Hall Museum**, 415 W. Gurley, Prescott, AZ 86301, tel: (520) 445-3122. Tuesday to Saturday 10am–4pm, Sunday 1–5pm.

**Titan Missile Museum**, PO Box 150, Green Valley, AZ 85622, tel: (520) 791-2929. Daily 9am–4pm.

**Tucson Museum of Art**, 140 N. Main Avenue, Tucson, AZ 85701, tel: (520) 624-2333. Monday to Saturday 10am–4pm, Sunday noon–4pm.

**Zane Grey Museum**, 408 W. Main Street, Suite 8, Payson, AZ 85547, tel: (520) 474-6243. Monday to Saturday 10am–4pm.

## Colorado

**Ouray Historical Museum**, 420 6th Avenue, Ouray, CO 81427, tel: (970) 325-4576. June to September daily 9am–6pm, October to May Friday to Monday 1–4pm.

**Ute Indian Museum**, 17253 Chipeta Road, Montrose, CO 81401, tel: (970) 249-3098. Call for hours.

## Nevada

**Las Vegas Art Museum**, 6130 W. Charleston Blvd, Las Vegas, NV 89102, tel: (702) 259-4458. Tuesday to Saturday 10am–3pm, Sunday noon–3pm.

**Liberace Museum**, 1775 E. Tropicana Avenue, Las Vegas, NV, tel: (702) 798-5595. Monday to Saturday 10am–5pm, Sunday 1–5pm.

**Museum of Natural History**, 900 N. Las Vegas Blvd, Las Vegas, NV 89101, tel: (702) 384-3466. Daily 9am–4pm.

**Nevada State Museum and Historical Society**, 700 Twin Lake Drive, Las Vegas, NV 89107, tel: (702) 486-5205. Daily 9am–5pm.

## New Mexico

**Albuquerque Museum**, 2000 Mountain NW, Albuquerque, NM 87102, tel: (505) 243-7255. Tuesday to Sunday 9am–5pm.

**Billy The Kid Museum**, 1601 E. Sumner Avenue, Fort Sumner, NM 88119, tel: (505) 355-2380. Monday to Saturday 8.30am–5pm, Sunday 11am–5pm.

**D.H. Lawrence Ranch and Memorial**, Route 3, San Cristobal, NM, tel: (505) 776-2245. Call for hours.

**El Rancho de las Golondrinas**, 334 Los Pinos Road, Santa Fe, NM 87505, tel: (505) 471-2261. June to September Wednesday to Sunday 10am–4pm, April to May and October by appointment only.

**Ernest L. Blumenschein Home**, 222 Ledoux Street, Taos, NM, tel: (505) 758-0330. Daily 9am–5pm.

**Fleming Hall Museum**, Western New Mexico University, Silver City, NM 88062, tel: (505) 538-6386. Monday to Friday 9.30-4.30, Saturday to Sunday 10am–4pm.

**Governor Bent Home and Museum**, 117A Bent Street, Taos 87571, tel: (505) 758-2376. Daily 10am–5pm.

**Indian Pueblo Cultural Center**, 2401 12th Street NW, Albuquerque, NM 87102, tel: (505) 843-6950. Daily 9am–5.30pm.

**Institute of American Indian Arts Museum**, 108 Cathedral Place, Santa Fe, NM 87501, tel: (505) 988-6211. Monday to Saturday 10am–5pm, Sunday noon–5pm.

**Kit Carson Home and Museum**, 113 E. Kit Carson Road, Taos, NM 87571, tel: (505) 758-4741. Daily 9am–5pm.

**Los Alamos County Historical Museum**, 1921 Juniper Street, Los Alamos, NM 87544, tel: (505) 662-4493, Monday to Saturday 10am–4pm, Sunday 1–4pm.

**Maxwell Museum of Anthropology**, University of New Mexico, Martin Luther King Blvd & Redondo Drive, Albuquerque, NM 87131, tel: (505) 277-4404. Weekdays 9am–4pm, Saturday 10am–4pm, Sunday noon–4pm.

**Millicent Rogers Museum**, 1504 Millicent Rogers Rd, Taos, NM 87571, tel: (505) 758-2462. November to March Tuesday to Sunday 10am–5pm, April to October daily 10am–5pm.

**Museum of Fine Arts**, 107 W. Palace Avenue, Santa Fe, NM 87501, tel: (505) 827-4455. March to December daily 10am–5pm, closed on Monday January to February.

**Museum of Indian Arts and Culture**, 710 Camino Lejo, Santa Fe, NM 87501, tel: (505) 827-6344. Daily 10am–5pm.

**Museum of Int. Folk Art**, 706 Camino Lejo, Santa Fe, NM 87503, tel: (505) 827-6350. Daily 10am–5pm.

**National Atomic Museum**, PO Box 5800, Albuquerque, NM 87185, tel: (505) 284-3243. Daily 9am–5pm.

**Palace of the Governors**, 105 W. Palace Avenue, Santa Fe, NM 87501, tel: (505) 827-6483. Daily 10am–5pm.

**Pinos Altos Museum**, 33 Main Street, Pinos Altos, NM 88053, tel: (505) 388-1882. Monday to Saturday 9am–6pm, Sunday 9am–5pm.

**Santa Fe Trail Museum**, Maxwell Avenue, Springer, NM 87747, tel: (505) 483-2341. June to September Monday to Saturday 9am–4pm.

**Silver City Museum**, 312 W. Broadway, Silver City, NM 88061, tel: (505) 538-5921. Tuesday to Friday 9am–4.30pm, weekends 10am–4pm.

**Wheelwright Museum**, 704 Camino Lejo, Santa Fe, NM 87501, tel: (505) 982-4636. Monday to Saturday 10am–5pm, Sunday 1–5pm.

## Texas

**El Paso Museum of Art**, 1211 Montana Avenue, El Paso, TX 79902, tel: (915) 541-4040. Tuesday to Saturday 9am–5pm, Thursday until 9pm, Sunday 1–5pm.

**El Paso Museum of History**, 12901 Gateway West, El Paso, TX 79927, tel: (915) 858-1928. Tuesday to Sunday 9am–4.50pm.

## Utah

**Brigham Young Winter Home**, 200 N. 100 West, St George, UT 84770, tel: (801) 673-2517. Daily 9am–5pm.

**Dan O'Laurie Museum**, 118 E. Center Street, Moab, UT 84532, tel: (801) 259-7985. Monday to Thursday 3–7pm, Friday to Saturday 1–7pm.

**Daughters of the Utah Pioneers Museum – St George**, 145 N. 100 East, St George, UT 84770, tel: (801) 628-7274. Monday to Saturday 10am–5pm.

**Jacob Hamblin House**, Route 91, Santa Clara, UT 84765, tel: (801) 673-2161. Daily 9am–5pm.

**John Wesley Powell River History Museum**, State Road 91, Green River, UT 84525, tel: (801) 564-3427. Daily 9am–5pm.

## Performing Arts

### Arizona

**Arizona Theater Company**, 403 E. 14th Street, Tucson, AZ 85701, tel: (520) 884-8210.

**Ballet Arizona**, 3645 E. Indian School, Phoenix, AZ 85018, tel: (602) 381-0184.

**Phoenix Symphony**, 3707 N. 7th Street, Phoenix, AZ 85014, tel: (602) 264-6363.

**Scottsdale Center for the Arts**, 7380 E. 2nd Street, Scottsdale, AZ 8525, tel: (602) 994-2787.

**Tucson Symphony**, 443 S. Stone Avenue, Tucson, AZ 85701, tel: (502) 792-9155.

### New Mexico

**Albuquerque Civic Light Opera Association**, 4201 Ellison NE, Albuquerque, NM 87109, tel: (505) 345-6577.

**New Mexico Symphony Orchestra**, 3301 Menaul Blvd, Albuquerque, NM 87107, tel: (505) 881-9590.

**Santa Fe Symphony Orchestra**, 200 W. Marcy, Santa Fe, NM 87501, tel: (505) 983-3530.

**Santa Fe Opera**, PO Box 2408, Santa Fe, NM 87504, tel: (505) 986-5900.

### Texas

**El Paso Symphony Orchestra**, 10 Civic Center Plaza, El Paso, TX 79901, tel: (915) 532-0632.

## Native American Cultures

Cultural sensitivity is vital in Indian Country. Because some Indian people may feel uncomfortable or ambivalent about the presence of outsiders, it is very important to be on your best behavior. Below are a few "dos" and "don'ts" to keep in mind.

• Don't use racist terms. Referring to an Indian as chief, redskin, squaw, buck, Pocahontas, Hiawatha or other off-color terms is highly offensive.

• Abide by all rules and regulations while on Indian land and at Indian events. These may include prohibitions on photography, sketching, taking notes, video and audio recording. In some cases a photography fee may be required. If you wish to take an individual's picture, you must ask permission first (a gratuity of $2 or $3 may be appropriate).

• Respect all restricted areas. These are usually posted, but ask permission before hiking into wilderness or archaeological areas, driving on back roads, wandering around villages, and entering ceremonial structures.

• Try to be unobtrusive. Remember that you are a guest at Indian communities and events. Be polite and accommodating. In general, it is better to be too formal than too casual.

• Don't ask intrusive questions or interrupt during Indian ceremonies or dances. Even if an Indian event is not explicitly religious (such as a powwow), it may have a spiritual component. Show the same respect at Indian ceremonies that you would at any other religious service. At all events, try to maintain a low profile. Do not talk loudly, push to the front of a crowd, block anyone's view, or sit in chairs that do not belong to you.

• Keep in mind that many Indian people have a looser sense of time than non-Indians. You may hear jokes about "Indian time." Prepare for long delays before ceremonies.

### Arizona

**Ak Chin Indian Community**, Route 2, Box 27, Maricopa, AZ 85239, tel: (520) 568-2227.

**Cocopah Tribe**, PO Bin G, Somerton, AZ 85250, tel: (602) 627-2102.

**Colorado River Indian Tribes**, Route 1, Box 23B, Parker, AZ 85344, tel: (520) 669-9211.

**Fort McDowell Mohave-Apache Indian Community**, PO Box 17779, Fountain Hills, AZ 85268, tel: (520) 990-0995.

**Gila River Pima-Maricopa Indian Community**, PO Box 97, Sacaton, AZ 85247, tel: (520) 562-3311.

**Havasupai Tribe**, PO Box 10, Supai, AZ 86435, tel: (520) 448-2961.

**Hopi Tribe**, PO Box 123, Kykotsmovi, AZ 86039, tel: (520) 734-2445.

**Hualapai Tribe**, PO Box 179, Peach Springs, AZ 86434, tel: (520) 769-2216.

**Kaibab Band of Paiute Indians**, Tribal Affairs Building, HC 65, Box 2, Fredonia, AZ 86022, tel: (520) 643-7245.

**Navajo Nation**, PO Box 308, Window Rock, AZ 86515, tel: (520) 871-6352.

**Pascua Yaqui Tribe**, 7474 S. Camino de Oeste, Tucson, AZ 85746, tel: (520) 883-5000.

**Quechan Tribe**, PO Box 11352, Yuma, AZ 85364, tel: (619) 572-0213.

**Salt River Pima-Maricopa Indian Community**, Route 1, Box 216, Scottsdale, AZ 85256, Tel: (602) 941-7277.

**San Carlos Apache Tribe**, PO Box 0, San Carlos, AZ 85550, tel: (520) 475-2361.

**Tohono O'odham Nation**, PO Box 837, Sells, AZ 85634, tel: (520) 383-2221.

**Tonto Apache Tribe**, Tonto Reservation No. 30, Payson, AZ 85541, tel: (520) 474-5000.

**White Mountain Apache Tribe**, PO Box 700, White River, AZ 85941, tel: (520) 338-4346.

**Yavapai-Apache Tribe**, PO Box 1188, Camp Verde, AZ 86322, tel: (520) 567-3649.

### Colorado

**Southern Ute Tribe**, PO Box 737, Ignacio, CO 81137, tel: (970) 563-4525.

**Ute Mountain Ute Tribe**, Towaoc, CO 81334, tel: (970) 565-3751.

### Nevada

**Duckwater Shoshone Tribe**, PO Box 68, Duckwater, NV 89314, tel: (702) 863-0227.

**Las Vegas Paiute Tribe**, 1 Paiute Drive, Las Vegas, NV 89106, tel: (702) 386-3926.

**Lovelock Paiute Tribe**, PO Box 878, Lovelock, NV 89419, tel: (702) 273-7861.

**Paiute-Shoshone Tribe**, 8955 Mission Road, Fallon, NV 89406, tel: (702) 423-6075.

**Pyramid Lake Paiute Tribe**, PO Box 256, Nixon, NV 89424, tel: (702) 574-0140.

**Summit Lake Paiute Tribe**, PO Box 1958, Winnemucca, NV 89445, tel: (702) 623-5151.

**Te-Moak Tribe of Western Shoshone Indians**, 525 Sunset Street, Elko, NV 89801, tel: (702) 738-9251.

**Walker River Paiute Tribe**, PO Box 220, Schurz, NV 89427, tel: (702) 773-2306.

**Washoe Tribe of Nevada**, 919 Highway 395, Garnerville, NV 89410, tel: (702) 265-4191.

## New Mexico

**Acoma Pueblo**, PO Box 309, Acomita, NM 87034, tel: (505) 552-6604.

**Cochiti Pueblo**, Po Box 70, Cochiti, NM 87041, tel: (505) 465-2244.

**Isleta Pueblo**, PO Box 317, Isleta, NM 87022, tel: (505) 869-3111.

**Jemez Pueblo**, PO Box 100, Jemez, NM 87024, tel: (505) 834-7359.

**Jicarilla Apache Tribe**, PO Box 507, Dulce, NM 87528, tel: (505) 759-3242.

**Laguna Pueblo**, PO Box 194, Laguna Pueblo, NM, tel: (505) 552-6654.

**Mescalero Apache Tribe**, PO Box 176, Mescalero, NM 88340, tel: (505) 671-4495.

**Nambe Pueblo**, PO Box 117, Santa Fe, NM 87501, tel: (505) 455-2036.

**Picuris Pueblo**, PO Box 127, Penasco, NM 87553, tel: (505) 587-2519.

**Pojoaque Pueblo**, Route 11, Box 71, Santa Fe, NM 87501, tel: (505) 455-2278.

**Sandia Pueblo**, PO Box 6008, Bernalillo, NM 87004, tel: (505) 867-3317.

**San Ildefonso Pueblo**, PO Box 315-A, Santa Fe, NM 87501, tel: (505) 455-2273.

**San Juan Pueblo**, PO Box 1099, San Juan, NM 87566, tel: (505) 852-4400.

**Santa Ana Pueblo**, Star Route Box 37, Bernalillo, NM 87532, tel: (505) 867-3301.

**Santa Clara Pueblo**, PO Box 580, Espanola, NM 87532, tel: (505) 753-7326.

**Santo Domingo Pueblo**, PO Box 99, Santo Domingo, NM 87052, tel: (505) 465-2214.

**Taos Pueblo**, PO Box 1846, Taos, NM 87571, tel: (505) 758-8626.

**Tesuque Pueblo**, Route 11, Box 1, Santa Fe, NM 87501, tel: (505) 983-2667.

**Zia Pueblo**, General Delivery, San Ysidro, NM 87053, tel: (505) 867-3304.

**Zuni Pueblo**, PO Box 339, Zuni, NM 87327, tel: (505) 782-4481.

## Utah

**Paiute Indian Tribe of Utah**, 600 North 100 East, Cedar City, UT 84720, tel: (801) 586-1111.

**Ute Tribe**, PO Box 190, Fort Duchesne, UT 84026, tel: (801) 722-5141.

## Parks & Historic Sites

### Arizona

**Alamo Lake State Park**, PO Box 38, Wenden, AZ 85356, tel: (520) 669-2088.

**Apache National Forest**, PO Box 640, Springerville, AZ 85938, tel: (520) 333-4301.

**Canyon de Chelly National Monument**, PO Box 588, Chinle, AZ 86503, tel: (520) 674-5436.

**Casa Grande National Monument**, 1100 Ruins Drive, Coolidge, AZ 85228, tel: (602) 723-3172.

**Chiricahua National Monument**, Dos Cabezas Route, Box 6500, Willcox, AZ 85643, tel: (520) 824-3560.

**Coronado National Forest**, Federal Building, 300 W. Congress, Tucson, AZ 85701, tel: (520) 670-5798.

**Coronado National Memorial**, 4101 E. Montezuma Canyon Road, Hereford, AZ 85615, tel: (520) 366-5515.

**Dead Horse Ranch State Park**, 675 Deadhorse Ranch Road, Cottonwood, AZ 86326, tel: (520) 634-5283.

**Fort Bowie National Historic Site**, PO Box 158, Bowie, AZ 85605, tel: (520) 847-2500.

**Fort Verde State Historic Park**, PO Box 397, Camp Verde, AZ 86322, tel: (520) 567-3275.

**Glen Canyon National Recreation Area**, PO Box 1507, Page, AZ 86040, tel: (520) 645-2471.

**Grand Canyon National Park**, PO Box 129, Grand Canyon, AZ 86023, tel: (520) 638-7888.

**Hubbell Trading Post National Historic Site**, PO Box 150, Ganado, AZ 86505, tel: (520) 755-3475.

**Jerome State Historic Park**, PO Box D, Jerome, AZ 86331, tel: (520) 634-5381.

**Lake Havasu State Park**, 1801 Highway 95, Lake Havasu, AZ 86406, tel: (520) 855-7851.

**Lost Dutchman State Park**, Apache Junction, AZ, tel: (520) 982-4485.

**Montezuma Castle National Monument**, PO Box 219, Camp Verde, AZ 86322, tel: (520) 567-3322.

**Monument Valley Navajo Tribal Park**, Box 93, Monument Valley, UT 84536, tel: (801) 727-3287.

**Navajo National Monument**, HC 71, Box 3, Tonalea, AZ 86044-9704, tel: (520) 672-2366.

**Organ Pipe Cactus National Monument**, Route 1, Box 100, Ajo, AZ 85321, tel: (520) 387-6849.

**Patagonia Lake State Park**, PO Box 274, Patagonia, AZ 85624, tel: (520) 287-6965.

**Petrified Forest National Park**, PO Box 2217, Petrified Forest, AZ 86028, tel: (520) 524-6228.

**Picacho Peak State Park**, PO Box 275, Picacho, AZ 85241, tel: (602) 466-3183.

**Pipe Spring National Monument**, HC 65, Box 5, Fredonia, AZ 86022, tel: (520) 643-7105.

**Prescott National Forest**, 344 S. Cortez, Prescott, AZ 86302, tel: (520) 771-4700.

**Riordan State Historic Park**, 1300 S. Riordan Ranch Street, Flagstaff, AZ 86001, tel: (520) 779-4395.

**Saguaro National Park**, 3693 S. Old Spanish Trail, Tucson, AZ 85730, tel: (520) 296-8576.

**San Xavier del Bac Mission**, 1950 W. San Xavier, Tucson, AZ 85706, tel: (520) 294-2624.

**Sunset Crater National Monument**, Route 3, Box 149, Flagstaff, AZ 86004, tel: (520) 556-7042.

**Tombstone Courthouse State Historic Park**, 219 Toughnut Street, Tombstone, AZ 85638, tel: (520) 457-3311.

**Tonto National Monument**, HC 02, Box 4602, Roosevelt, AZ 85545, tel: (520) 467-2241.

**Tumacacori National Historical Park**, PO Box 67, Tumacacori, AZ 85640, tel: (520) 398-2341.

**Tuzigoot National Monument**, PO Box 68, Clarkdale, AZ 86324, tel: (520) 634-5564.

**Yuma Territorial Prison State Historic Park**, PO Box 10792, Yuma, AZ 85366, tel: (520) 783-4771.

**Walnut Canyon National Monument**, Walnut Canyon Road, Flagstaff, AZ 86004-9705, tel: (520) 526-3367.

**Wupatki National Monument**, HC 33, Box 444A, Flagstaff, AZ 86004, tel: (520) 556-7040.

## Colorado

**Black Canyon of the Gunnison National Monument**, 2233 E. Main Street, Suite 2, Montrose, CO 81401, tel: (970) 249-7036.

**Great Sand Dunes National Monument**, 11500 Highway 150, Mosca, CO 81146, tel: (719) 378-2312.

**Hovenweep National Monument**, McElmo Route, Cortez, CO 81321, tel: (970) 529-4465.

**Mesa Verde National Park**, PO Box 8, Mesa Verde National Park, CO 81330, tel: (970) 529-4465.

**Ute Mountain Tribal Park**, Ute Mountain Ute Tribe, Towaoc, CO 81334, tel: (970) 565-3751.

## Nevada

**Great Basin National Park**, Baker, NV 89311, tel: (702) 234-7331.

**Lake Mead National Recreation Area**, 601 Nevada Highway, Boulder City, NV 89005, tel: (702) 293-8907.

**Old Mormon Fort**, 908 N. Las Vegas Blvd, Las Vegas, NV, tel: (702) 486-3511.

## New Mexico

**Aztec Ruins National Monument**, PO Box 640, Aztec, NM 87410, tel: (505) 334-6174.

**Bandelier National Monument**, HCR 1, Box 1, Suite 15, Los Alamos, NM 87544-9701, tel: (505) 672-3861.

**Capulin Volcano National Monument**, PO Box 40, Capulin, NM 88414, tel: (505) 278-2201.

**Carlsbad Caverns National Park**, 3225 National Parks Highway, Carlsbad, NM 88220, tel: (505) 785-2232.

**Carson National Forest**, Forest Service Building, Taos, NM 87571, tel: (505) 758-6200.

**Cathedral of St Francis of Assisi**, 131 Cathedral Plaza, Santa Fe, NM 87501, tel: (505) 982-5619.

**Chaco Culture National Historical Park**, Star Route 4, Box 6500, Bloomfield, NM 87413, tel: (505) 786-7014.

**Cibola National Forest**, 10308 Candelaria NE, Albuquerque, NM 87112, tel: (505) 761-4650.

**Coronado State Monument and Park**, PO Box 95, Bernalillo, NM 87004, tel: (505) 867-5351.

**Cristo Rey Church**, 1120 Canyon Road, Santa Fe, NM 87501, tel: (505) 983-8528.

**El Malpais National Monument**, PO Box 939, Grants, NM 87020, tel: (505) 285-4641.

**El Morro National Monument**, Route 2, Box 43, Ramah, NM 87321, tel: (505) 783-4226.

**Fort Selden State Monument**, c/o New Mexico State Parks, 408 Galisteo, Santa Fe, NM 87501, tel: (505) 827-7465.

**Fort Sumner State Monument**, PO Box 356, Fort Sumner, NM 88119, tel: (505) 355-2573.

**Fort Union National Monument**, PO Box 127, Watrous, NM 87753, tel: (505) 425-8025.

**Gila Cliff Dwellings National Monument**, Route 11, Box 100, Silver City, NM 88061, tel: (505) 536-9461.

**Gila National Forest**, 3005 E. Camino del Bosque, Silver City, NM 88061, tel: (505) 388-8201.

**Jemez State Monument**, Route 4, Jemez, NM, tel: (505) 829-3530.

**Kit Carson Memorial State Park**, c/o New Mexico State Parks, 408 Galisteo, Santa Fe, NM 87501, tel: (505) 827-7465.

**Lincoln National Forest**, Federal Building, Alamogordo, NM 88310, tel: (505) 434-7200.

**Lincoln State Monument and National Landmark**, PO Box 36, Lincoln, NM 88388, tel: (505) 653-4372.

**Loretto Chapel**, 211 Old Santa Fe Trail, Santa Fe, NM 87501, tel: (505) 984-7971.

**Pancho Villa State Park**, c/o New Mexico State Parks, 408 Galisteo, Santa Fe, NM 87501, tel: (505) 827-7465.

**Pecos National Historical Park**, PO Box 418, Pecos, NM 87552, tel: (505) 757-6414.

**Petroglyph National Monument**, PO Box 1293, Albuquerque, NM 87103, tel: (505) 768-3316.

**Puye Cliff Dwellings**, Santa Clara Pueblo, PO Box 580, Espanola, NM 87532, tel: (505) 753-7326.

**Salinas Pueblo Missions National Monument**, PO Box 496, Mountainair, NM 87036, tel: (505) 847-2585.

**San Francisco de Asis Church**, PO Box 72, Rancho de Taos, NM 87557, tel: (505) 758-2754.

**San Miguel Mission**, 401 Old Santa Fe Trail, Santa Fe, NM, tel: (505) 983-3974.

**Santa Fe National Forest**, 1220 St Francis Drive, Santa Fe, NM 87501, tel: (505) 988-6940.

**Santuario de Chimayo**, PO Box 235, Chimayo, NM 87522, tel: (505) 351-4889.

**Santuario de Guadalupe**, 100 Guadalupe, Santa Fe, NM, tel: (505) 988-2027.

**White Sands National Monument**, PO Box 1086, Holloman Air Force Base, NM 88330, tel: (505) 479-6124.

## Utah

**Anasazi Indian Village State Park**, PO Box 1329, Boulder, UT 84716-1329, tel: (801) 335-7308.

**Arches National Park**, PO Box 907, Moab, UT 84532, tel: (801) 259-8161.

**Bryce Canyon National Park**, Bryce Canyon, UT 84717, tel: (801) 834-5322.

**Canyonlands National Park**, 2282 SW Resource Blvd, Moab, UT 84532, tel: (801) 259-7164.

**Capitol Reef National Park**, Torrey, UT 84775, tel: (801) 425-3791.

**Cedar Breaks National Monument**, 82 N. 100 East, Cedar City, UT 84720, tel: (801) 586-9451.

**Coral Pink Sand Dunes State Park**, PO Box 95, Kanab, UT 84741, tel: (801) 874-2408.

**Dead Horse Point State Park**, PO Box 609, Moab, UT 84532, tel: (801) 259-6511.

**Edge of the Cedars State Park**, 660 W. 400 North, Blanding, UT 84511, tel: (801) 678-2238.

**Fremont Indian State Park**, 11550 Clear Creek Canyon Road, Sevier, UT 84766, tel: (801) 527-4631.

**Glen Canyon National Recreation Area**, PO Box 1507, Page, AZ 86040, tel: (602) 645-2471.

**Golden Spike National Historic Site**, PO Box 897, Brigham City, UT 84302-0923, tel: (801) 471-2209.

**Iron Mission State Park**, 585 N. Main, Cedar City, UT 84720, tel: (801) 586-9290.

**Natural Bridges National Monument**, Box 1, Lake Powell, UT 84533, tel: (801) 259-5174.

**Zion National Park**, Springdale, UT 84767-1099, tel: (801) 772-3256.

## Texas

**Big Bend National Park**, TX 79834, tel: (915) 477-2251.

**Guadalupe Mountains National Park**, HC 60, Box 400, Salt Flat, TX 79847, tel: (915) 828-3251.

## Zoos

**Phoenix Zoo**, 455 N. Galvin Parkway, Phoenix, AZ 85008, tel: (602) 273-1341.
**Rio Grande Zoological Park**, 903 10th Street SW, Albuquerque, NM 87102, tel: (505) 843-7413.

## Historic Railroads

**Cumbres & Toltec Scenic Railroad**, PO Box 789, Chama, NM 87520, tel: (505) 756-2151. Daily late May to mid October.
**Durango & Silverton Narrow Gauge Railroad**, 479 Main Avenue, Durango, CO 81301, tel: (303) 247-2733. Daily year-round.
**Grand Canyon Railway**, 123 N. San Francisco Street, Suite 210, Flagstaff, AZ 86001, tel: (520) 773-1976. Daily year-round.

## Other Attractions

**Old Tucson Studios**, 201 S. Kinney Road, Tucson, AZ 85746, tel: (520) 883-0100.

## Casinos

There are over 50 casinos in Las Vegas. Below are some of the largest.
**Bally's**, 3645 Las Vegas Blvd S, Las Vegas 89109, tel: (702) 739-4111 or toll free 800-634-3434.
**Barbary Coast**, 3595 Las Vegas Blvd S, Las Vegas, NV 89109, tel: (702) 737-7111 or toll free 800-634-6755.
**Caesars Palace**, 3570 Las Vegas Blvd S, Las Vegas, NV 89109, tel: (702) 731-7110 or toll free 800-634-6661.
**Circus Circus**, 2880 Las Vegas Blvd S, Las Vegas, NV 89109, tel: (702) 734-0410 or toll free 800-634-3450.
**Excalibur**, 3850 Las Vegas Blvd S, Las Vegas, NV 99109, tel: (702) 597-7777 or toll free 800-937-7777.
**Flamingo**, 3555 Las Vegas Blvd S, Las Vegas, NV 89109, tel: (702) 733-3111 or toll free 800-732-2111.
**Four Queens**, 202 Fremont Street, Las Vegas, NV 89101, tel: (702) 385-4011 or toll free 800-634-6045.
**Golden Nugget**, 129 E. Fremont Street, Las Vegas, NV 89101, tel: (702) 385-7111 or 800-634-3454.
**Harrah's**, 3475 Las Vegas Blvd S, Las Vegas, NV 89109, tel: (702) 369-5000 or toll free 800-634-6785.

**Jackie Gaughan's**, 1 Main Street, Las Vegas, NV 89101, tel: (702) 386-2110 or toll free 800-634-6575.
**Luxor**, 3900 Las Vegas Blvd S, Las Vegas, NV 81119, tel: (702) 262-4000 or toll free 800-288-1000.
**MGM Grand**, 3799 Las Vegas Blvd S, Las Vegas, NV 89109, tel: (702) 891-7777 or toll free 800-929-1111.
**Mirage**, 3400 Las Vegas Blvd S, Las Vegas, NV 89109, tel: (702) 791-7111 or toll free 800-627-6667.
**Sands**, 3355 Las Vegas Blvd S, Las Vegas, NV 89109, tel: (702) 733-5000 or toll free 800-634-6901.
**Showboat**, 2800 Fremont Street, Las Vegas, NV 89104, tel: (702) 385-9123 or toll free 800-826-2800.
**Treasure Island**, 3300 Las Vegas Blvd S, Las Vegas, NV 89109, tel: (702) 894-7111 or toll free 800-944-7444.
**Tropicana**, 3801 Las Vegas Blvd S, Las Vegas, NV 89109, tel: (702) 739-2222 or toll free 800-634-4000.

## Calendar of Events

### JANUARY

**Arizona National Livestock Show**, 1826 W. McDowell Road, Phoenix, AZ 85007, tel: (602) 258-8568.
**Parada del Sol and Rodeo**, Scottsdale Chamber of Commerce, 7343 Scottsdale Mall, Scottsdale, AZ 85251, tel: (602) 945-8481.
**Phoenix Open Golf Tournament**, Scottsdale Chamber of Commerce, 7343 Scottsdale Mall, Scottsdale, AZ 85251, tel: (602) 945-8481.
**San Ildefonso Feast Day**, San Ildefonso Pueblo, PO Box 315-A, Santa Fe, NM 87501, tel: (505) 455-2273.
**Snowdown in Durango and Purgatory**, Durango Chamber Resort Association, 111 S. Camino del Rio, Durango, CO 81301, tel: (970) 247-0312.
**Southwestern Livestock Show and Rodeo**, PO Box 10239, El Paso, TX 79993, tel: (915) 532-1401.
**Turtle Dance**, Taos Pueblo, PO Box 1846, Taos, NM 87571, tel: (505) 758-8626.

### FEBRUARY

**Las Vegas International Marathon**, Las Vegas Convention and Visitors Authority, Convention Center, 3150 Paradise Road, Las Vegas, NV 89109, tel: (702) 892-0711 or toll free 800-332-5333.

**Los Comanches Dance**, Taos Pueblo, PO Box 1846, Taos, NM 87571, tel: (505) 758-8626.
**O'odham Tash Indian Celebration**, Tohono O'odham Nation, PO Box 837, Sells, AZ 85634, tel: (520) 383-2221.
**Tucson Rodeo – La Fiesta de los Vaqueros**, Tucson Convention & Visitors Bureau, 130 S. Scott Avenue, Tucson, AZ 85701, tel: (520) 624-1817.

### MARCH

**Heard Museum Indian Fair and Market**, 22 E. Monte Vista Road, Phoenix, AZ 85004, tel: (602) 252-8848.
**San Jose Feast Day**, Laguna Pueblo, PO Box 194, Laguna Pueblo, NM, tel: (505) 552-6654.
**St George Arts Festival**, Color Country, 906 N. 1400 West, St George, UT 84771, tel: (801) 628-4171 or toll free 800-233-8824.

### APRIL

**Albuquerque Founder's Day**, Albuquerque Convention and Visitors Bureau, PO Box 26866, Albuquerque, NM 87125, tel: (505) 243-3696 or toll free 800-284-2282.
**Gathering of Nations Powwow**, Albuquerque Convention and Visitors Bureau, PO Box 26866, Albuquerque, NM 87125, tel: (505) 243-3696 or toll free 800-284-2282.
**Institute of American Indian Arts Powwow**, 1369 Cerrillos Road, Santa Fe, NM 87501, tel: (505) 988-6463.
**San Xavier Pageant and Fiesta**, Tucson Convention & Visitors Bureau, 130 S. Scott Avenue, Tucson, AZ 85701, tel: (520) 624-1817.

### MAY

**Buckskinner Rendezvous**, Arizona Office of Tourism, 1100 W. Washington Street, Phoenix, AZ 85007, tel: (602) 542-8687 or toll free 800-842-8257.
**Cinco de Mayo Celebration**, Albuquerque Convention and Visitors Bureau, PO Box 26866, Albuquerque, NM 87125, tel: (505) 243-3696 or toll free 800-284-2282.
**Fiesta de Santa Fe Baile de Mayo**, Santa Fe Convention & Visitors Bureau, PO Box 909, Santa Fe, NM 87501, tel: (505) 984-6760.
**Iron Horse Bicycle Classic**, Durango Chamber Resort Association, 111 S. Camino del Rio, Durango, CO 81301, tel: (970) 247-0312.

**Santa Cruz Feast Day**, Taos Pueblo, PO Box 1846, Taos, NM 87571, tel: (505) 758-8626.

**Telluride Mountain Film Festival**, Telluride Chamber Resort Assocation, 666 W. Colorado Avenue, Telluride, CO 81435, tel: (970) 728-3041.

## JUNE

**Durango Pro. Rodeo Series**, Durango Chamber Resort Association, 111 S. Camino del Rio, Durango, CO 81301, tel: (970) 247-0312.

**Fort Union Trading Post Rendezvous**, Fort Union Trading Post National Historic Site, RR 3, Box 71, Williston, ND 58801, tel: (701) 572-9083.

**Old Fort Days**, Fort Sumner State Monument, PO Box 356, Fort Sumner, NM 88119, tel: (505) 355-2573.

**Old Miners Day, Chloride**, Arizona Office of Tourism, 1100 W. Washington Street, Phoenix, AZ 85007, tel: (602) 542-8687 or toll free 800-842-8257.

**San Antonio Feast Day–Comanche Dance**, San Ildefonso Pueblo, PO Box 315-A, Santa Fe, NM 87501, tel: (505) 455-2273.

**San Felipe Fiesta**, Albuquerque Convention and Visitors Bureau, PO Box 26866, Albuquerque, NM 87125, tel: (505) 243-3696 or toll-free 800-284-2282.

**San Juan Feast Day**, Taos Pueblo, PO Box 1846, Taos, NM 87571, tel: (505) 758-8626.

**Santa Fe Trail Rendezvous**, Raton Chamber of Commerce, PO Box 1211, Raton, NM 87740, tel: (505) 445-3689.

**Telluride Bluegrass Festival**, Telluride Chamber Resort Association, 666 W. Colorado Avenue, Telluride, CO 81435, tel: (970) 728-3041.

**Territorial Days**, Prescott Chamber of Commerce, 117 W. Goodwin Street, Prescott, AZ 86302, tel: (520) 445-2000.

## JULY

**Days of '47 Celebrations**, Utah Travel Council, Council Hall, Capitol Hill, Salt Lake City, UT 84114, tel: 800-200-1160.

**Dixie Folkfest**, Color Country, 906 N. 1400 West, St George, UT 84771. (801) 628-4171 or toll free 800-233-8824.

**Durango Cowgirl Classic**, Durango Chamber Resort Association, 111 S. Camino del Rio, Durango, CO 81301, tel: (970) 247-0312.

**El Paso Festival**, El Paso Arts Alliance, 333 E. Missouri Street, El Paso, TX 79901, tel: (915) 533-1700.

**Frontier Days and World's Oldest Rodeo**, Prescott Chamber of Commerce, 117 W. Goodwin Street, Prescott, AZ 86302, tel: (520) 445-2000.

**Mescalero Festival**, Mescalero Apache Tribe, PO Box 176, Mescalero, NM 88340, tel: (505) 671-4495.

**Soldiering on the Santa Fe Trail**, Fort Union National Monument, PO Box 127, Watrous, NM 87753, tel: (505) 425-8025.

**Spanish Market**, Spanish Colonial Arts Society, PO Box 1611, Santa Fe, NM 87504, tel: (505) 983-4038.

**Taos Fiesta**, Taos County Chamber of Commerce, PO Drawer I, Taos, NM 87571, tel: (505) 758-3873 or toll free 800-732-8267.

**Taos Pueblo Powwow**, PO Box 1846, Taos, NM 87571, tel: (505) 758-8626.

**Utah Shakespearean Festival**, Southern Utah University, Cedar City, UT, tel: (801) 586-7878.

## AUGUST

**Fiesta de San Agustin**, Tucson Convention & Visitors Bureau, 130 S. Scott Avenue, Tucson, AZ 85701, tel: (520) 624-1817.

**Flagstaff Festival in the Pines**, Flagstaff Convention and Visitors Bureau, 211 W. Aspen Avenue, Flagstaff, AZ 86001, tel: (520) 779-7611.

**Indian Market**, Santa Fe Convention & Visitor Bureau, PO Box 909, Santa Fe, NM 87501, tel: (505) 984-6760.

**Old Lincoln Days**, New Mexico Tourism, Lamy Building, 491 Old Santa Fe Trail, Santa Fe, NM 87503, tel: toll-free 800-545-2040.

**Palace Mountain Man Rendezvous and Buffalo Roast**, Museum of New Mexico, Palace of the Governors, 105 W. Palace Avenue, Santa Fe, NM 87501, tel: (505) 827-6483.

**Santa Clara Feast Day**, Santa Clara Pueblo, PO Box 580, Espanola, NM 87532, tel: (505) 753-7326.

**Telluride Chamber Music Festival**, Telluride Chamber Resort Assocation, 666 W. Colorado Avenue, Telluride, CO 81435, tel: (970) 728-3041.

## SEPTEMBER

**Fiesta de Santa Fe**, Santa Fe Convention & Visitor Bureau, PO Box 909, Santa Fe, NM 87501, tel: (505) 984-6760.

**Ghost Dancer All-Indian Rodeo**, Durango Chamber Resort Association, 111 S. Camino del Rio, Durango, CO 81301, tel: (970) 247-0312.

**Navajo Nation Fair**, Navajo Nation Tourism Office, PO Box 663, Window Rock, AZ 86515, tel: (520) 871-6436.

**New Mexico State Fair and Rodeo**, New Mexico Tourism, Lamy Building, 491 Old Santa Fe Trail, Santa Fe, NM 87503, tel: toll free 800-545-2040.

**Old Taos Trade Fair**, Taos County Chamber of Commerce, PO Drawer I, Taos, NM 87571, tel: (505) 758-3873 or toll free 800-732-8267.

**San Esteban Feast Day**, Acoma Pueblo, PO Box 309, Acomita, NM 87034, tel: (505) 552-6604.

**San Geronimo Feast Day**, Taos Pueblo, PO Box 1846, Taos, NM 87571, tel: (505) 758-8626.

**Southern Utah Folklife Festival**, Zion National Park, Springdale, UT 84767-1099, tel: (801) 772-3256.

**Telluride Hang Gliding Festival**, Telluride Chamber Resort Assocation, 666 W. Colorado Avenue, Telluride, CO 81435, tel: (970) 728-3041.

## OCTOBER

**Albuquerque International Balloon Fiesta**, Albuquerque Convention and Visitors Bureau, PO Box 26866, Albuquerque, NM 87125, tel: (505) 243-3696 or toll free 800-284-2282.

**Apache Days**, Globe, San Carlos Apache Tribe, PO Box 0, San Carlos, AZ 85550, tel: (520) 475-2361.

**Arizona State Fair**, Phoenix & Valley of the Sun Convention and Visitor Bureau, 400 E. Van Buren #600, Phoenix, AZ 85004, tel: (602) 254-6500.

**Helldorado Days**, Tombstone Office of Tourism, PO Box 917, Tombstone, AZ 85638, tel: (520) 457-3929 or toll free 800-457-3423.

**La Fiesta de los Chiles**, Tucson Convention & Visitors Bureau, 130 S. Scott Avenue, Tucson, AZ 85701, tel: (520) 624-1817.

**Las Vegas Invitational Golf Tournament**, Las Vegas Convention and Visitors Authority, Convention Center, 3150 Paradise Road, Las Vegas, NV 89109, tel: (702) 892-0711 or toll free 800-332-5333.

**Northern Navajo Fair**, Shiprock, Navajo Nation Tourism Office, PO Box 663, Window Rock, AZ 86515, tel: (520) 871-6436.

Old West Rodeo, Durango Chamber Resort Association, 111 S. Camino del Rio, Durango, CO 81301, tel: (970) 247-0312.

Tucson Heritage Experience Festival, Tucson Convention & Visitors Bureau, 130 S. Scott Avenue, Tucson, AZ 85701, tel: (520) 624-1817 or toll free 800-638-8350.

Utah State Chili Competition, Color Country, 906 N. 1400 West, St George, UT 84771. 801-628-4171 or toll free 800-233-8824.

### NOVEMBER

Celebrity Golf Tournament, Color Country, 906 N. 1400 West, St George, UT 84771, tel: (801) 628-4171 or toll free 800-233-8824.

Indian National Finals Rodeo, New Mexico Tourism, Lamy Building, 491 Old Santa Fe Trail, Santa Fe, NM 87503, toll free tel: 800-545-2040.

Telluride Winter Festival (through December), Telluride Chamber Resort Assocation, 666 W. Colorado Avenue, Telluride, CO 81435, tel: (970) 728-3041.

Thunderbird Balloon Classic, Phoenix & Valley of the Sun Convention and Visitor Bureau, 400 E. Van Buren #600, Phoenix, AZ 85004, tel: (602) 254-6500.

### DECEMBER

Indian Market, Phoenix & Valley of the Sun Convention and Visitor Bureau, 400 E. Van Buren #600, Phoenix, AZ 85004, tel: (602) 254-6500.

National Finals Rodeo, Las Vegas Convention and Visitors Authority, Convention Center, 3150 Paradise Road, Las Vegas, NV 89109, tel: (702) 892-0711 or toll free 800-332-5333.

Red Rock Balloon Rally, Gallup Convention and Visitors Bureau, PO Drawer Q, Gallup, NM 87305, tel: (505) 863-3841.

Sun Carnival, El Paso Convention and Visitors Bureau, 1 Civic Center Plaza, El Paso, TX 79940, tel: (915) 534-0658.

Winter Spanish Market, Santa Fe Convention & Visitors Bureau, PO Box 909, Santa Fe, NM 87501, tel: (505) 984-6760.

Ye Merry Olde Christmas Faire, Albuquerque Convention and Visitors Bureau, PO Box 26866, Albuquerque, NM 87125, tel: (505) 243-3696 or toll free 800-284-2282.

# Sports & Leisure

## Outfitters & Horse Riding

Adrift Adventures, 378 N. Main Street, Moab, UT, tel: (801) 259-8594. Float trips on the Colorado and Green rivers and Jeep tours of Canyonlands National Park.

Adventure River Expeditions, 185 S. Broadway, Green River, UT, tel: (801) 564-3648. Float trips on the Colorado, Green and San Juan rivers.

ARA Lake Powell, Wahweap Lodge, Page, AZ 86040, tel: (520) 278-8888. Motorboat and houseboat rentals on Lake Powell.

Arizona River Runners, PO Box 47788, Phoenix, AZ 85068, tel: (602) 867-4866. Float trips on the Colorado River through the Grand Canyon.

Canyonlands Field Institute, PO Box 68, Moab, UT 84532, tel: (801) 259-7750. Guided nature-trips into Canyonlands and Arches national parks and surrounding wilderness areas.

Canyon Trail Rides, PO Box 128, Tropic, UT 84736, tel: (801) 679-8665. Trail rides in the national parks and red-rock country of southern Utah and northern Arizona.

Four Corners Rafting, PO Box 1032, Buena Vista, CO 81211, tel: (719) 395-4137 or toll free 800-332-7238. Raft trips on the Arkansas, Gunnison and Dolores rivers.

Goulding's Lodge Monument Valley Tours, Highway 163, Goulding, UT 84536, tel: (801) 727-3231. Tours of Monument Valley by four-wheel-drive.

Kokopelli River Tours, 100 E. San Francisco Street, Santa Fe, NM, tel: (505) 983-6556. Float trips on the Rio Grande and Rio Chama.

Monument Valley Navajo Tribal Park, Box 93, Monument Valley, UT 84536, tel: (801) 727-3287. Inquire about horseback riding tours at visitors center.

Pack Creek Ranch, PO Box 1270, Moab, UT 84532, tel: (801) 259-5505. Pack trips around La Sal Mountains.

Wilderness Adventures, PO Box 63282, Phoenix, AZ 85082, tel: (602) 220-1414. Instruction in rock climbing, mountain climbing and other outdoor skills.

## Skiing

### Arizona

Arizona Snowbowl, tel: (520) 779-1951.

Mount Lemmon Ski Valley, tel: (520) 576-1400.

Sunrise Ski Area, tel: (520) 735-7669.

### Colorado

Purgatory-Durango, tel: (970) 247-9000 or toll free 800-525-0892.

Telluride Skier Services, tel: (970) 728-4424.

### New Mexico

Angel Fire, tel: 800-633-7463.

Pajarito Ski Area, tel: (505) 662-5725.

Red River Ski Area, tel: (505) 754-2382.

Sandia Peak Ski Area, tel: (505) 242-9133.

Santa Fe Basin, tel: (505) 982-4429.

Sipapu Ski Area, tel: (505) 587-2240.

Ski Apache, tel: (505) 336-4356.

Snow Canyon Ski Area, tel: (505) 682-2333.

Taos Ski Valley, tel: (505) 776-2291.

### Utah

Brianhead Ski Resort, tel: (801) 677-2035.

Elk Meadows Ski Resort, tel: 800-248-7669.

## Hunting & Fishing

Hunting and fishing licenses are needed at nearly all times and places and are generally available at local marinas, bait shops, sporting-goods shops and trading posts. Regulations change, so contact state authorities for up-to-date information.

Arizona Game and Fish Department, 2222 W. Greenway Road, Phoenix, AZ 85023, tel: (602) 942-3000.

Colorado Division of Wildlife, 6060 N. Broadway, Denver, CO 80216, tel: (303) 297-1192.

New Mexico Department of Fish and Game, PO Box 25112, Santa Fe, NM 87504, tel: (505) 827-7911.

**Utah Division of Wildlife Resources**, 1095 W. Motor Avenue, Salt Lake City, UT 84116, tel: (801) 538-4700.

## Hiking

Avoid solitary hiking. The best situation is to hike with at least two other partners. If one person is injured, one member of the party can seek help while the other two remain behind. If you must hike alone, be sure to tell someone your intended route and time of return. Backcountry hiking may require a permit. Ask a ranger before setting out.

Use common sense on the trail. Don't attempt routes that are too strenuous for your level of fitness. Concentrate on what you're doing and where you're going. Even well-trod and well-marked trails can be dangerous. Be careful near cliffs, rocky slopes, ravines, rivers and other hazards. Don't attempt anything you're not comfortable with or anything that's beyond your level of skill.

### ENVIRONMENTAL ETHICS

The old saw is good advice: "Take nothing but pictures, leave nothing but footprints." The goal of low-impact/no-impact backpacking is to leave the area in the same condition as you found it, if not better. If you're camping in the backcountry, don't break branches, level the ground or alter the landscape in any way. Make fires in designated places only. Otherwise, use a portable stove. When nature calls, dig a hole 6 inches (15 cm) deep and at least 100 feet (30 meters) from water, campsites and trails. Take away all trash, including toilet paper.

### WILDLIFE

Never approach wild animals. Don't try to feed or touch them, not even the "cute" ones like chipmunks, squirrels and prairie dogs (they may carry diseases). Some animals, such as bison, may seem placid and slow-moving but will charge if irritated. People who have tried to creep up on bison in order to get a better photograph have been seriously injured by the animals. If you want close-ups, buy a telephoto lens.

## Spectator Sports

The only big-league teams in the region are in Phoenix.
**Basketball**: Phoenix Suns, American West Arena, tel: (620) 379-7900.
**Football**: Arizona Cardinals, Sun Devil Stadium, tel: (602) 379-0101.
**Baseball**: In addition, several major-league baseball teams come to the Phoenix and Tucson areas for spring training.

# Armchair Travel

## Movies/Videos

*Bugsy*, 1991. Warren Beatty portrays mobster Ben "Bugsy" Seigel, founder of the Flamingo Hotel, the first big-time casino in Las Vegas.
*Casino*, 1995. A Martin Scorsese film about the Las Vegas underworld with Robert De Niro, Sharon Stone and Joe Pesce.
*The Dark Wind*, 1991. This adaptation of a Tony Hillerman mystery takes place on the Navajo and Hopi reservations.
*Gunfight at the OK Corral*, 1957, and *High Chaparral* (television series). Just two of the many Westerns filmed at the Old Tucson Studios.
*Geronimo*, 1994. Yet another telling of Geronimo's story, much of it shot in southern Utah.
*Honeymoon in Vegas*, 1992. Las Vegas provides the backdrop for this off-the-wall comedy.
*Milagro Beanfield War*, 1988. John Nichols' novel is thoughtfully adapted to the screen by director Robert Redford. An interesting look at the people and land of Hispanic northern New Mexico.
*My Darling Clemetine*, 1946. John Ford's version of the infamous gunfight at the O.K. Corral with Henry Fonda as Wyatt Earp and Victor Mature as Doc Holliday.
*Stagecoach*, 1939, and *Fort Apache*, 1948. The stunning landscape of Monument Valley is featured in countless Westerns, most notably in John Ford's classic Westerns.
*Wyatt Earp*, 1995. Kevin Costner takes a shot at the classic gunfighter with rather lackluster results.

## Further Reading

### Nonfiction

*The Arizona Rangers*, by Bill O'Neal. Austin, TX: Eakin Press, 1986.
*Art of the Golden West*, by Alan Axelrod. New York, Abbeville Press, 1990.
*Best of the West: An Anthology of Classic Writing from the American West*, edited by Tony Hillerman. New York, Harper Collins, 1991.
*Beyond the Hundredth Meridian*, by Wallace Stegner. New York: Penguin, 1953.
*Billy the Kid: A Short and Violent Life*, by Robert M. Utley. Lincoln: University of Nebraska Press, 1989.
*Book of the Hopi*, by Frank Waters. New York: Penguin, 1963.
*Book of the Navajo*, by Raymond Locke. Los Angeles: Mankind Publishing, 1976.
*Buckaroo*, edited by Hal Cannon and Thomas West. New York, Callaway, 1993.
*Dancing Gods*, by Erna Ferguson. Albuquerque: University of New Mexico, 1931.
*Desert Notes: Reflections in the Eye of a Raven*, by Barry Holstun Lopez. New York: Avon, 1981.
*Desert Solitaire: A Season in the Wilderness*, by Edward Abbey. New York: McGraw-Hill, 1968.
*The Desert Year*, by Joseph W. Krutch. Tucson: University of Arizona, 1990.
*Earthtones: A Nevada Album*, by Ann Ronald and Stephen Trimble. Reno: University of Nevada Press, 1995.
*The Exploration of the Colorado River and its Canyons*, by John Wesley Powell. New York: Penguin, 1987.
*500 Nations*, by Alvin Josephy. New York, Knopf, 1994.
*Fighting Men of the Indian Wars*, by Bill O'Neal. Stillwater, OK, Barbed Wire Press, 1991.
*Geronimo: The Man, His Time, His Place*, by Angie Debo. Norman: University of Oklahoma, 1976.
*Ghost Towns of the American West*, by Bill O'Neal. Lincolnwood, IL, Publications International, 1995.
*Grand Canyon: An Anthology*, by Bruce Babbitt. Flagstaff: Northland Press, 1978.
*Grand Canyon: A Traveler's Guide*, by Jeremy Schmidt. Jackson Hole: Free Wheeling Travel Guides, 1991.

*Grand Canyon National Park: A Natural History Guide*, by Jeremy Schmidt. Boston: Houghton Mifflin Company, 1993.

*Grand Canyon: Today and All Its Yesterdays*, by Joseph Wood Krutch. Tucson: University of Arizona, 1989.

*The Guide to National Parks of the Southwest*, by Nicky Leach. Tucson: Southwest Parks & Monuments Association, 1992.

*In the House of Stone and Light: A Human History of the Grand Canyon*, by Donald J. Hughes. Grand Canyon: Grand Canyon Natural History Association, 1978.

*Indian Villages of the Southwest*, by Buddy Mays. San Francisco: Chronicle Books, 1985.

*Killing Custer: The Battle of the Little Bighorn and the Fate of the Plains Indians*, by James Welch. New York, Norton, 1994.

*The Man Who Walked Through Time*, by Colin Fletcher. New York: Random House, 1989.

*Masked Gods*, by Frank Waters. Athens: Swallow Press, 1950.

*Native America*, by Christine Mather, photographs by Jack Parsons. New York: Clarkson Potter, 1991.

*The People: Indians of the American Southwest*, by Stephen Trimble. Santa Fe: School of American Research Press, 1993.

*Santa Fe Style*, by Christine Mather, photographs by Jack Parsons. Rizzoli, 1986.

*True West: Arts, Traditions, and Celebrations*, by Christine Mather, photographs by Jack Parsons. New York, Clarkson Potter, 1992.

*The West: A Treasury of Art and Literature*, edited by T.H. Watkins and Joan Watkins. New York, Hugh Lauter Levin Associates, 1994.

## Fiction & Poetry

*Almanac of the Dead*, by Leslie Marmon Silko. New York: Simon & Schuster, 1991.

*Anything for Billy*, by Larry McMurtry. New York: Simon & Schuster, 1988.

*Ceremony*, by Leslie Marmon Silko. New York: Viking, 1977.

*The Dance Hall of the Dead*, by Tony Hillerman. New York: Harper & Row, 1973.

*The Dark Wind*, by Tony Hillerman. New York: Harper & Row, 1982.

*Death Comes for the Archbishop*, by Willa Cather. New York: Knopf, 1927.

*Milagro Beanfield War*, by John Nichols. New York: Holt, Rinehart, Winston, 1974.

*Riders of the Purple Sage*, by Zane Grey. New York: Penguin, 1990.

*Skinwalkers*, by Tony Hillerman. New York: Harper & Row, 1987.

## Other Insight Guides

The 190 books in the *Insight Guide* series cover every continent and include 40 titles devoted to the US. Companion books to this title include:

*Insight Guide: The Rockies* takes the reader through Colorado, Wyoming, Montana and Utah while exploring the beauty of the national parks and the rich culture and history of the area and the people.

Glorious color photographs and a perfect read whether on the trail or in an armchair, *Insight Guide: Wild West* explores the history, culture, romance and actual sites of the American West.

*Insight Guide: National Parks West.* Park rangers and experts write all about the West, from Texas to North Dakota, from Colorado to California and then on to the national parks of Alaska and Hawaii.

*Insight Guide: Native America* provides absorbing text about the Native Americans' culture and a detailed guide to Indian reservations, historic sites, festivals and ceremonies, from the Southwest to the East Coast.

## Art/Photo Credits

**Photography by**

**Academy of Motion Picture Arts and Sciences** 100/101, 103

**Ellis Armstrong** 35, 211, 223L, 234, 238, 239, 240, 257, 261

**Suzi Barnes** 96, 140, 148

**Courtesy of Colorado Historical Society** 133

**Kathleen N. Cook** 22, 110, 120/121, 150/151, 159, 163, 166, 180

**Sam Curtis** 139, 189

**Richard Erdoes** 28, 30, 32/33, 36, 37, 46, 80, 82, 83, 84, 89, 93, 94, 95, 112, 172/173, 213, 220, 221, 222, 223R, 231, 233, 262

**Richard Erdoes**/painting by **Widmar** 45

**Glyn Genin** 196/197, 202

**Grand Canyon National Park** 48/49

**John Gattuso** 31

**Dallas and John Heaton** 195, 198, 199, 201, 204

**Jack Hollingsworth** 9, 58, 77, 264

**Karl Kernberger** 178, 232, 235, 252, 256

**Dick Kent** 212

**Las Vagas News Bureau** 205

**Library of Congress** 53, 55, 104, 105, 179

**Lee Marmon** 87, 174, 210

**Buddy Mays** 38, 39, 61, 68, 70, 71, 72, 73, 74, 76, 79, 111, 113, 115, 124, 136/137, 162, 165, 169, 208/209, 214, 215, 236/237, 241, 242, 243, 249, 258, 259R, 176L&R, 263

**Terrence Moore** 66/67, 88, 114, 128, 130, 131, 132, 135, 138, 142, 143, 147, 153, 154, 157, 158, 224/225, 227, 228, 230, 251

**Allan C. Morgan** 60, 99, 141, 146, 155, 156, 167, 259

**Courtesy of Museum of New Mexico** 34, 40/41, 43, 44, 47

**National Archives** 50

**Mark Nohl** 218

**Jack Parsons** 216/217, 244, 253

**Ronnie Pinsler** 18, 59, 86, 229

**Frank Randall/Harvey Caplin** 42

**David Ryan** 145

**Harald Sund/Image Bank** Cover

**Tom Till** 26, 246/247

**Stephen Trimble** 1, 12/13, 14/15, 16/17, 56/57, 184/185

**US Postal Service** 149

**Vautier-de Nanxe** 2, 10/11, 20/21, 29, 63, 64/65, 90, 92, 108/109, 177, 118/119, 160/161, 181, 186, 190, 194, 200, 202, 203, 206, 207, 170, 254/255

**Joseph Viesti** 182, 183, 191, 192

**Donald Young** 24/25, 171, 175, 193

---

**Maps** Berndston & Berndston

**Visual Consultant** V. Barl

# Index